Competition and Concentration

The Economics of the Carbonated Soft Drink Industry

By

Robert D. Tollison
George Mason University

David P. Kaplan
Capital Economics

Richard S. Higgins
Capital Economics

LEXINGTON BOOKS
An Imprint of Macmillan, Inc.
NEW YORK

Maxwell Macmillan Canada
TORONTO

Maxwell Macmillan International
NEW YORK   OXFORD   SINGAPORE   SYDNEY

As for Seven-Up, it is, as I've said, a failing brand, and I would have liked to help save it.
— Roger Enrico, The Other Guy Blinked: How Pepsi Won the Cola Wars

Copyright © 1991 by Lexington Books
An Imprint of Macmillan, Inc.

Lexington Books
An Imprint of Macmillan, Inc.
866 Third Avenue, New York, N.Y. 10022

Maxwell Macmillan Canada, Inc.
1200 Eglinton Avenue East
Suite 200
Don Mills, Ontario M3C 3N1

Macmillan, Inc. is part of the Maxwell Communication Group of Companies.

Printed in the United States of America

printing number

2 3 4 5 6 7 8 9 10

Library of Congress Cataloging-in-Publication Data

Tollison, Robert D.
    Competition and concentration : the economics of the carbonated soft drink industry / by Robert D. Tollison, David P. Kaplan, Richard S. Higgins.
        p.   cm.
    Includes index.
    ISBN 0-669-27139-X
    1. Soft drink industry—United States. 2. Industrial concentration—United States. 3. Competition—United States.
I. Kaplan, David P.   II. Higgins, Richard S.   III. Title.
HD9349.S633U67   1991
338.4'766362'0973—dc20   90-44544
                                                         CIP

Contents

Figures

Tables

Preface

This book is a contribution to the economics of industry, an old and honorable subdiscipline in economics. Its purpose is to analyze the state of competition in the carbonated soft drink industry. The conventional wisdom about this industry is that it is very concentrated (PepsiCo and Coca-Cola) and hence must be viewed with suspicion by the antitrust community. We grant that the industry is concentrated. The puzzle is, why does the industry perform so well? By answering this question, we hope to offer a better understanding of the carbonated soft drink industry, as well as to provide a useful framework for antitrust analysis of the industry.

We thank PepsiCo for partial support of this project. In addition, we thank the following individuals for their help in our efforts: Susan Manning, Kristy Mathews, Sara Hudson, Patti Walsh, Susan Mora, William Shughart, and Kevin Grier. In particular, we thank William Myslinski for the development of some of the material in the chapter on entry. We also thank Richard Tedlow for his thoughtful comments on an earlier draft of the manuscript. We, of course, are responsible for any errors or omissions in this book.

1
Introduction

By any traditional measure, the carbonated soft drink industry in the United States is highly concentrated. In 1988 the two largest firms, the Coca-Cola Company and PepsiCo, Inc., represented 71.3 percent of total sales, as measured by retail sales (grocery stores, drugstores, and so forth), fountain accounts, and vending machines. The four largest firms, including Dr Pepper/Seven-Up and Cadbury Schweppes, accounted for 85.1 percent of these categories. The Herfindahl-Hirshman Index (HHI) stood at 2,713 in 1988.[1] The industry is also characterized by increasing concentration. In 1981 the same two firms represented 64.1 percent of sales, four-firm concentration was 75.7 percent, and the HHI was 2,184.

Particular distribution channels are even more concentrated. In 1987 Coca-Cola and PepsiCo accounted for over 85 percent of fountain sales, and the top four firms represented roughly 97 percent of such sales. In the vending channel, Coca-Cola and PepsiCo represented almost 80 percent of sales, and the top four firms accounted for approximately 91 percent.

The industry has also been characterized by consolidations at both the concentrate and bottler levels. In the 1980s, Dr Pepper and Seven-Up combined, and Cadbury Schweppes now controls Schweppes, Canada Dry, Sunkist, Sun-Drop, Crush, and Hires. A&W owns the Squirt and Vernors brands and licenses the Country Time Lemonade brand. Bottler consolidation has been even more dramatic. The number of bottlers declined from 2,398 in 1975 to 1,102 in 1986 and approximately 1,000 at the end of 1988. Moreover, concentrate companies, particularly PepsiCo and Coca-Cola, purchased bottlers at an increased pace in the 1980s.

The conventional antitrust paradigm (structure-conduct-performance) would predict from these numbers that the carbonated soft drink industry would not be competitive and would be characterized by poor performance in which price increases outstripped costs, there was little price discounting, no new product development occurred, production inefficiencies abounded, and demand was stagnant or falling. This same paradigm would predict that

PepsiCo and Coca-Cola would perceive their mutual interest to be served by nonaggressive, nonthreatening behavior, particularly toward each other.

But this conventional wisdom does not hold up here. The carbonated soft drink industry performs exceptionally well and is characterized by intense competition, particularly between PepsiCo and Coca-Cola. Gallons of soft drinks consumed grew from 2.1 billion in 1960, to 4.6 billion in 1970, and to 12.4 billion in 1988, an increase of almost 500 percent (almost 7 percent a year). Each distribution channel (retail, fountain, and vending) has participated in this phenomenal growth. Per capita consumption of carbonated soft drinks has more than doubled over the past twenty years, currently at almost 50 gallons per capita, and is predicted to reach 60 gallons per capita in the 1990s.

As consumption has grown, real prices have substantially declined. Real prices (adjusted for inflation) declined from $6.19 per case (288 ounces) in 1965 to $3.99 per case in 1988. These results are not affected if costs are held constant. Declining soft drink prices have been driven largely by increasing trade deals and discounts. Soft drinks are on deal more often in the grocery store than any other product, with upwards of 80 percent of all soft drinks sold at discounted prices. Soft drink end-aisle displays and special promotional prices are commonplace.

Concentrate producers have also moved to reduce production costs, particularly by consolidating bottling facilities and specializing production facilities. These facts and others, such as private label competition, strong regional competition, new product introductions, and new packaging innovations, are basically inconsistent with theories of monopoly or collusion. On a performance scorecard, the soft drink industry is one of the leaders in the United States economy. Consumers have expressed their satisfaction with products and prices by purchasing more soft drinks than any other beverage.

Much of this competition is generated by PepsiCo and Coca-Cola. The so-called "Cola Wars" are not a figment of a writer's imagination; they are a real behavioral phenomenon in the daily life of the industry. Perhaps the best example of this competition was the introduction of "New Coke" in 1985. In an event that received much publicity, Coca-Cola changed the formula for its flagship brand but within months was forced to reintroduce the original formula as Classic Coke. This marketing mistake was motivated by Coca-Cola's attempt to compete better with the Pepsi brand, which had been gaining sales. Roberto Goizueta, chairman of the Coca-Cola Company, saw the "value of the Coca-Cola trademark . . . going downhill" as the "product and the brand had a declining share in a shrinking segment of the market."[2]

The 1986 PepsiCo–Seven-Up and Coca-Cola–Dr Pepper proposed acquisitions represent another example of this competition between PepsiCo and Coca-Cola. In January 1986 PepsiCo announced its intention to acquire Seven-Up from Philip Morris. PepsiCo argued to the Federal Trade Commission (FTC) that it intended to increase the sales of Seven-Up by lowering prices and aggressively marketing the brand. The firm that would have suffered most directly from an invigorated Seven-Up was Coca-Cola because, during the 1980s, Seven-Up was losing substantial sales to Sprite, a product marketed by Coca-Cola.

In response, Coca-Cola countered with an announcement in February 1986 that it planned to acquire Dr Pepper. On June 20, 1986, the FTC voted 4–0 to oppose the acquisitions of Seven-Up by PepsiCo and Dr Pepper by Coca-Cola.[3] As a result of the vote, Philip Morris terminated the transaction with PepsiCo.[4] A federal judge in Washington, D.C., subsequently granted an injunction against Coca-Cola's proposed acquisition of Dr Pepper.[5]

Coca-Cola reacted to the possibility of increased competition from a combined PepsiCo–Seven-Up by initiating its attempt to purchase Dr Pepper, as indicated in Coca-Cola's corporate documents, which were produced during the Washington federal court proceedings. One document stated that the "primary objective" of Coca-Cola's proposed acquisition of Dr Pepper "should be an attempt to stop" PepsiCo's bid for Seven-Up.[6] Coca-Cola has in fact benefited from the demise of the PepsiCo–Seven-Up transaction: Seven-Up has continued to lose share and is struggling competitively. In 1988 Sprite overtook Seven-Up in sales of lemon-lime soft drinks. This is but one dramatic example of the intense competitive struggle between PepsiCo and Coca-Cola, a struggle that takes many forms, including lower prices, new products, and cost reductions.[7]

Why does this industry perform so well despite high concentration and recent consolidation?[8] We offer some suggestions.[9] First, carbonated soft drinks do not compete only with other carbonated soft drinks. Some may argue with the significance and magnitude of interproduct competition, but its existence cannot be reasonably disputed. Soft drinks actively compete, in differing degrees, for a share of the consumer's beverage purchases with powdered soft drinks (such as Kool-Aid and Crystal Light), iced tea, fruit juice, bottled water, coffee, and others. Consumers are never confronted with a harsh alternative in choosing among beverages and in fact switch regularly among carbonated soft drinks and a host of other beverages. Among the factors suggesting that carbonated soft drinks compete with other beverages are the efforts and perceptions of the sellers of soft drinks and other beverages (Pepsi A.M. aimed at morning coffee consumption), the targeting of advertising messages, including direct comparative advertising (Kool-Aid as the "third largest selling soft drink brand"), the introduction of new products that are blurring distinctions among beverage products (such as flavored water), evolving tastes and preferences, such as the trend toward healthier foods, and the growth of carbonated soft drink consumption at the expense of other beverages. Interproduct competition is also supported by econometric analysis of beverage prices.

If beverage products beyond carbonated soft drinks are included in the relevant market, concentration statistics based only on carbonated soft drinks are misleading. Some may object to any other beverage product being included in the product market for the purpose of calculating market share statistics. The question, however, is not whether these other beverage products are technically in or out of the market for purposes of calculating market shares but whether they limit the ability of carbonated soft drink producers to raise prices above competitive levels. It is clear that these alternative beverage products provide significant competitive pressure on soft drink producers.

A second factor that helps explain the competitive nature of this industry involves entry and expansion by fringe competitors. Entry would not appear to be difficult in this industry or, put another way, supply elasticity would appear high. Carbonated soft drinks are a simple product to produce; they are flavored water with bubbles. No patents or other types of government regulation restrict entry.[10] There are no raw material restrictions. Concentrate and bottling capacity is available and can be easily expanded. No production or process secrets serve as significant obstacles. Distribution does not appear to create an insurmountable barrier. Numerous firms, including other large beverage and food companies, already distribute and sell products in the same outlets as carbonated soft drinks, and these and other firms have access to capital to fund marketing campaigns. Consumers' willingness to try new brands is evidenced by the success (and failures) of Coca-Cola, PepsiCo, and other companies, such as A&W, in the introduction and expansion of beverage products. The industry has seen new entry and expansion over the years regionally and nationally.

At least as measured in national share levels, no new brand or firm has approached the size of Coca-Cola or PepsiCo. A reason for this is the intense degree of competition among existing competitors, particularly Coca-Cola and PepsiCo. As a result of this competition, an entrant of equal dimensions has never materialized. Existing competitors, particularly PepsiCo and Coca-Cola, appreciate how vulnerable their competitive position is to new entry and expansion, and this fear, in part, explains their competitive behavior.

A third reason that helps explain the competitive behavior of the carbonated soft drink industry springs from the fact that the industry is much more than its two most prominent members. The industry is characterized by numerous firms, multiple brands, even more package sizes, new product introductions, complex pricing schemes, regional and local differences in competition, and sophisticated buyers. Each of these factors limits the ability of soft drink concentrate firms to collude successfully.

Another reason that helps explain the competitive nature of this industry is its social framework, particularly as it relates to PepsiCo and Coca-Cola. The rivalry between Coca-Cola and PepsiCo is so intense and well entrenched historically that the suggestion that these concentrate firms would collude to raise prices is unlikely. The competition between them includes lower prices, new products, new packaging, cost reductions, and many forms of nonprice competition.

Of course, the preceding analysis reflects a general model or approach to industry behavior. PepsiCo and Coca-Cola have invested heavily in their trademarks over time and continue to do so. Their trademarks have come to represent a ready supply of high-quality products at competitive prices. The consequences of an attempt to raise prices above competitive levels could be ominous. Consumers, many of whom switch among brands, would no longer take it for granted that PepsiCo and Coca-Cola were providing products at competitive prices. Many would switch to other carbonated drinks or other beverages; significant entry, perhaps by a large food or beverage company, would become more feasible; and so on. Thus, although PepsiCo and Coca-Cola are highly successful firms, they are, in fact, intense competitors, with such competition being driven by their reputational capital and by the tenuous nature of their hold on a substantial number of consumers.[11] Viewed in this way, the extremely competitive nature of this industry is more easily understood.

The organization of this volume is straightforward. Section II is mainly descriptive, providing an identification of the actors. Section III addresses competition and performance in the carbonated soft drink industry. Section IV analyzes the relevant market in which carbonated soft drinks compete. Section V reviews entry conditions. Section VI represents an overview of why collusion is not likely in this industry. This section also addresses recent bottler price-fixing allegations and their impact on our conclusions. Section VII addresses vertical integration in the industry and its impact on competition and entry. Section VIII revisits issues associated with PepsiCo's attempt to acquire Seven-Up, and, finally, Section IX presents our conclusions.

Notes

1. The HHI is calculated by squaring the shares of individual firms and then aggregating these figures. An industry with ten firms, each representing 10 percent of sales, would have an HHI of 1,000. An industry with two firms, each having 50 percent of sales, would have an HHI of 5,000.

2. *Wall Street Journal,* April 24, 1986.

3. For a discussion of the FTC's deliberations, see *Legal Times,* July 7, 1986. On the same day, a federal judge in Columbus, Georgia, issued a temporary restraining order against the same two transactions at the request of attorneys for Royal Crown.

4. Philip Morris did, however, sell the international operations (including Canada) of Seven-Up to PepsiCo later.

5. Federal Trade Commission v. The Coca-Cola Company, Civil Action No. 86–1764, July 31, 1986. The FTC continues to pursue an administrative action against the Coca-Cola–Dr Pepper transaction despite the fact that both parties walked away from the deal approximately four years ago.

6. *Washington Post,* July 29, 1986. RC's lawsuit may also suggest that PepsiCo's proposed acquisition of Seven-Up was procompetitive. RC would benefit if the acquisition led to higher prices and restricted output but possibly suffer if increased competition resulted.

7. Further evidence of Coca-Cola's intent to stop the PepsiCo–Seven-Up combination by announcing its plan to purchase Dr Pepper is discussed by Roger Enrico, president and chief executive officer of PepsiCo Worldwide Beverages, in his book, *The Other Guy Blinked: How Pepsi Won the Cola Wars* (New York: Bantam Books, 1986). Enrico points out (p. 267) that at a purchase price of $470 million, Coca-Cola was offering up to two and a quarter times more per case for Dr Pepper than PepsiCo had offered for Seven-Up.

8. For a recent and interesting historical analysis of the evolution of competition in the industry, see Richard Tedlow, *New and Improved: The Story of Mass Marketing in America* (New York: Basic Books, 1990).

9. Our logic here is based on the rationale put forth by the FTC in its "Statement of Merger Principles" and the Merger Guidelines adopted by the Department of Justice, *Department of Justice Merger Guidelines,* Federal Register, 26,823, June 29, 1984; and *Statement of Federal Trade Commission Concerning Horizontal Mergers,* 42 Antitrust & Trade Regulation Reporter, Special Supplement, June 17, 1982.

10. There are, of course, some famous trade secrets in the industry, the most prominent being the well-kept secret formulas for Pepsi and Coca-Cola. The evidence in this book shows that their secrets have not retarded entry or competition in the industry. In fact, protection of formulas appears to be basically a way to protect brand-name capital by firms.

11. The substantial problems Perrier faces as it attempts to recover from product formulation problems is a prime example of how quickly a trademark can be damaged.

2
The Carbonated Soft Drink Industry

The carbonated soft drink industry is made up of a number of different actors: concentrate or syrup producers, bottlers, distributors, and at the retail level, grocery stores, convenience stores, fountain outlets (restaurants, hotels, institutions, and so forth), and vending companies. Numerous combinations of these actors are used to make products available to the consumer. Generally, however, the following functions are performed:

1. *Concentrate or syrup producers:* Firms that produce concentrate or syrup, the raw material used to produce the finished soft drink products.
2. *Bottlers:* Firms that purchase concentrate or syrup and manufacture finished soft drink products by mixing the concentrate or syrup with carbonated water and other ingredients.
3. *Distributors:* Firms that deliver finished soft drink products to the retail trade. Many different types of firms provide this service, including bottlers, beer distributors, wine and spirit distributors, independent food wholesalers, warehouses owned or operated by retail grocery chains, and food brokers.
4. *Retailers:* Firms such as grocery stores, convenience stores, fountain establishments, and vending companies, which make soft drinks available to consumers.

Different firms use different methods to provide their product to consumers. PepsiCo, for example, manufactures concentrate, which it sells to independent franchise bottlers, as well as to bottlers it owns and operates throughout the United States. The bottlers manufacture, distribute, and market finished soft drink products under various PepsiCo trademarks, including Pepsi, Diet Pepsi, Mountain Dew, and Slice. PepsiCo bottlers distribute PepsiCo and other soft drink products through retail stores, vending machines, and food service outlets, including restaurants and fountains.[1]

Shasta manufactures its own finished soft drink products at twelve canning plants. The finished product is delivered to warehouses owned or operated by retail chains, such as Safeway, which put the product on the retail shelf. Many private label producers, such as Safeway, Giant, and Kroger, produce finished products in plants they own or operate or have the product bottled or canned under contract by a third party and then deliver the finished products to their own warehouses for ultimate delivery to consumers. These retailers either make their own concentrate or buy it from independent flavor houses.

Coca-Cola manufactures syrup, which it sells to bottlers, which, in turn, manufacture, distribute, and market finished soft drink products principally to grocery stores, convenience stores, and vending machines.[2] Coca-Cola, however, largely uses independent food wholesalers rather than its bottlers to distribute its syrup to food service outlets. It also sells directly to certain fountain accounts.

Other companies use bottlers or contract packers to manufacture finished products but rely on firms such as beer distributors to distribute the product to the retail trade. Many firms use various combinations of these actors to provide products to the consumer.

Notes

1. PepsiCo bottlers, whether independently owned or company owned, generally hold bottling and syrup appointments from other concentrate or syrup manufacturers, in addition to PepsiCo, under which they are authorized to manufacture and distribute soft drinks under the trademarks owned by those other companies.

2. Coca-Cola also owns 49 percent of the stock of Coca-Cola Enterprises (CCE), a publicly owned bottler.

3
Competition and Performance

C oncentrate is sold to bottlers, who mix it with carbonated water and sweetener to produce finished soft drinks, which they deliver (themselves or through distributors) for final sale to consumers. The price at which concentrate is sold to bottlers is a list price. Since concentrate producers provide substantial funds to bottlers to make them more competitive, the actual transaction price for concentrate normally is substantially below the list price. The bottler uses these funds, along with its own resources, to promote and discount carbonated soft drinks. The magnitude of price incentives is immense. These incentives exist because the output of concentrate producers—the concentrate itself—depends on the amount of product sold by local bottlers. As a result, the concentrate company has a strong incentive to expand output at the bottling level by maintaining competitive pricing.

The competitive effect of national and regional advertising by PepsiCo and other soft drink competitors is also experienced at the retail level. As a result, the following analysis focuses on the level of industry involvement that matters most: the prices and product quality experienced by consumers of carbonated soft drinks.

In 1987 carbonated soft drink sales to food stores represented 42.6 percent of total sales; other retail outlets, such as drugstores, represented 22.4 percent; fountain accounts represented 22.0 percent; and vending sales represented 13.0 percent.[1] The first section below will focus primarily on retail-type stores (collectively accounting for 65 percent of retail sales), while the second section will analyze the fountain and vending channels (accounting for 35 percent of retail sales). Certain subject areas, such as advertising and new product competition, which impact all types of outlets, are discussed in the first section. The third section discusses profits in the industry, while the last section addresses future prospects.

The Competitive Venue

Based on all the evidence we have obtained, the carbonated soft drink industry is intensely competitive by any reasonable measure. As recently stated by
Royal Crown:

> The soft drink business is highly competitive. RCC competes not only
> directly for consumer acceptance but also for shelf space in supermarkets
> and for maximum marketing efforts by multibrand licensed bottlers. RCC's
> soft drink products compete with all liquid refreshments, and with the prod-
> ucts of numerous nationally known producers of soft drinks such as "Coca-
> Cola," "Pepsi-Cola" and "Seven-Up". RCC also competes with regional pro-
> ducers and "private label" suppliers. Competition may take many forms,
> including pricing, packaging, the introduction of new products and advertis-
> ing campaigns.[2]

Our analysis of the competition among soft drink competitors included
a review of sales patterns, price and non-price factors, entry, and performance.

Price and Volume

The trend in prices of carbonated soft drinks, illustrated by the solid line segment in figure 3–1, is quite remarkable. "Price" here is computed as the dollar
value of carbonated soft drink case volume (288 ounces per case). This price
is, in effect, a wholesale, or bottler-to-retailer, price. The price series (the
solid line) is deflated by the consumer price index (CPI), and begins at a level
of $6.19 in 1965 and ends at $3.99 in 1988—over a 30 percent reduction in
the real price of carbonated soft drinks in twenty-four years, or more than a
1 percent price reduction per year over this period.

Even when costs are held constant, the real price of carbonated soft
drinks also declined between 1965 and 1986. This is shown by the dotted line
segment in figure 3–1 and by the regression results in table 3–1. Essentially,
the regression in table 3–1 seeks to explain carbonated soft drink prices over
time with a time trend (T) and a measure of material and labor costs per unit
of carbonated soft drink volume.[3] In other words, how much of the time
series of soft drink prices is explained by costs? As the results show, the coefficient on T is negative and strongly significant, holding cost factors constant.
Price has been falling over time independently of the behavior of industry
costs. This is shown by the dotted line in figure 3–1, which begins at $3.60
and ends at $1.97, a 45.3 percent reduction in the real price of carbonated
soft drinks after accounting for cost changes over the 1965–1986 period.

The steep decline in the price of carbonated soft drinks is therefore not

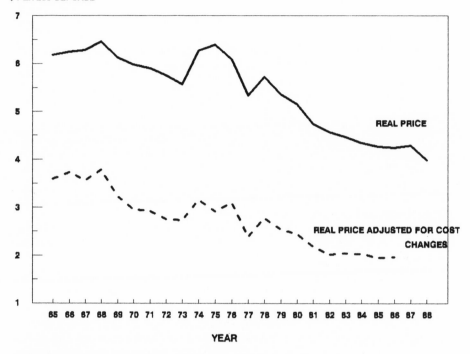

$ PER 288 OZ.-CASE

REAL PRICE

REAL PRICE ADJUSTED FOR COST CHANGES

YEAR

Source: *Beverage Industry/Annual Manual* (Cleveland, OH: Edgell Communications, Inc., 1989/1990).
Note: Cost information was unavailable for 1987 and 1988.

Figure 3–1. Price of Carbonated Soft Drinks, Adjusted for Inflation and Costs, 1965–1988

solely attributable to cost reductions in the industry. The source of this decline, among other things, is the intense competition that prevails in the industry. One of the primary purposes of this book is to examine the nature and extent of this competition.

The low prices of soft drinks combined with a high-quality product have fueled tremendous growth in the consumption of soft drinks. A 1989 report by Standard & Poor's concluded that "overall soft drink pricing has been roughly flat for at least three years, which, combined with heavy marketing, has contributed significantly to per capita consumption growth."[4] Figure 3–2 reflects per capita growth of carbonated soft drinks from 1965 to 1988.

The prices of carbonated soft drinks have risen at a much lower rate than many other beverage products in the last few years. For example, between

Table 3–1
Regression Results for Carbonated Soft Drink Prices, 1965–1986

Independent Variable	Coefficient	T-statistic
Constant	4.358	7.76
Time trend	−0.086	−10.75
Cost/volume	0.866	5.75
R^2 adjusted	0.93	
F-statistic	122.36	
N	22	

Source: *Beverage Industry/Annual Manual* (Cleveland, OH: Edgell Communications, Inc., 1989/1990).

1981 and 1988, the prices of soft drinks rose 10.9 percent based on CPI data published by the United States Department of Labor. The prices of other products grew at much faster rates; noncarbonated drinks rose 20.8 percent, fruit juices and frozen fruit drinks 33.5 percent, coffee 19.5 percent, and beer 25.9 percent.[5]

Such disparate price histories are roughly consistent with volume trends. Over this same time period, per capita consumption of carbonated soft drinks increased over 30 percent, while coffee fell roughly 8 percent and juices 19 percent (figure 3–3). The day-to-day price history and growth of carbonated soft drink consumption are indicative of a healthy competitive industry.

Price Competition

The day-to-day pricing of carbonated soft drinks is consistent with intense competition in the industry. One recent study concluded that "in 1988, the highly competitive soft drink industry's situation was highlighted by extensive price wars."[6] Soft drink pricing is competitive, in part, because if a particular soft drink price is too high, consumers can buy an alternative soft drink or beverage. Many consumers also purchase soft drinks often and as a result are unwilling to pay prices they consider to be excessive.[7] In response to a market research inquiry, one consumer stated that if "Pepsi is 30, 40, 50 cents more for the two-liter bottle, I'll buy the Coke. They [her family] can go through a couple of bottles a day. I'm not out to spend that kind of money on soda."[8]

The role of trade promotions is important to the pricing of carbonated soft drinks and the price sensitivity of soft drink consumers.

Trade Promotions. Soft drink companies heavily promote their products by providing funds to bottlers for such purposes. Bottlers also spend sums independently for trade promotions.[9] A typical trade promotion might include an

GALLONS PER CAPITA

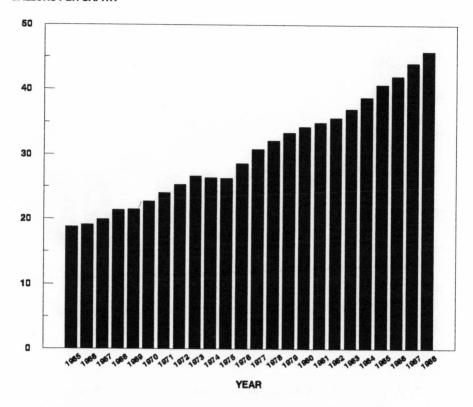

Source: *Maxwell Report* (Richmond, VA: Wheat First Securities, 1985, 1989).

Figure 3–2. Per Capita Consumption of Carbonated Soft Drinks, 1965–1988

end aisle or other secondary display in a grocery store, with the price of the product significantly reduced. The price reduction will frequently be publicized by an advertisement in the local newspaper.

Expenditures on soft drink promotions are large. One report concluded that "throughout the 1980s" consumer soft drink "prices were moderated by an overall policy of competitive price discounting."[10] Another observer has concluded that "promotions in the soft drink industry are beginning to explode as producers and bottling operators take a more imaginative and aggressive approach to local market activities."[11] Price discounting is not new to the industry, however. Royal Crown's 1981 *Annual Report* stated:

PERCENTAGE CHANGE

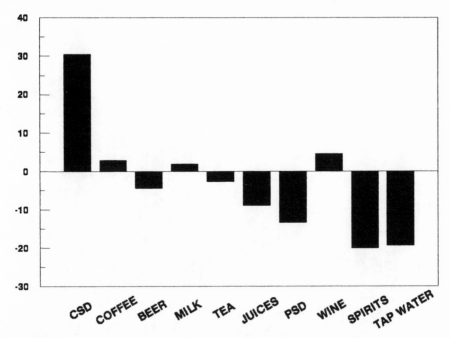

Source: Ibid.
Note: CSD = carbonated soft drinks; PSD = powdered soft drinks.

Figure 3–3. Percentage Change in Per Capita Beverage Consumption, 1981–1988

Industrywide there was a sharp increase in the level of discounting in the struggle for market share by the leading soft drink companies in 1981. Consumers were constantly exposed to cents-off promotions, under the cap contests and a host of other discounts. The results of these programs are difficult to measure since the net effect has been to weaken brand loyalties. People who formerly bought only one soft drink brand now buy whatever is on sale, often switching brands each time they make a purchase.[12]

Carbonated soft drinks are the most heavily promoted item sold in grocery stores. They rank first out of 344 product categories, with 75 percent of the product sold on some type of trade deal.[13] Table 3–2 compares trade promotion activity in carbonated soft drinks with an average of all 344 categories.[14] Carbonated soft drinks are also more heavily promoted than any other beverage product (figure 3–4).

Price Sensitivity. It is not unusual for the volume of a carbonated soft drink to increase twofold to fourfold when it is on deal at the retail level. We investigated the responsiveness of consumers to changes in the prices of Coke and Pepsi brands across various package sizes using Nielsen Scantrack data from January 1988 through September 1989. The sales figures represent regular, nondiet brands. These data consist of weekly observations on volumes and scanner prices per case for 2-liter and 3-liter bottles, 12-ounce cans (twelve pack), 12-ounce cans (singles), and 16-ounce nonreturnable bottles (singles).

Simple correlation coefficients between price and volume are shown in table 3–3. The coefficients derive from a statistical procedure that allows a determination of the direction of the relationship between price and volume. In general, the two variables are inversely related; that is, higher prices are associated with lower volumes, and vice versa. For example, the price-volume

Table 3–2
Average Trade Promotion: Carbonated Soft Drinks versus 344 Categories, 1988.

Percentage of Volume with Specified Deal	Carbonated Soft Drinks	Average of All 344 Categories
Any trade deal	75.0	24.5
Print ad feature	38.0	8.5
In-store display	51.0	8.5
Shelf price reduction	61.0	19.5
Store coupon	2.0	0.7
Manufacturer coupon	5.0	10.8
Average percentage off on price deals	30.0	25.2

Source: *The Marketing Factbook Annual Report* (Chicago, IL: Information Resources, Inc., 1989).

Table 3–3
Correlation Coefficients: Price versus Volume

Package Type	Pepsi-Cola	Coca-Cola Classic
2-liter bottles	−0.639	−0.597
3-liter bottles	−0.796	−0.654
12-ounce cans, twelve pack	−0.958	−0.929
12-ounce cans, singles	−0.917	−0.938
16-ounce nonreturnable bottles, singles	−0.747	−0.898

Source: Nielsen, *Nielsen Scantrack* (Chicago, IL: Nielsen, 1988–1989).

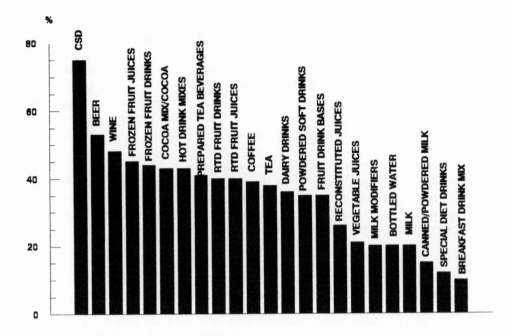

Source: *The Marketing Factbook Annual Report* (Chicago, IL: Information Resources Inc., 1989).
Note: CSD = carbonated soft drinks; RTD = ready to drink.

Figure 3–4. Percentage of Volume on Any Trade Deal, 1988

data for Pepsi 2-liter bottles are contained in figure 3–5 and plotted against one another in figure 3–6. Notice in figure 3–5 that the volume series in the upper panel generally moves in the opposite direction from the price series in the lower panel. (The horizontal axis in the figure represents the same time period for both panels.) Figure 3–6 merges the price and volume data in one graph; that is, each dot in figure 3–6 represents a weekly observation.

All of these data suggest an inverse relationship between price and quantity. To confirm this, we fitted simple linear regression lines to the data. In lay terms, a regression analysis moves beyond the statistical procedure of simple correlation by assuming a direction of causation and by attempting to hold other factors constant. In the case of the price and volume examined here, it is assumed that price drives or causes variations in volume, which are to be explained by a regression with the price data in it. The RHO-variables represent a statistical procedure for correcting in the regression for a condition known as autocorrelation, and the R^2 statistic shows how much of the variation in volume is explained by the price-based regression. The regression results for Pepsi and Coke brands are shown in tables 3–4 and 3–5.

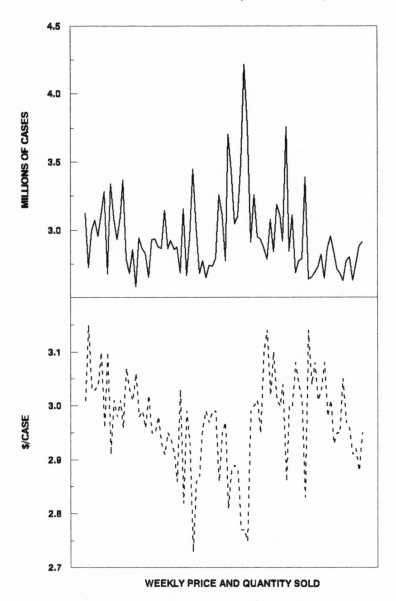

Source: Nielsen, *Nielsen Scantrack* (Chicago, IL: Nielsen, 1988–1989).

Figure 3–5. Pepsi 2-Liter Bottles, Price versus Volume, January 1988–September 1989

In all cases, we found a statistically significant negative relationship between price and volume. The estimated price elasticities are given in table 3–6. These numbers measure the responsiveness of volume to changes in price. The results across both brands suggest that a 1 percent price increase leads to a 2.37 and 3.41 percent decrease in volume, depending on container type. In other words, a 10 percent price increase would lead to a 23–34 percent loss of volume.

Cooperative Merchandising Agreements. Cooperative merchandising agreements (CMAs) between grocery stores and bottlers are used to promote soft drinks. (These agreements originated and are still in use with other grocery products.) The agreements cover a schedule of promotional activities over the period of, say, three to six months in the chain's stores in a given area. For example, a CMA might call for PepsiCo products to be attractively featured and discounted in a chain's food ads for specified weekends over the specified period. In addition, PepsiCo products would be attractively promoted in the store, with end-of-aisle displays, and so forth. In return, the chain receives a payment from the PepsiCo bottler that services the chain's stores. CMAs invariably result in lower prices to consumers.[15]

Sellers, Brands, and Packages

Approximately sixty franchise companies in the United States sell soft drink products under some 200 different brand names. (*See* appendix A. A small number of the firms listed in this directory sell powdered soft drinks.) Not included in this count are other firms selling brands of soft drinks, such as private label suppliers. Among the many companies selling branded soft drink products are PepsiCo, Coca-Cola, Cadbury Schweppes, Seagrams, Royal Crown, Shasta, and Treesweet (Faygo). Firms selling private label products include Safeway, Kroger, Giant, and most other major retail chains. There are also regional soft drink companies (Big Red). In addition, many firms sell a number of different brands. Both Coca-Cola and PepsiCo, for example, sell over ten different brands, and many other firms also sell a large number of brands. The brands represent various flavors (cola, root beer, and so on), diet and caffeine-free products, and different package types and sizes (cans, bottles, plastic, 16 ounces, 32 ounces, and so on). (Appendix B contains data on the size of these product groupings and package sizes.)

The large number of brands and the variety associated with their existence would appear to be in response to consumer demand for variety in flavor (cola, root beer), calorie reduction (diet), health (caffeine free), and convenience (large plastic bottles). The response of the industry to consumer demands appears to be consistent with a healthy, competitive industry.

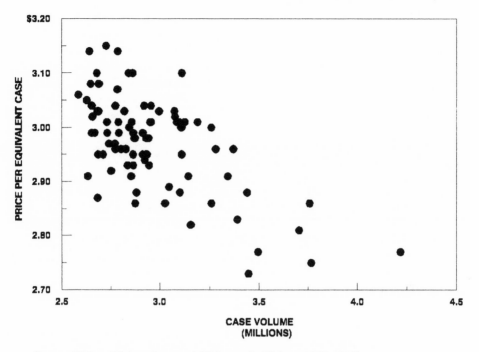

Source: Nielsen *Nielsen Scantrack* (Chicago, IL: Nielsen, 1987–1989).

**Figure 3–6. Pepsi 2-Liter Bottles, Price versus Volume, April 1987–
September 1989**

New Products

Another important way that carbonated soft drink firms compete is by developing new products. The 1989 Standard & Poor's Industry Survey concluded that the soft drink industry "continues to benefit from increased competition, much of which can be attributed to new products and flat pricing for about three years."[16] Another report noted that in 1988, the industry "continued to successfully market innovative products."[17] The 1985 *Beverage Marketing and Packaging Report* wrote that the

> U.S. soft drink industry historically has been characterized by continuous change and innovation. Its intense competitive climate required franchise companies to quickly respond to competitive activity, technological changes and evolving consumer tastes. . . . The rate of change within the industry has recently been accelerating, placing increased pressure and demands upon franchise company management. 1984 was a year marked by tremen-

Table 3–4
Regression Results: Volume on Price, Pepsi-Cola

Independent Variables	2-Liter Bottles	3-Liter Bottles	12-Ounce Cans, 12 Pack	12-Ounce Cans, Singles	16-Ounce Nonreturnable Bottles, Singles
INTERCEPT	17.88	15.49	18.70	17.65	15.92
OWN-PRICE	−2.75	−2.37	−3.27	−2.38	−2.54
	(−11.23)	(−17.16)	(−16.21)	(−25.72)	(−13.99)
RHO1	0.42	0.59	0.57	0.52	0.76
	(4.00)	(5.38)	(5.43)	(4.92)	(10.76)
RHO2	0.30	0.24	0.27	0.25	——
	(2.38)	(2.20)	(2.66)	(2.39)	——
R^2 adjusted	0.63	0.84	0.94	0.93	0.80
F-statistic	49.43	140.75	492.17	341.76	166.91

Note: T-statistics are listed in parentheses below the coefficient values.

Table 3–5
Regression Results: Volume on Price, Coca-Cola

Independent Variables	2-Liter Bottles	3-Liter Bottles	12-Ounce Cans, 12 Pack	12-Ounce Cans, Singles	16-Ounce Nonreturnable Bottles, Singles
INTERCEPT	18.35	15.98	18.60	18.12	16.96
OWN-PRICE	-3.41	-2.62	-3.26	-2.61	-3.21
	(-9.58)	(-10.06)	(-18.89)	(-27.18)	(-18.39)
RHO1	0.38	0.56	0.56	0.42	0.23
	(3.83)	(5.15)	(5.40)	(4.04)	(2.06)
RHO2	0.39	0.28	0.34	— —	— —
	(3.81)	(2.54)	(3.30)		
R^2 adjusted	0.65	0.74	0.95	0.93	0.84
F-statistic	52.96	81.79	576.04	609.20	221.53

Note: T-statistics are listed in parentheses below the coefficient values.

Table 3–6
Own-Price Elasticity Using Using Scantrack Data

Package Type	Pepsi Elasticity	Coca-Cola Elasticity
2-liter bottles	− 2.75	− 3.41
3-liter bottles	− 2.37	− 2.62
12-ounce cans, twelve pack	− 3.27	− 3.26
12-ounce cans, singles	− 2.38	− 2.61
16-ounce nonreturnable bottles, singles	− 2.54	− 3.21

dous change within the soft drink industry, with new flavors, ingredients, packaging, health claims, and advertising claims appearing every few weeks.[18]

New products introduced in the 1980s now represent over 20 percent of total carbonated soft drink sales.[19] Diet Coke was introduced in 1982; in 1988, it represented the third largest soft drink brand, with over 1 million gallons sold. PepsiCo's Slice was also a significant new product introduction. Diet drinks and caffeine-free products have changed the industry dramatically.[20]

Another area where the industry has experienced great change is in packaging. Plastic containers (2- and 3-liter bottles) were introduced in 1978 and now represent 32 percent of all sales of packaged products (see appendix B). The introduction of these new package types has resulted in lower prices for carbonated soft drinks.

Sales Patterns

Another area of interest was whether firms take sales away from each other. We initiated our analysis by reviewing the share of overall case sales (at all retail outlets, fountain, and vending) across the United States represented by a number of the larger producers of concentrate. The following list shows the change in share of case sales for each firm over the period 1981–1988 (these figures represent sales for all brands combined of the individual companies):[21]

> Coca-Cola, + 4.2.
>
> PepsiCo, + 3.0.
>
> Dr Pepper, − 0.3.
>
> Royal Crown, − 1.1.
>
> Seven-Up, − 1.3.

These share changes reflect the aggregate of all brands sold by each company and therefore mask a good deal of competitive give and take. A review of the sales history of certain individual brands over the same time period also exhibits divergent sales patterns (illustrated in appendix C). For example, a number of smaller brands have grown at a much higher rate than more established products. Squirt sales grew by 47 percent over the period, for instance, while the Seven-Up brand declined 2.9 percent. The A&W brand (owned by the company that sells Squirt) grew over 50 percent during this same time period.[22]

Even individual brand sales at the national level mask industry turbulence at the local and regional levels. Figure 3–7 reflects the change in share of sales through grocery and convenience stores (as measured by Nielsen) located in Chicago, for instance, over the period 1985–1988.

The situation in Chicago is not atypical, and because it reflects changes over a four-year period, it also masks competitive interplay. Table 3–7 reflects percentage changes in share of sales from one two-month period to another for San Francisco. These data are reflected graphically in figure 3–8.

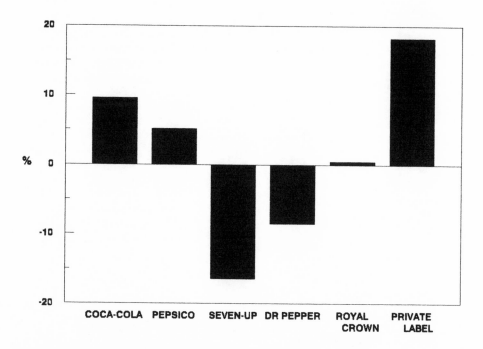

Source: Nielsen, *Nielsen Audit Data* (Chicago, IL: Nielsen 1985–1988).

Figure 3–7. Percentage Change in Share of Sales, Chicago, 1985–1988

Table 3–7
Percentage Change in Share of Sales, San Francisco

	PepsiCo	Coca-Cola	7Up	Dr Pepper	RC	Private Label
December 1984–January 1985	—	—	—	—	—	—
February–March 1985	4.13	3.17	−23.00	1.88	30.47	13.58
April–May 1985	−6.25	5.94	−2.22	−5.90	−21.52	−5.65
June–July 1985	9.07	−8.03	−15.93	−7.03	0.78	26.46
August–September 1985	−1.66	9.80	−5.74	2.73	−12.84	−9.83
October–November 1985	9.00	−1.08	6.87	6.64	1.63	−14.52
December–January 1986	−7.84	3.57	18.08	−6.50	16.45	16.72
February–March 1986	16.15	−2.42	−19.49	7.28	23.36	−11.26
April–May 1986	−1.90	−3.48	−8.02	−12.25	−1.35	20.92
June–July 1986	−5.16	−1.25	−12.82	−1.59	6.37	23.63
August–September 1986	−7.53	0.39	5.05	9.43	−1.74	0.75
October–November 1986	2.84	11.29	21.60	−1.56	−3.46	−29.84
December–January 1987	3.55	−7.30	8.60	−5.07	3.01	13.09
February–March 1987	4.75	2.93	12.82	22.08	29.94	−17.22
April–May 1987	−6.48	4.96	18.41	−11.55	−29.03	6.79
June–July 1987	5.18	−4.36	−17.90	−10.50	27.74	15.20
August–September 1987	2.14	4.59	2.03	−5.11	−26.91	−14.04
October–November 1987	−2.26	2.36	11.17	5.64	7.17	−17.11
December–January 1988	−4.00	−6.33	20.65	−4.54	61.52	21.00
February–March 1988	4.98	10.89	−25.65	11.24	3.65	−16.27
April–May 1988	−5.50	−8.13	6.60	5.33	13.80	37.83
June–July 1988	22.26	−2.85	−19.42	−22.63	−19.77	11.83
August–September 1988	−9.55	8.36	−6.32	1.53	−18.20	13.62
October–November 1988	−0.25	−6.91	0.68	18.16	−12.27	8.42
December–January 1989	0.80	4.92	13.00	−12.71	−25.63	−4.41
February–March 1989	−6.05	−2.16	−0.25	23.56	85.45	5.00
April–May 1989	6.50	1.04	−9.48	−14.84	−5.94	−21.24
June–July 1989	0.90	−9.31	4.24	4.01	17.88	34.71

Source: Nielsen, *Nielsen Audit Data* (Chicago, IL: Nielsen, 1985–1989).

PERCENTAGE CHANGE

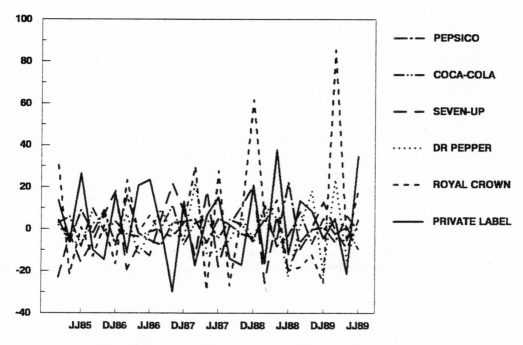

Source: Nielsen, *Nielsen Audit Data* (Chicago, IL: Nielsen, 1985–1989).

Figure 3–8. Percentage Change in Share of Sales, San Francisco

Such sales patterns are reflective of a healthy state of competition. (Appendix D contains similar examples from across the United States.)

PepsiCo versus Coca-Cola

The so-called Cola Wars are real.[23] The Cola Wars and the competitive ethic in the soft drink industry serve consumers well. The intense competition between PepsiCo and Coca-Cola, in particular, yields lower prices, greater product variety, reliable and safe products, ready availability of products, and good service for soft drink consumers. There is indeed a sociology of the executive suite that is relevant to competition in this industry.

Coca-Cola sells more total soft drinks in the United States than PepsiCo, primarily because of its substantial lead in the vending and food service channels. In supermarkets, however, the Pepsi-Cola brand is the most popular product, outselling its closest rival, Coca-Cola Classic, by some 10 percent.[24] Roger Enrico, president and chief executive officer of PepsiCo Worldwide

Beverages, has stated that PepsiCo's "long-term goal is to be the No. 1 beverage company in the country."[25]

Coca-Cola and PepsiCo's continual efforts to take sales from each other are successful. If share changes are analyzed on a bimonthly basis, Coca-Cola and PepsiCo are moving in opposite directions (when PepsiCo increased share, Coca-Cola lost share, and vice versa) 66 percent of the time (table 3–8). Moreover, many of the changes from one two-month period to the next are significant movements of 3 to 6 percentage points.

Coca-Cola and PepsiCo compete through price, packaging, advertising, and new product introduction, among other methods.[26] They are fierce competitors in grocery and convenience stores, which represent roughly 60 percent of total soft drink consumption, and also in the fountain and vending channels.

Table 3–8
Change in Share Performance, Coca-Cola versus PepsiCo,
December 1984–January 1985 through June–July 1989 (Bimonthly)

Nielsen Area	Total Number of Changes in Share	Coca-Cola and PepsiCo Share Movement	
		Same Direction	*Different Direction*
New England	27	11	16
New York/New Jersey	27	9	18
Philadelphia	27	10	17
Pittsburgh	27	7	20
Chesapeake	27	8	19
Cincinnati	27	10	17
Southeast Michigan	27	12	15
Out-state Michigan	27	12	15
Indianapolis	27	6	21
Chicago	27	9	18
Minneapolis	27	11	16
St. Louis	27	8	19
Charlotte	27	7	20
Orlando	27	10	17
Atlanta	27	3	24
South Texas	27	7	20
North Texas	27	13	14
Tulsa	27	7	20
Wichita	27	7	20
Seattle	27	9	18
San Francisco	27	14	13
Los Angeles	27	14	13
Denver	27	9	18
Phoenix	27	7	20
TOTAL	648	220	428

Source: Ibid.

Private Label and Regional Competitors

Private label brands are another competitive force in the soft drink industry. The following list shows the share of sales of private label brands in 1988 in specified areas:[27]

Buffalo, 17.6 percent.

Rochester, 16.6 percent.

San Francisco, 13.4 percent.

Denver, 12.4 percent.

Pittsburgh, 11.7 percent.

Nashville, 10.9 percent.

New York, 10.3 percent.

Philadelphia, 9.9 percent.

Los Angeles, 9.5 percent.

Chicago, 9.4 percent.

Other competitors play an important role in this industry on a regional basis too. For example, Shasta represented only 1.2 percent of total U.S. sales, as measured by Nielsen in 1988, but 5.0 percent in Seattle. Faygo represented 1 percent nationally in 1988 but over 10 percent in Detroit. Similarly, Big Red represented 4.7 percent in Louisville. (Big Red recently announced plans to expand into New England and other parts of the East Coast.) These data are reflected in table 3–9.

In addition to regional competitors, companies that sell on a nationwide basis are larger in certain geographic areas, as illustrated in table 3–9. For example, the Canada Dry brand has a 1.8 percent share of sales nationally but 3.7 percent in Rochester, 5.5 percent in New York, and 4.7 percent in Philadelphia. Similarly, Royal Crown has a 3.5 percent share nationally but garners 9.4 percent in Nashville, 8.1 percent in Chicago, and 7.9 percent in Louisville.[28]

Advertising

Producers of soft drinks use advertising in an attempt to generate demand for their products. Table 3–10 lists advertising expenditures per gallon for selected producers. These statistics represent expenditures by the concentrate producers for national media advertising; they do not include the substantial local feature advertising, supported by both the concentrate producers and bottlers.

Table 3–9
Regional Strength of Selected Competitors, 1988

Brand	Total U.S. Share	Nielsen Area	Share
Royal Crown	3.5	Nashville	9.4
		Chicago	8.1
		Louisville	7.9
Canada Dry	1.8	New York	5.5
		Philadelphia	4.7
		Rochester	3.7
Shasta	1.2	Seattle	5.0
		Los Angeles	2.3
		Fresno	2.2
Faygo	1.0	Detroit	10.2
		Out-state Michigan	7.6
		Buffalo	3.4
Sun-Drop	0.2	Charlotte	2.0
Big Red	0.2	Louisville	4.7
Vernor's	0.2	Detroit	5.7
Squirt	0.5	Out-state Michigan	2.4
		Detroit	1.8

Source: Ibid.

Consumers tend to switch from one product to another fairly frequently, suggesting that advertising does not create significant brand loyalty to products priced above competitive levels. Rather, media advertising is used to facilitate sale of the product when it is on deal at the local level.

Competition from Other Beverages

Carbonated soft drinks face competition from a broad range of alternative beverage products, each of which also uses price and marketing programs to gain sales, thereby adding to the intensely competitive nature of rivalry among producers of carbonated soft drinks.

Fountain and Vending

Less information is available concerning the sale of carbonated soft drinks to fountain and vending accounts than is available for grocery and other retail trade. The data suggest nevertheless that these segments also exhibit healthy competition.

Table 3–10
Advertising Cents per Gallon, 1982–1988

Year	Coca-Cola	PepsiCo	Dr Pepper/Seven-Up	Cadbury Schweppes	Royal Crown	A&W
1982	2.8	2.8	4.8	4.3	5.0	7.9
1983	3.5	3.5	5.5	5.0	4.9	6.4
1984	4.2	3.6	5.2	5.0	3.5	6.5
1985	3.8	3.9	5.2	5.7	2.9	6.0
1986	3.4	4.1	5.7	4.8	3.3	6.7
1987	3.2	4.0	6.1	3.7	3.2	4.9
1988	3.7	4.0	6.5	3.3	2.7	5.8

Source: "U.S. Soft Drink Market and Packaging Report, 1989," *Beverage Marketing* (August 1989): 240.

Fountain

Coca-Cola, with roughly 60 percent of carbonated soft drink sales, is by far the largest firm in the fountain area. PepsiCo has roughly 25 to 30 percent of fountain sales.

Competition for fountain accounts is intense.[29] One recent review concluded that the "fountain channel remains fiercely competitive" and is characterized by "significant everyday discounting to national and local customers."[30] Although price data on sales of soft drink fountain products are limited, the overall price increase for the producer price index (PPI) that includes fountain sales has risen at a much slower rate than overall inflation (as measured by the gross national product implicit price deflator).

Volume of fountain sales has risen at a faster pace than packaged sales, indicating a healthy growth record (table 3–11).[31]

Coca-Cola and PepsiCo also compete by the introduction and use of fountain equipment, such as service dispensers.[32] For example, in 1988 Coca-Cola introduced the Breakmate system, a soft drink dispenser designed for small offices (generally fewer than fifty employees). Coca-Cola claimed it placed 20,000 such units in 1988. PepsiCo countered with its Omnitron fountain machine, which offers advantages unavailable in competing machines, including quicker dispensing (without foaming), and control of the sweetness/syrup to carbonation ratio (ensuring a product more consistent with that offered in cans and bottles). Both Coca-Cola and PepsiCo spent millions developing these systems, with the investment designed to gain a greater share of overall fountain sales. Additional competition at fountain accounts is indicated by the increasing number of spigots at many fountain accounts and "free refill" programs, such as those at Burger King.

Table 3–11
Packaged and Fountain Gallonage, 1980–1988
(millions of gallons)

| Year | Packaged | | Fountain | |
	Actual	Percent Change	Actual	Percent Change
1980	6,555.6	————	1,892.3	————
1981	6,790.5	3.6	1,987.0	5.0
1982	6,987.6	2.9	2,088.3	5.1
1983	7,344.0	5.1	2,222.0	6.4
1984	7,752.1	5.6	2,421.2	9.0
1985	8,193.5	5.7	2,641.1	9.1
1986	8,557.4	4.4	2,786.4	5.5
1987	8,933.9	4.4	2,945.2	5.7
1988	9,317.5	4.3	3,096.2	5.1
Change, 1980–1988	2,761.9	42.1	1,203.9	63.6

Source: Ibid.

Carbonated soft drink companies appear to have little market power over the restaurants to which they sell fountain syrup. Chains such as McDonald's and Burger King are large enough that if PepsiCo, Coca-Cola, or any other soft drink firm tried to increase prices above competitive levels, the restaurants would switch suppliers or products.[33] These restaurants, in the business of satisfying the wants of consumers at low prices, have a strong incentive to search for alternatives to achieve that goal. Recently, for example, Burger King decided to switch to Coca-Cola from PepsiCo.[34]

If a fountain syrup supplier raises prices above competitive levels, the restaurant chain can quickly and with little cost switch suppliers. Besides switching to a syrup that consumers prefer or that is cheaper, the restaurant chain may wish to buy syrup concentrate from an independent flavor house and produce its own carbonated soft drink, as McDonald's does with its orange concentrate. McDonald's could, for example, create its own "McCola" if it believed that the development of such a brand would improve its overall competitive position.

Carbonated soft drinks also compete with other beverages in the fountain area—ice tea, coffee, milk, juices, milkshakes, hot chocolate and sometimes beer and wine. Thus, carbonated soft drinks must maintain a competitive relationship with alternative beverages in the fountain channel.

Vending

Coca-Cola and PepsiCo are the largest suppliers of soft drinks to the vending channel. Vending does include, however, firms other than PepsiCo and Coca-Cola. So-called third-party vending companies, such as ARA and Canteen Corporation, purchase soft drinks from bottlers and canners, own, place, and stock the machines, and sell to consumers. The owners of the property on which vending equipment is located usually receive a sales commission.

The growth of the vending industry over the past forty years indicates an industry that has served consumers well. Vending of soft drinks and other goods developed for the sole purpose of offering consumers convenience. The machines are placed in readily accessible locations, and products are offered in attractive and convenient packages. Recently, more attractive and efficient machines have become available, and they provide a wider selection than in the past.[35]

Soft drink sales through vending machines are being threatened by fountain accounts as improved machines that use a tap to dispense the soft drink are being installed in offices and similar settings in addition to and in place of vending machines. Some of this development is explained by improved dispensing machines.

Vending machine sales are also being adversely affected by the sale of competing beverages in vending machines, such as juice, tea, and lemonade.

Sometimes these other products are being supplied in vending machines previously dedicated to soft drinks and sometimes by separate machines that sell only one type of product—say, juice. William E. Buckholz of Goodman Vending Service, located in Pennsylvania, has seen lemonade outselling his leading soft drink and finds excellent results from juice products, particularly in 12-ounce cans. Similarly, Wayne Hood of Hood Services, located in California, recently stated that "juice is flying".[36] The competition between soft drinks and other beverages in the vending channel also says something about the relevant product market.

Profits

Like any other industry, the soft drink business is characterized by winners and losers. PepsiCo and Coca-Cola have been quite successful; Seven-Up has not fared well. The issue here is the reason for these successes and failures. Are soft drink profits the result of superior competitive performance or some monopolistic design? Our analysis of profits in the soft drink industry suggests the former.

The issue of profits in the soft drink industry is important. Later, we shall estimate a residual demand elasticity for soft drinks and use this elasticity to discuss whether soft drink firms, acting jointly, could profitably increase prices by 10 percent or less. Critical to this analysis is the use of soft drink contribution margins as a competitive benchmark from which to assess the costs and benefits of hypothetical collusive price increases. As documented throughout this study, the carbonated soft drink industry earns high marks for its competitive framework and good performance. This section shows by both factual and theoretical discussion that soft drink profits are generated by superior competitive performance.

Available Evidence

To gain some perspective on profits in the soft industry, we examined several sources of data.

SIC Food and Beverage Industries. Appendix E lists the median rate of return on sales, assets, and net worth for thirty-six four-digit SIC industry classifications that relate to food and beverages as reported in the *Dun and Bradstreet Industry Norms and Key Business Ratios* for 1987–1988. SIC 2086 and 2087 represent roughly the manufacturing and wholesale components of the soft drink industry. The rates of return for these classifications hover around average values in sales and assets but fall well below the average in net worth (table 3–12). Soft drink bottlers and concentrate producers show a slightly

Table 3–12
Industry Profit Data, 1987–1988

Median After-Tax Return	Extract Syrup (SIC 2087)	Bottling (SIC 2086)	Average for Thirty-six Four-Digit SIC Codes[a]
Sales	4.3%	3.0%	2.5%
Assets	5.7	4.7	5.4
Net worth	10.0	7.8	13.1

Source: *Industry Norms and Key Business Ratios* (Murray Hill, NJ: Dun & Bradstreet Credit Services, 1987 and 1988).

[a]Excludes SIC 2086 and 2087 and industries with a negative rate of return.

above average rate of return on sales, a rate of return approximately equal to average on assets, and a substantially lower than average rate of return on net worth. To the extent that data such as the SIC profit computations are to be taken into account (discussed below), soft drink bottling and concentrate producers appear to be approximately at or below the average of the various calculated rates of return for other food and beverage industries.[37]

Company-Specific Accounting Rates of Return. There is no question that Coca-Cola, PepsiCo, and certain other firms earn positive rates of return in the sale of carbonated soft drinks. Calculating company-specific rates of return, however, is difficult, particularly for Coca-Cola and PepsiCo. Both sell other products, so financial summaries derived from annual reports may not be particularly informative. PepsiCo had worldwide sales of over $13 billion and operating profits of almost $1.5 billion in 1988, but soft drinks represented only 36 percent of sales and 31 percent of operating profits on a worldwide basis.[38] Coca-Cola had worldwide net sales of $8.3 billion in 1988, with domestic soft drink sales representing $2.3 billion or 27 percent of this total, and 22 percent of Coca-Cola's operating income.[39]

With these limitations, we report the 1988 after-tax return on sales, assets, and stockholders' equity in table 3–13 for PepsiCo and Coca-Cola and for a category "food and kindred products."

These data are of limited use when addressing the issue of only carbonated soft drink profitability. However, they suggest that PepsiCo's performance is similar to the reported yardstick, while Coca-Cola does better.[40] Even this tentative statement assumes that one can infer economic or monopoly profits from accounting rates of return, an issue we discuss below.

Company-Specific Stock Market Rates of Return. To clarify company-specific performance, we used the CRISP tapes to calculate rates of return on holding the shares of individual companies for the years 1972 through 1986 and compared them to the Standard & Poor's (S&P) 500.[41] The annual rates of

Table 3–13
Company Profit Data, 1988

After-Tax Return	Coca-Cola	PepsiCo	Food and Kindred Products
Sales	12.4%	5.9%	5.5%
Assets	13.9	6.8	8.2
Stockholders' equity	31.0	24.1	21.0

Sources: U.S. Department of Commerce, *Quarterly Financial Report* (Washington, D.C.: Government Printing Office, 1988); Coca-Cola, *Annual Report* (1988); and PepsiCo, Inc., *Annual Report* (1988).

return show an investor's gain or loss on stock bought on January 1 of the given year and sold on December 31; it encompasses dividends and share price appreciation or depreciation. Table 3–14 presents the results year by year, as well as the summary statistics covering the whole period. Average return over the whole period, as well as the standard deviation of the average return (a measure of its variability), is given at the bottom of the table.

The average yearly rate of return for the S&P 500 computes to .0675. Over the same period, the yearly return from holding PepsiCo or Coca-Cola stock was .1435 and .1121, respectively. Thus, the two companies showed a higher than average rate of return for this period as compared to the S&P 500. Of course, financial markets determine a rate of return that is comparable across industries. However, the returns on the S&P 500 (or treasury bills) may only set a lower bound on what capital owners can receive for their investments. Such investments may offer relatively low returns compared to other investments but at much less risk. For more risk, investors can earn higher returns. Financial markets therefore do not necessarily set a normal rate of return for all industries.

It is instructive to note the performance of other companies over this same period. The table also reports the results for a variety of firms ranging from industrial firms, such as Exxon and Dow, to other food companies, such as General Mills and Hershey. In all cases, the rates of return from holding the other stocks exceeded that for PepsiCo and Coca-Cola. Thus, when placed in the context of competing with other companies, the two soft drink firms earn lower rates of return.[42]

Profits and Antitrust Analysis

The available evidence on profits in the soft drink business must be viewed carefully because interpreting profit data for antitrust purposes is a difficult task, with a number of factors to consider and assess.

Table 3-14
Annual Stock Returns for Selected Companies, 1972–1986

Year	S&P 500	PepsiCo	Coca-Cola	Exxon	Dow	General Mills	Hershey	Marriott	Ralston
1972	.1485	.2404	.2209	.2305	.2827	.4784	-.0953	.4011	.2713
1973	-.1782	-.1936	-.1284	.1410	.1977	-.1071	-.5181	-.5002	-.0154
1974	-.3287	-.4398	-.7517	-.2726	.0403	-.2118	-.0991	-.8508	-.0344
1975	.2864	.6147	.5214	.3960	.5580	.4416	.7711	1.0788	.2935
1976	.1814	.1693	.0114	.2576	-.0047	.1996	.2626	-.0888	.1456
1977	-.1180	.1055	-.0008	-.0397	-.4213	-.0756	-.0381	-.0844	-.1666
1978	.0184	-.0265	-.2260	.1072	.0250	.0292	.1215	.1059	-.1598
1979	.1220	.0360	-.1719	.2165	.3382	-.1056	.2699	.4291	.0463
1980	.2430	.1807	.0643	.4895	.1071	.1695	.0468	.6877	.0653
1981	-.0933	.3590	.1295	-.1476	-.1030	.3686	.5133	.1332	.2343
1982	.1543	.0729	.5093	.0753	.1219	.3861	.5196	.5394	.4678
1983	.1682	.1395	.1099	.3370	.3598	.1325	.1870	.2288	.5333
1984	.0219	.1734	.2163	.2907	-.0955	.0357	.2724	.0879	.3288
1985	.2390	.5796	.3593	.2888	.4695	.3939	.3423	.3854	.3224
1986	.1473	.1421	.3661	.3236	.4222	.4186	.4310	.3408	.4610
Average return	.0675	.1435	.1121	.1777	.1532	.1702	.1991	.1929	.1862
Standard deviation	.1706	.2545	.3051	.1982	.2512	.2260	.3047	.4514	.2167

Source: Center for Research in Security Prices, University of Chicago Business School, Chicago, IL.

Accounting versus Economic Profits. Accounting profits (like the SIC data) are not the same as economic profits and cannot be easily adjusted to conform to them. Capital owners have choices among possible investments. The potential return on these alternative investments generally must be covered in order for capital to remain employed in an industry. Accountants' balance sheets do not consider this so-called opportunity cost of capital as an item to be subtracted from profits. Instead, this part of the return to capital owners is included in the accountants' profit measure. The result is that accounting profits generally overstate economic profits.[43]

The extent to which accounting profits overstate economic profits generally cannot be determined by a simple formula. It is not sufficient to calculate some normal rate of return derived from the entire economy and then subtract this normal return from the accounting profit data in a particular industry to obtain economic profits. The normal competitive rate of return in any one industry may not conform to a normal return aggregated across all industries. The competitive rate of return in a specific industry depends on factors peculiar to that industry: the amount of capital used, the salvageability and substitutability of the capital, the relative riskiness of the investment, the type of capital used, the relative ability of the capital owners, and others.[44]

Clearly the data on profits for PepsiCo and Coca-Cola must be interpreted cautiously. We do not know the normal rate of return for this industry, so even high rates of return may result from such factors as the relative ability of the capital owners and managers in the industry. Understandably, however, the accounting rates of return most likely overstate the economic profits of these two companies.

Trademarks and Profits. One implication of the difference between accounting and economic profits is that even in the absence of monopoly power and market disequilibrium, profits may appear on the books of competitive firms. Such profits may arise not because of the exercise of market power by the firm in question but rather because of the treatment accorded to various assets of the firm under accepted accounting practices. One illustration of the tendency for accounting techniques to overstate the economic rate of return concerns the valuation of intangible assets such as goodwill, brand-name capital, or reputation. Such assets are typically assigned a minimum value on the firm's accounts, but the reputation of a firm is an important capital asset.

Intangible assets are clearly important for companies such as PepsiCo and Coca-Cola, which have invested heavily (and continue to do so) in their trademarks. The following analysis will show why standard accounting treatment of the PepsiCo and Coca-Cola brand-names, which generally ignores the capitalization or expensing over time of brand-name capital assets, will lead to an overstatement of the economic profits of these two firms.

To assess the consequences for profitability of this accounting practice, compare the rates of return earned by two representative firms—one that identifies the output it sells in a product-differentiated market by a company trademark (company A) and one that operates in an industry selling a homogeneous (undifferentiated) good (company B). In the absence of capitalization of the brand-name, company A earns accounting profits of 10 and has capital worth 25, with capital measured by original cost of equipment and other tangible assets minus depreciation. The accounting rate of return is accordingly 10/25, or 40 percent. Company B enjoys a seemingly lower rate of return of 20 percent (10/50).

In this situation, the firm selling a homogeneous product may have little incentive to advertise or engage in any other promotional activities because consumers are indifferent as to which seller they deal with. The trademark firm, however, will continually engage in advertising, promotion, and customer relations in order to keep its name before current and potential buyers. It makes these expenditures to establish and, later, to preserve the value of the firm's brand-name, an asset that may have taken years to build.

Expenditures to build goodwill and reputation represent capital invested in assets in the same way capital is invested for plant and equipment. Accounting practices recognize that a firm's reputation should be capitalized, but such assets are routinely assigned a minimum value such as $1 when the more accurate value to be assigned may be much more. In our example, if goodwill in reputation is worth, say, 25, then the trademark firm's (company A) rate of return should be 10/50, or 20 percent, the same as company B. This illustration shows the general problem of dealing with intangible assets in adjusting an accounting rate of return to reflect the appropriate economic magnitudes. Although such adjustments are straightforward in principle, in practice assigning values to the firm's brand-name capital and choosing an appropriate depreciation rate are difficult.

For trademark firms, therefore, accounting rates of return may provide little or no information about the relevant economic rates of return and may be misleading as a guide to assessing the presence or absence of market power.

Economic Profits in Competitive Disequilibrium. The presence of economic profits taken in isolation from other factors is not proof of monopoly. Economic profits can be indicative of a very dynamic industry in which firms are innovative and responsive to consumer preferences. For economic profits to be considered as evidence of monopoly, product demand and costs of production must remain constant for an extended period of time. Economic profits will equal zero only in an industry that has reached its long-run competitive equilibrium, by definition, a situation in which all firms have made optimal adjustments to demand and cost conditions. All firms are at the most cost-efficient size, and all entry and exit of firms have taken place so that all economic profits have been competed away. Thus, the presence of economic profits in an industry is not enough to infer monopoly power. One must also be able to say that the economic profits are accruing when the industry is in a state of long-run equilibrium. Innovation, for example, cannot be an aspect of industry behavior in long-run equilibrium.

In the absence of these auxiliary conditions, the presence of economic profits has a completely different interpretation. When demand and costs constantly change, no long-run equilibrium position can be attained. An increase in demand for the industry's product makes profits available to firms already engaged in production. An increased demand for a product such as carbonated soft drinks says that consumers value it more highly relative to other goods; they are, for example, willing to shift some income from other goods to purchase more carbonated soft drinks. As it becomes clearer to firms that consumers value their product more highly, incumbent producers will increase output, and new suppliers might enter the industry.

The profits will not go to all producers equally. Firms that are the most alert to higher demand for older products or demand for new products will innovate and respond first, and they will gain profits first. Profits in this case go to the firms that are best at recognizing and anticipating consumers' wants. In this dynamic setting of changing demand, firms with the most profits are the best competitors.

Similarly, firms that decrease costs by technological improvements can still receive the same price for their products as other firms. When other firms imitate the new technology, market supply increases, and profits will fall as the market price is driven down. As in the case of a demand shift, profits go first to firms that are best at reducing costs. These cost reductions eventually lead to lower prices for consumers.

The carbonated soft drink industry is characterized by dynamic demand and cost conditions and competition among producers. Profit opportunities exist because demand and costs are constantly changing, not as the result of a market in or near long-run equilibrium in which firms raise prices to monopoly levels to attain profits. The carbonated soft drink industry has responded many times to the desires of consumers. Indeed, many of the demand increases in the industry are due to innovation. For example, new brands are developed in an attempt to meet consumer preferences more effectively. The firms most sensitive to consumer desires have gained the highest profits over time by developing brands that consumers value the highest. In essence, the firms that found previously unmet demand located new profit opportunities by serving consumers better.

Carbonated soft drink firms' technological innovations in packaging also led to cost reductions. The fact that many consumers switched from other types of containers to plastic indicates that they valued the new containers more highly. The profits from this involvement in containers went first to the producers that were the earliest in developing the new packages. It is the alert firms that make profits in a dynamic competitive environment.

Far from symptoms of monopolization, profits play a vital role in a dynamic industry, such as carbonated soft drinks. The failure of New Coke is a primary instance. Firms in this industry cannot afford to produce Edsels or to have their products (in competition with other beverages) go the way of Pabst Blue Ribbon, for example, in the beer industry. Firms do not know with certainty that consumers will purchase a new type of product. They can only apply their best entrepreneurial foresight to what consumers will purchase. Without profits, they receive no reward for undertaking the risks and costs of product and technological innovation. In a dynamic industry, profit opportunities are not evils of monopolization; they are the driving force behind innovation. Firms that are the best entrepreneurs receive profits. Clearly, concentrate producers are not engaged in output restrictions. They are expanding output in old product lines and introducing new lines, behavior indicative of a situation where profits are playing a socially productive role.

Summary

The available evidence that we have adduced suggests that PepsiCo's and Coca-Cola's profit performances are based on their superior competitive performances. It is also true that this kind of behavior, over the history of both firms, has been correlated with an increase in the share of carbonated soft drink sales captured by both firms.

Some other producers of carbonated soft drinks are successful, and some are not, a further indication of the intense competition among carbonated soft drink producers.

Projections

The carbonated soft drink industry is characterized by healthy competition and good performance. Its future prospects appear bright; the available data suggest more growth, lower costs, and overall good performance for the industry, with the increase in per capita consumption of soft drinks projected to continue (figure 3–9).[45]

This section has focused almost exclusively on competitive activities within the carbonated soft drink industry. The next chapter will discuss how carbonated soft drinks interact competitively with other beverage products.

GALLONS PER CAPITA

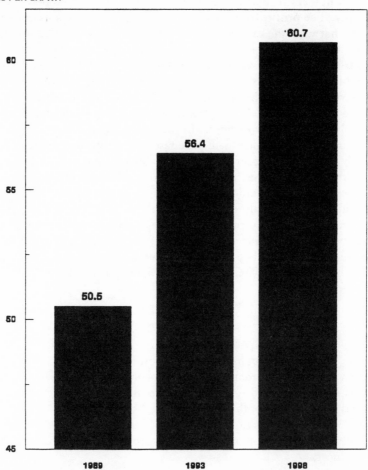

Source: *Beverage Marketing,* p. 295.

**Figure 3–9. Projected Per Capita Consumption of Carbonated
Soft Drinks**

Notes

1. "U.S. Soft Drink Market and Packaging Report, 1989," *Beverage Marketing* (August 1989): 192.
2. DWG Corporation, Form 10-K, August 3, 1989.
3. Cost information used in this analysis includes material and labor costs. Both cost items were for Standard Industrial Code 2086, which represents bottled and canned soft drinks.

4. Industry Surveys," *Standard & Poor's,* February 2, 1989, p. F-23. Another report suggests that certain nominal wholesale prices have actually declined in recent years. An article published in *Business Week* reported that Coca-Cola Enterprises' net wholesale prices declined 2.5 percent in 1987 and 2.5 percent in 1988. "Bottling Is Hardly a Classic for Coke," *Business Week,* December 11, 1989.

5. This time period represents the longest available trend on a consistent basis for the products listed.

6. *Beverage Marketing,* p. 138.

7. This is obviously a statement about relevant market discussed in more detail in chapters 4 and 5.

8. *Wall Street Journal,* May 13, 1985.

9. Concentrate producers generally provide funds for newspaper advertisements concerning special low prices, display space in the store, and other promotional activities. Bottlers generally share in these expenditures.

10. *Beverage Marketing,* p. 171.

11. "Promotions Add Fizz in Soft Drink Business," *Advertising Age,* August 15, 1985.

12. Royal Crown, *Annual Report* (1981).

13. These data are based on statistics published by Information Resources Inc. (IRI). This organization collects purchase data from approximately 40,000 households in twenty-seven metropolitan areas across the country. All data are based on purchases made in stores with scanner equipment.

14. The all-product "categories" reported by Information Resources Inc. in the *Marketing Factbook* represent products sold through grocery stores—carbonated soft drinks, coffee, tuna, pasta, ready-to-eat cereals, paper towels, and many others.

15. Some argue that CMAs exclude certain competitors or make competition more difficult. This issue is discussed in more detail in chapter 5.

16. "Industry Surveys," *Standard & Poor's,* February 2, 1989, p. F–15.

17. *Beverage Marketing,* p. xxi.

18. "U.S. Soft Drink Market and Packaging Report, 1985," *Beverage Marketing* (August 1985).

19. *Maxwell Report* (Richmond, VA: First Wheat Securities, 1989).

20. Diet drinks now represent almost 30 percent of total soft drink sales, up from 9 percent in 1972. *Beverage Marketing,* p. 41.

21. *Maxwell Report* (Richmond, VA: First Wheat Securities, 1989).

22. For a discussion of A&W's recent success, see "Root Beer Float," *Forbes,* December 11, 1989.

23. J.C. Louis and Harvey Yazijian, *The Cola Wars* (New York: Everest House, 1980).

24. Based on Nielsen Audit Data.

25. *AD Week,* May 26, 1986.

26. Recently, Ernst & Young dropped PepsiCo as an audit client as a result of an apparent conflict with Coca-Cola. PepsiCo had been an audit client of Arthur Young since 1965, which merged with Ernst & Young in 1989. Ernst & Young has audited Coca-Cola since 1921. Allegedly, Coca-Cola forced Ernst & Young to drop PepsiCo. *Wall Street Journal,* January 26, 1990.

27. Nielsen, *Nielsen Audit Data* (Chicago, IL: Nielsen, 1988).

28. Royal Crown has introduced plans designed to increase its national share of

carbonated soft drink sales from 3.5 percent to 8.0 percent in the next five years. "RC Ready for Laughs," *Advertising Age,* May 1, 1989.

29. Certain national accounts, such as McDonald's, are sold directly by PepsiCo or Coca-Cola, with individual locations serviced by local bottlers or distributors. Other accounts are sold directly by the bottler.

30. "Climb Every Fountain," *Beverage World* (February 1989).

31. Many are projecting that fountain sales will continue to grow. "The Fast Food Current," *Beverage World* (February 1988).

32. In September 1988 legislation was introduced in the U.S. Senate (S.2347) to prevent fountain and vending equipment giveaways, behavior labeled as anticompetitive in the proposed legislation. There has been an initial hearing on the bill but no subsequent action. A few small distributors testified that this practice harmed competition and excluded them from competing. The National Restaurant Association argued that the bill would raise retail prices. A Coca-Cola distributor explained that the equipment was loaned primarily to small accounts—those that probably could not afford the equipment to produce a quality product. The FTC did not support the bill because it did not view the giveaways as anticompetitive. Instead, they were seen as an additional way to discount prices. *Antitrust and Trade Regulation Report,* March 1, 1990.

33. In certain situations, the equipment the franchise companies use is leased from the bottler and/or concentrate producer; in others, it is owned by the franchise company or local retail establishment.

34. For a discussion of this episode, see "The Fast Food Corral," *Beverage World* (February 1988); and *Washington Post,* May 2, 1990. In 1986 Wendy's International announced a switch from PepsiCo products to Coca-Cola products in company-owned Wendy's stores. After a number of lawsuits concerning contractual issues, Wendy's decided to stay with PepsiCo products at company-owned stores (roughly 1,200 in number). Interestingly, the majority of Wendy's franchises (about 2,500 stores) use Coca-Cola products. See "Mending Fences: The Pepsi-Wendy's Relationship," *Beverage World* (February 1989).

35. In an effort to increase vending sales, concentrate companies may subsidize the purchase and placement of vending units by their bottlers.

36. *Vending Times* (May 1989).

37. These results for carbonated soft drinks are consistent with those published in 1986 by the National Soft Drink Association in a report entitled "Soft Drink Industry Financial Statistics." This report used Internal Revenue Service data to track profits at the bottling level for the years 1980–1983. The average after-tax returns for these years, as reported in this study, were 3.24 percent on sales, 6.60 percent on assets, and 14.11 percent on owner equity.

38. PepsiCo, Inc., *Annual Report* (1988). PepsiCo's soft drink data include both domestic and international sales.

39. Coca-Cola Company, *Annual Report* (1988).

40. A comparison of other years, such as 1987, results in similar findings.

41. CRISP stands for the Center for Research in Security Prices, located at the University of Chicago Business School. The CRISP tapes provide data on security prices, as well as certain aggregate information about security prices across stock exchanges.

42. These data are also rates of return before (individual) income taxes. Adjusting these figures for the tax consequences of holding the stocks from 1972 to 1986 and then selling them would cause rates of return on the soft drink stocks to fall further.

43. This problem of economic versus accounting profits persists whether profit levels or profit rates are used. Profits are often divided by sales, assets, or some other denominator to obtain profits as a percentage of something. Profit rates obtained in this way are subject to the shortcomings already identified.

44. For a discussion on this and related issues, see Franklin Fisher and John McGowan, "On the Misuse of Accounting Rates of Return to Judge Monopoly Profits," *American Economic Review* 73 (March 1983): 82–97; and Franklin Fisher, John McGowan, and Michael Greenwood, *Folded, Spindled, and Mutilated: Economic Analysis of U.S. v. IBM* (Cambridge: MIT Press, 1983).

45. *Beverage Marketing,* p. 295. See also Department of Commerce, *U.S. Industrial Outlook, 1989* (Washington, D.C.: Government Printing Office, 1989), pp. 39–24.

4
The Market Setting

A central question about the nature of competition in the carbonated soft drink industry is the degree to which soft drinks compete in a wider universe of beverages. In other words, what is the market for understanding the competitive process in the case of carbonated soft drinks? One response to this question is that carbonated soft drinks compete only with other carbonated soft drinks. This, however, is a testable hypothesis, and the tool kit of modern economics and econometrics offers the means to shed light on this important issue. Moreover, other types of data and information pertain to this issue.

Product Market

Economic common sense and empirical evidence strongly support the proposition that carbonated soft drinks compete with other beverage products. This section examines the evidence supporting this proposition. The discussion analyzes both qualitative factors, such as seller and buyer recognition of competing beverage products, and quantitative evidence, consisting of the estimation of a residual demand function for carbonated soft drinks.

Switching among Alternative Beverages

The consumption of soft drinks and other beverages has a demography indicative of competition among a broad range of beverages.

Quantitative Data. Share-of-intake (SIP) data represent consumer purchase diary information on consumption patterns of a wide range of beverage products. The SIP data are an extremely rich data set concentrating on the characteristics of individuals who consume beverages.

Among individuals who consume carbonated soft drinks, significant percentages drink a variety of other beverages: 48.9 percent coffee, 52 percent tea, 71.6 percent milk, 64.4 percent fruit juice, 36.8 percent fruit drinks, and 29.7 percent powdered soft drinks. (Moreover, a significant percentage of each of these beverage users also consumes carbonated soft drinks.) These data show no unique group of people in the economy who consume only carbonated soft drinks.

Every day consumers drink a variety of beverages, both at and away from home. This switching during a day illustrates competition among beverages. Table 4–1 (based on SIP data), which displays information on beverage consumption patterns during the course of a day, shows the interaction of carbonated soft drinks with other beverages at all times and occasions (for example, 12.8 percent of the individuals who consume a beverage before breakfast consume carbonated soft drinks). Moreover, this interaction has been increasing (table 4–2).

There are other examples of consumer switching among beverage categories during the course of a day. For example, most consumers keep a variety of beverages on hand to satisfy preferences for different drinks at different times. This beverage inventory naturally invites competition among beverages because purchases to stock the home inventory will be made in batches during trips to grocery stores. Comparison shopping and switching are promoted by such inventory trips.

Not all beverage consumption takes place at home. Eating out in the United States has increased as the opportunity cost of homemaker time rises and the female labor force participation rate increases. The Crest data, published by National Purchase Diary, which track beverage consumption away from home, confirm competition among beverages. At family-style restaurants, where coffee is consumed and is convenient to reorder, soft drinks have low shares of beverage consumption, for example, 20.6 percent at Big Boy, 11.1 percent at Denny's, and 20.5 percent at Lum's. At McDonald's and Burger King, by contrast, soft drink consumption ranks at or above 40 percent of beverage consumption.[1] Thus, beverage consumption is a function of where one goes out to eat; that is, beverages compete across places of sale.

Qualitative Data. A variety of related evidence indicates that other beverages feel competitive pressure from carbonated soft drinks. For example, industry analysts have increasingly come to view soft drinks as part of a larger beverage market. Impact Research, a marketing consulting firm, concluded that each of the beverages they studied, including carbonated soft drinks, is

> closely inter-related, each offering a refreshment alternative. For the truth of this statement, one has only to look at the effect of high coffee prices on tea sales, or the effect of white wine cocktails on distilled spirits, or notice someone at a party opt for a glass of sparkling water over either.

Table 4–1
Percentage of Individuals Consuming Beverages, Breakdown by Time of Day, 1988

Beverage Category	Before Breakfast	At Breakfast	Between Breakfast and Lunch	At Lunch	Between Lunch and Dinner	At Dinner	After Dinner	Late Night
Carbonated soft drink	12.8%	9.2%	41.4%	68.8%	67.6%	65.8%	61.2%	49.4%
Powdered soft drink	3.0	3.7	9.0	17.1	15.7	18.7	11.9	6.7
Iced tea	4.5	4.9	10.4	26.7	16.9	31.0	14.4	9.0
Fruit drink	6.5	11.5	10.2	17.1	14.4	12.0	11.0	6.2
Fruit juice	30.0	49.5	20.8	20.7	20.1	16.5	16.6	12.8
Coffee	50.0	44.1	37.7	21.8	20.0	19.6	18.7	15.9
Hot tea	7.4	9.2	7.5	7.8	6.2	8.3	7.4	6.7
Milk	17.3	44.3	15.0	44.5	19.0	46.6	25.7	24.0
Beer	0.9	0.2	1.9	4.5	11.8	10.0	13.5	15.8
Wine	0.3	0.2	0.6	2.0	4.4	8.3	4.0	4.9

Source: *Share of Intake Panel* (Greenwich, CT: Share of Intake Panel, 1988).
Note: The conclusions do not change if measured by total volume. See appendix F.

Table 4–2
Percentage of Individuals Consuming Carbonated Soft Drinks, Breakdown by Time of Day, 1980–1988

Year	Before Breakfast	At Breakfast	Between Breakfast and Lunch	At Lunch	Between Lunch and Dinner	At Dinner	After Dinner	Late Night
1980	7.5%	5.1%	36.0%	60.6%	64.7%	55.3%	57.9%	50.4%
1981	8.4	5.1	37.7	60.0	64.3	54.9	58.1	50.7
1982	8.9	6.5	36.9	62.4	65.0	57.6	58.4	51.5
1983	N.A.	N.A.	N.A.	N.A.	N.A.	N.A.	N.A.	N.A.
1984	9.6	7.1	39.4	64.6	67.2	60.4	60.4	49.2
1985	11.1	8.3	39.2	64.6	66.4	62.2	61.4	52.2
1986	12.2	8.7	42.3	67.6	67.7	63.7	60.5	52.6
1987	11.7	9.6	40.5	68.2	67.4	63.0	61.0	49.6
1988	12.8	9.2	41.4	68.8	67.6	65.8	61.2	49.4

Source: Ibid.

Note: N.A. = Not available.

Moreover, trends in marketing, product segmentation and advertising positioning tend to cross boundaries between beverage types. . . . Another example is the indication that health and diet considerations are playing an ever-expanding role in consumer buying decisions for all beverages.[2]

Bottled water and seltzer brands are increasingly competing more directly with carbonated soft drinks. Much of the recent growth in sales of carbonated water and flavored seltzers has come at the expense of carbonated soft drinks. Perrier claims to be "earth's first soft drink." A buyer for the Wetterau retail chain in Pittsburgh identifies a typical purchaser of bottled water and seltzer products as "most likely to be a parent who wants to give his or her child something a little better than plain soda."[3] At Marsh Supermarkets, located in Indiana, 13 percent of the soft drink department "is allocated to flavored seltzer and carbonated bottled water such as Perrier and Evian."[4] A representative of G. Heileman Brewing Co., which has sold La Croix and Cold Spring bottled water, finds that bottled water producers are "gaining soft drink users" and could not be "successful without them."[5] The *Beverage Industry Annual Manual (1989/1990)* concluded:

> Bottled water marketers are likely to receive increasing levels of competition from soft drink and fruit juice/fruit drink producers who will capitalize on the same health concerns that have promoted flavored waters. These companies have been introducing new fruit-flavored seltzers and new fruit juice and sparkling water products as well as increasing the "all natural" aspects of their existing products to compete more effectively in the multiple, U.S. beverage marketplace.[6]

Coffee sales, in contrast, have been declining for twenty to thirty years in the United States. George Boecklin, president of the National Coffee Association identifies soft drinks as the "reason that coffee has lost ground" and "that's been the trend for a long time."[7] Average daily coffee consumption peaked in 1962 at 2.12 cups a person but is now down to roughly 1.70 cups. Industry officials, particularly stung by the loss of students and other young consumers as coffee drinkers, have been developing strategies to interest younger consumers in coffee (coffee houses in college student unions, for example).[8] The interaction between coffee and other beverage products, particularly carbonated soft drinks, is further highlighted by a comparison of consumption trends across beverages reported in a study published by the International Coffee Organization. Particularly illuminating is a chart which shows the degree to which coffee consumption has fallen and carbonated soft drink consumption has risen since 1960.[9]

The increasing competition between coffee and carbonated soft drinks is highlighted by attempts by both Coca-Cola and PepsiCo to increase soft drink consumption in the morning—Coca-Cola through its "Coke in the morning campaign" and PepsiCo through a similar program and Pepsi A.M., an extra-caffeine cola aimed at morning consumption that it began test marketing in 1989. Jorge Cardenas, general manager for the National Federation of Coffee Growers in Colombia, recently stated: "As we all know, breakfast is the time when close to 48 percent of coffee is consumed. If the soft drink campaigns succeed, the effect on coffee consumption could have grave repercussions." And a major coffee broker concluded that "if there is any degree of success and more soft drink companies join in, an industry-wide movement could be a real threat."[10] Steven L. Gregg, program coordinator for the Coffee Development Group, is concerned about these efforts; the "fact that Coke is promoting cola in the morning will only serve to boost its position in that segment and take [sales] away from coffee."[11] And Boecklin, in a 1988 speech, concluded that the soft drink morning campaigns are a "serious threat" and a "frontal attack to the very heart" of the coffee industry.[12]

Milk is in a similar position. In the summer of 1986, the American Dairy Association (ADA) attempted to convince the FTC to alter a consent order restricting the ADA's ability to advertise the nutritional value and fat content of milk. In support of its petition, the ADA argued that over the last ten years, soft drink advertising claims had become increasingly vital marketing tools and that "such claims have made these beverage products increasingly competitive substitute items for milk."[13] Roger W. Miller, a beverage analyst, concluded that an "important factor in milk's drop in popularity is competition from other beverages, especially soft drinks, which are now America's favorite type of beverage."[14]

The dairy industry is attempting to develop new products to compete with other beverages, including carbonated soft drinks:

> IN THE FUTURE . . . Both new packaging and products may influence the traditional consumption of milk. Brick-shaped cartons—called "aseptic" packaging—enable consumers to easily carry milk to events such as picnics and outings. One possible new product is a carbonated, flavored milk drink, which would contain the same nutritional benefits of skim milk and be available in a variety of fruit flavors.[15]

Powdered soft drinks represent a similar competitive situation. Much of powdered soft drink consumption comes at the expense of carbonated soft drinks. Kool-Aid is marketed as the nation's "third largest selling soft drink brand," with direct comparisons to Pepsi and Coca-Cola. Crystal Light is marketed in much the same way, with direct comparisons to soft drinks. The interaction of ice tea products (representing some 80 percent of all tea consumption) and carbonated soft drinks is similarly obvious: "Companies like Lipton and Tetley offer single-serve teas with sugar or NutraSweet, in cans or glass bottles, to compete with soft drinks and juices in vending, convenience store and other typical single-serve sales opportunities."[16] Nevertheless, powdered soft drinks are losing sales because of the "aggressive promotional and pricing environment generated by the soft drink industry"; "with the forecast of continued price wars and increased consumption in the soft drink segment the powdered beverage industry will probably see both volume and dollar declines in 1989."[17]

Juice and juice drinks products have been marketed directly against soft drinks for years, with some success: "Consumers seem to want convenience without sacrificing quality, and the juice industry is getting better and better at achieving this. Refrigerated, ready-to-drink juices are gaining shelf space in the dairy cases of supermarkets and single serve cans and bottles of juice are making inroads in vending and convenience stores, right next to soft drinks."[18] Of increasing competitive significance are sales of juice drinks in single-serve, aseptic packages, which grew 17 percent in 1988. These drinks are popular with children and sell as three packs for as little as 69 to 79 cents.[19]

Are these developments in the broader beverage category relevant to PepsiCo and Coca-Cola? Obviously the two companies pay most attention to one another. Historically and currently, this has resulted in intense competition between them. But this is by no means the end of the matter. Data on consumer purchases of all beverage products are quite important to the soft drink leaders. It is from such data that they can attempt to divine the existing state of consumer behavior with respect to beverages and the future of beverage consumption.

In a variety of fundamental ways, carbonated soft drink companies keep track of, monitor, and conduct research on other beverage products. They behave in a manner that indicates they compete with other beverage products.[20] Competition is a fact of life among beverage companies, as Donald Keough, president and chief operating officer of Coca-Cola, observed in 1976: " 'We must never forget that the real competition facing soft drinks is first and foremost other types of liquid refreshment.' "[21]

Growth of Carbonated Soft Drinks

Figure 4–1 suggests that soft drinks have been growing at the expense of other products. Explaining this trend in beverage consumption involves some assumptions about physiology. If consumers are simply drinking more liquids over time, the growth of a beverage category such as carbonated soft drinks can be purely incremental. No doubt there is some tendency in this direction. But most observers think the growth of carbonated soft drinks has been at the expense of other sources of liquid refreshment, such as coffee, milk, and water. In other words, there has been both growth in aggregate beverage con-

PERCENTAGE CHANGE

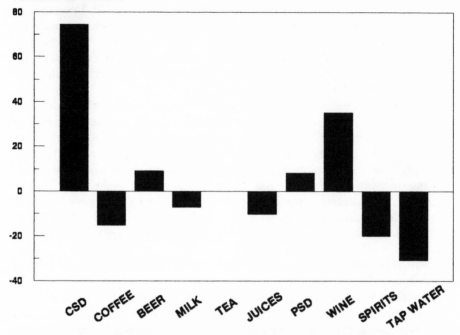

Source: *Maxwell Report* (Richmond, VA: First Wheat Securities, 1985, 1989).
Notes: CSD = carbonated soft drinks; PSD = powdered soft drinks.
   The time period reflected is the longest for which consistent data are available. Tea remained flat over this period. SIP data also show this substitution. Over the period 1985–1988, carbonated soft drinks increased their share of consumption of all beverages—almost 3 percentage points—while, for instance, milk lost 1.3 percentage points and hot tea 2 percentage points. See appendix G.

Figure 4–1. Percentage Change in Per Capita Beverage Consumption, 1975–1988

sumption over the last twenty years and switching among beverages. The latter clearly shows competition among beverages.

Fundamentally, competition and demographic changes are the basic causes of change in beverage consumption patterns over time. Competition focuses on the relative prices and qualities of beverages. If carbonated soft drinks are heavily discounted (they are), they will gain sales at the expense of other beverages. If carbonated soft drinks are of better quality than competing beverages ("Don't drink the water!"), they will gain share points in the market. Liquid is liquid; consumers will shop for low-cost, flavorful liquids.

Demographic changes also play a role in beverage consumption. As the population gets older, carbonated soft drink consumption may decline as older people increasingly choose other beverages. However, will the carbonated soft drink industry become "grayer," as younger soft drink consumers carry their drinking habits with them into old age as recent evidence suggests?

The future is unknown to beverage producers, as it is to all other producers. Will soft drink consumption continue to rise? Will coffee consumption continue to fall? Evolving tastes and preferences make it imperative for beverage companies to keep abreast of the market with research and development, consumer surveys, and other methods. This process of identifying what people want to drink cuts across all beverages and goes to the heart of the survival of these companies. To survive and to prosper, they must compete against all participants in the beverage market.

New Product Developments

A beverage can be defined by various characteristics. A carbonated soft drink, for example, can be defined by such features as carbonation, taste, color, sweetness, flavor, and caffeine. The nature of research and development and marketing in the soft drink business is to find a successful combination of these characteristics. At the same time, however, it is impossible to identify a carbonated soft drink in terms of its basic characteristics without intersecting and overlapping with the characteristics of other beverages—for example, the caffeine in coffee and in some carbonated soft drinks.

Only by looking at the multitude of characteristics inherent in the products is one able to define the breadth of the market. One characteristic common to all members of the beverage market is that they are liquids, indeed, mostly water. In the most general sense, then, one beverage is a substitute for another as an alternative source of water. But we can also look at the bundle of other characteristics that define each beverage.

Carbonated soft drinks compete not just against themselves but also against other beverages with some of the same characteristics. Consider PepsiCo's introduction of Slice, a carbonated soft drink line with real juices. In a limited sense, Slice competes only with other juice-added carbonated soft drinks; in the larger sense, Slice competes with other soft drinks and other beverages as well. Because of its juice content, Slice competes with fruit juices and fruit drinks, including Kool-Aid and other powdered drinks. And because it is also marketed as a diet drink, it competes with other diet and health drinks. In other words, Slice is a beverage, possessing certain characteristics, in competition with other beverages possessing similar characteristics.

Every carbonated soft drink has a flavor characteristic. Slice has orange and lemon-lime flavors. Lemon-lime Slice competes with other lemon-lime soft drinks (Sprite, Seven-Up, Bubble Up, Faygo, Shasta, SoHo, Rock Creek, and others), powdered soft drinks in lemon and lime flavors (Kool-Aid, Wylers, Country Time, Cragmont, and others), lemon and lime juice drinks

(HiC, lemonade, limeade, Lemon-lime, Ssips, and others), bottled waters flavored with lemon and lime (Perrier, Poland Spring, and others), and tea with lemon and lime flavors (Nestle Ice Teasers, Twinings, Lipton Herbal Tea Lemon Soother, and others).

The point is that beverages possess a multitude of characteristics, and it is these characteristics in certain combinations that consumers desire. The line defining the beverage market is blurred; substitution occurs over many, if not all, beverage characteristics.

How important is this blurring phenomenon? Today, trademarks once associated only with juices (Minute Maid, Sunkist) appear on carbonated soft drinks. Carbonated soft drinks are vitamin enriched (Squirt, Minute Maid) and decaffeinated (Pepsi Free) to compete with other beverages for health-conscious consumers. Traditional distinctions among beverages have virtually disappeared: juices are carbonated (Popple, Apple Annie Soda Juice); bottled waters are fruit flavored (Perrier, Geyser, Poland Spring); carbonated soft drinks contain juice (Slice, Minute Maid, Orangina); tea is mixed with juice, both liquid (Knudsen Mint Tea Cooler) and powdered (Crystal Light Fruit Tea); coffees are flavored (General Foods International Coffee) or sold as iced coffee; carbonated soft drinks contain coffee flavors (Manhattan Special); milk contains fruit flavors; and wine is mixed with fruit juice and carbonated water to make wine coolers. All of this blurring and mixing is strong evidence of competition among beverage producers across a spectrum of beverage characteristics.

Targeting of Advertising Messages

The print and television advertising of beverage companies reflects competition among beverages. The advertising has a similarity of execution and message that is astounding: sellers clearly believe that buyers perceive beverage products as substitutes for one another.

Directly Comparative Advertising. Much of beverage product advertising is directly comparative; that is, the virtues of competitive beverage products are referred to explicitly. In one of the most striking ads in this category, a bike rider/racer has worked up a sweat on the road. He rides up to a vending area, first passing Coca-Cola and Pepsi machines and shaking his head slowly in the negative. Then he pulls up to a juice vending unit, has a delicious drink of juice, and jets off on his bike. The message is that health-conscious consumers are switching to juice from carbonated soft drinks; juice competes with carbonated soft drinks. (This and other examples of direct comparative advertising are included in appendix H.)

Powdered soft drinks also use explicitly comparative advertising to compete with carbonated soft drinks. For example, General Foods uses advertising that presents vague images of Coke and Pepsi in the background of a pitcher of Kool-Aid. The advertisement also asks rhetorically, "Guess who's the third largest-selling soft drink in America?" and then lists reasons why Kool-Aid is so successful in competing with Pepsi and Coke ("no caffeine" and "only 1/2 the price of soda"). Other advertisements for Kool-Aid highlight the competition between Kool-Aid and carbonated soft drinks—Mother says "I could open a soda, but they wouldn't get those fruity flavors and Vitamin C" and "Soda is about twice the price"—and Crystal Light uses pictures of diet soft drinks when marketing its product.

The advertisements for Perrier are strongly comparative in nature, positioning Perrier as "earth's first soft drink."

Similarity of Message and Execution. Beverage ads are highly similar in design, message, and execution. Advertisements for diet beverage products emphasize health and weight control. Those for such products as Crystal Light and diet soft drinks are essentially trying to reach the same consumers: weight-conscious adults.

A large number of beverage advertisements are set in or near water as a backdrop or prop. The idea being conveyed is clearly liquid refreshment. And these examples are but the tip of the iceberg. Close examination of beverage advertisements reveals even more commonalities of approach, suggesting an intense degree of competition among beverages.

Competition in Beverage Outlets

A person can buy or consume beverages at a number of locations—restaurants, grocery stores, convenience stores, vending machines, and others. And at each location, a variety of choices is available.

Restaurants. All restaurants offer a multitude of beverages, typically at comparable prices and grouped together on the menu. The choices available vary by type of restaurant. For example, at a fast food chain, selections include soft drinks, juice, coffee, tea, milkshakes, milk, and water. Other restaurants offer beer, wine, and alcoholic drinks.

Grocery Stores. Grocery shoppers are faced with a different decision than when going to a restaurant. They usually consume the product not at the point of purchase but at another location, typically the home. In other words, the consumer makes an inventory decision, stocking up on beverage products to be consumed at a later date at a different locale.

Grocery stores stock a diverse selection of beverages consumers can purchase for later consumption. All beverages in a store may not be stocked in one specific area. Soft drinks, mineral water, fruit drinks, iced tea, and low-alcohol beers may well be found on one aisle; in the refrigerated section are found milk and cartons of fruit juices and drinks; in the freezer section are found frozen juices and drinks; another area of the store may be stocked with powdered soft drinks such as Kool-Aid, Crystal Light, and Wyler's Lemonade.

Although beverages are found throughout the store, their prices are clearly posted and can be easily compared. Moreover, products such as juices and powdered soft drinks, among others, are increasingly found in the same aisle as carbonated soft drinks. In most convenience stores, carbonated soft drinks are sold along with other beverages in the same cooler.

Vending Machines. In the vending channel of beverage sales, the trend is toward a more competitive choice. In earlier years, many vending machines that dispensed soft drinks were isolated. Today, vending machines are more and more contained in clusters. Those that dispense carbonated soft drinks are placed together with machines for fruit juice, fruit drinks, an assortment of milk products, coffee, and iced tea. The wider assortment of beverage vending machines is a reflection of a competitive beverage market.

Packaging and Distribution

The competition among beverages is further manifested in the similarity of packages in which they are sold. The following examples underscore the competition among beverages to position themselves, through packaging, as alternatives. Carbonated soft drinks, fruit punch, lemonade, and fruit juice are sold in 12-ounce containers. Producers of powdered drinks, like Crystal Light and Lipton Fruit Tea, also pack their products in containers that appear to be 12 ounces. Carbonated soft drinks, fruit drinks, bottled water, and even wine coolers are sold in 2-liter plastic containers. Increasingly, juices are being sold in single-serve containers—both glass bottles and aseptic packages—in direct competition with carbonated soft drinks.

The way products reach retail markets can indicate to some extent the degree of competition among them. There are many avenues to retail markets, such as food brokers and beverage distributors, and in virtually all cases, channels of distribution are populated by multiple beverages.

Production of Beverage Products

Soft drinks bottlers produce other beverages in addition to carbonated soft drinks.[22] Each year, a trade show, InterBev, attracts beverage producers from around the world. Examination of the exhibits and literature generated by these trade shows demonstrates that many beverage producers share similar competitive interests and that certain producers utilize the same or similar equipment. Many brewers are producing nonalcoholic beers, distillers are expanding into soft drinks, soft drink bottlers are developing fruit juices, and fruit juice producers are adding bottled water. In economic terms, this trend means that supply-side substitutability across beverage products is increasing, intensifying the competition in the industry.

Statistical Analysis

We now turn from qualitative to quantitative analysis. Statistical analysis of the product market issue is pursued using a microeconomic data set. Using the Nielsen data and data from public sources, the analysis estimates a residual demand function for carbonated soft drinks. Residual demand analysis provides a conceptual framework for econometric market definition in antitrust analysis. In this section, statistical estimation of residual demand coefficients is used to provide evidence of the scope of the product market containing carbonated soft drink firms. The statistical estimates suggest that collusion among carbonated soft drink firms would not be profitable because of competition from a variety of noncarbonated substitute products.[23]

The statistical results that follow must be seen in the light of the discussion of the qualitative aspects of the product market. The statistical results are basically a corroboration of what common sense and qualitative evidence suggest. The statistical results are also consistent with other quantitative evidence. For example, the statistical results discussed below are consistent with the beverage substitution patterns observed using the SIP and Crest data sets. These statistical results therefore support the conclusion to which all the other evidence points: that an analysis of competition cannot be limited to carbonated soft drinks.

Residual Demand. The concept of residual demand is best explained by contrasting it with ordinary demand. Ordinary demand relates the rate of consumption of a particular commodity (or group of commodities) and the price of the commodity, holding constant the prices of substitute commodities and other demand factors. The own-price elasticity of demand that results from statistical estimation of ordinary demand measures the percentage volume loss that would result when the own commodity's price is raised by a hypothetical percentage if other demand factors—particularly the prices of substitute commodities—remained unchanged.

In contrast, residual demand relates a commodity's rate of consumption and price while allowing for the competitive responses of suppliers of substitute products. Specifically, substitutes' prices are not held constant as own-price elasticity is estimated. Thus, own-price elasticity of residual demand measures the percentage volume loss that would actually result when price is raised by a hypothetical percentage. Residual demand elasticity measures actual volume loss because estimation of residual demand elasticity subsumes the actual pricing response of competitive products.

Because residual demand elasticity measures the ability to raise actual price, residual demand elasticity is important to market definition. For example, the *Department of Justice Merger Guidelines* prescribe a hypothetical price test for market definition. The hypothetical scenario asks whether currently competing suppliers acting jointly could profitably raise prices by a small but significant amount (such as 5 to 10 percent) above competitive levels. In the example that follows, we assume market performance at the competitive level.

Suppose ordinary demand elasticity at the competitive price were known to be equal to −2.5 for the products in a provisional market. Based on an elasticity of −2.5, the suppliers as a group could achieve a 10 percent price increase but only at the expense of a 25 percent volume loss, provided the prices of substitute products not included in the provisional market remained constant. Often firms' contribution margins are sufficiently high so that even when the market is performing well, the loss of income net of variable cost over 25 percent of the volume in the provisional market would exceed the gain from a 10 percent premium over the competitive price for the remaining volume sold. Thus, if the magnitude of the ordinary demand elasticity were the appropriate criterion, the provisional market may be defined too narrowly in our example.

In the example, however, if prices were raised 10 percent in the provisional market, demand would shift to substitute products. Under some forms of competitive interaction, the increase in demand for these substitute products would lead their suppliers to raise their prices. This competitive response would feed back to the provisional market, raising the demand for the products there. The demand elasticity that more correctly predicts the volume response to the hypothetical price increase is thus residual demand elasticity, not ordinary demand elasticity.

In our example, residual demand elasticity may equal only −1.5, while ordinary demand elasticity is significantly more elastic. An elasticity of −1.5 may in fact be small enough relative to applicable contribution margins to justify treating the provisional market as a relevant market for competitive analysis. The critical residual demand elasticity depends on the specific circumstances of the case. Without case-specific evidence, one can only say that residual demand elasticity generally will be smaller (in absolute magnitude) than ordinary demand elasticity.

Residual Demand and Market Definition. There is substantial evidence that consumers switch among cola brands, among colas and flavored carbonated soft drinks, and among carbonated soft drinks and other beverages. The important issue for market definition is the volume of product sold to marginal or swing consumers, given a provisional market. Doubtless some consumers have acquired a taste for Coke Classic ("old Coke") and would not switch from it if its price were 25 percent higher. Just as certain, however, is that some consumers will buy the cheaper of Pepsi and Coke brand colas, that some consumers will buy the cheapest of products available, and that others will switch to noncarbonated products depending on relative price. Residual demand analysis estimates the actual extent of substitution between one product group and others.

In the empirical section below, we estimate the residual demand for all carbonated soft drinks to determine whether all such suppliers together could profitably raise prices a significant percentage.[24] The market definition test is implemented in the following way. The first step is to estimate the elasticity of residual demand for all carbonated soft drinks. We then calculate the profitability of a 10 percent price increase: residual demand elasticity for carbonated soft drinks implies an overall volume restriction necessary to raise average prices 10 percent. If all suppliers jointly restricted volume by the necessary amount, income would be foregone on the units not sold. The latter is estimated based on the average percentage contribution margin on carbonated soft drink units sold in the competitive situation and the volume restriction evaluated at the average competitive market price. The gain from restricting output is the price premium (10 percent of the competitive price) times the volume sold at the higher price. If the net gain is negative, the provisional market of all carbonated soft drinks is too narrowly defined.

Two fundamental issues underlie application of the market definition exercise. First, since the profitability of a joint price increase depends critically on the size of the percentage price increase used in the test, the magnitude of the critical price increase is important to market definition. We therefore use a number of different test levels in our analysis. The second issue concerns the current state of competition among carbonated soft drink suppliers. The current state is important because it is the benchmark against which the profitability of hypothetical collusion among suppliers is assessed.

Based on the evidence we have presented so far, it is our opinion that the carbonated soft drink industry is competitive. Thus, in our implementation of the market definition test, we use an estimate of the current percentage contribution margin that in our opinion reflects competitive returns in the soft drink industry. By using existing contribution margins to evaluate the cost of a joint price increase, we are not assuming that the carbonated soft drink industry is perfectly competitive. Our study of this industry suggests that competition here is an example of competition among brands differentiated to varying degrees in the eyes of consumers with different tastes. However, sufficient numbers of consumers view carbonated soft drinks as perfectly substitutable so that no brand or brands can command a price significantly in excess of marginal cost.[25]

Statistical Estimation of Residual Demand. To determine whether all carbonated soft drinks (CSDs) is a relevant product market, we estimated the inverse residual demand function for all CSDs sold in the United States.[26] We specified a log-linear regression model and applied a two-stage least-squares estimation method.

To replicate statistically the residual demand experiment already described, we included cost variables for several non-CSD categories among the demand shifters. These cost variables include cost factors specific to non-CSD production and distribution and cost factors common to CSD and non-CSD supply. For example, since sucrose is used in making CSDs as well as in making powdered soft drinks, fruit drinks, and juices and is complementary to tea and coffee consumption, the price of sucrose must be included in the residual demand for CSDs. In contrast, the hourly earnings of brewery workers, which is specific to non-CSD production, is included to hold constant beer marginal cost. To complete the residual demand experiment, we included several CSD-specific cost variables in the first-stage regression but not in the residual demand for all CSDs.

Nielsen Scantrack data provide actual dollars and volume purchased in Nielsen's sample of supermarkets for numerous brands, package sizes, and brand characteristics (diet, decaffeinated, and so on).[27] For the several product groupings defined, we created a weighted average price by dividing dollars by 192-ounce case-equivalent volume for overall carbonated soft drinks. Nielsen Scantrack prices reflect the retail price as scanned by a computer used by the retailer. The price data Nielsen used represent weekly observations beginning April 4, 1987, and ending September 2, 1989.

Consumers purchase CSDs from drugstores, convenience stores, "mom and pop" grocery stores, and supermarkets, the last representing the large majority of CSD sales made through those channels. (Nielsen Scantrack surveys only supermarkets.) CSDs are also sold to final consumers through fountain services at restaurants and bars and from vending machines. Although our statistical demand analysis is based on supermarket sales alone, there is no reason to expect the relevant market containing fountain and vending sales of CSDs to be any narrower than the relevant market containing retail sales of CSDs. At restaurants, patrons typically have the same variety of beverage options as they do in supermarkets, and in vending areas, consumers can buy coffee, fruit drinks, and fruit juices, as well as CSD products.

Following is a list of the definitions and sources of the data used to estimate residual demand for several regression variable categories (all variables except the seasonal variables are included in the regressions as logged variables):[28]

Direct Demand Factors

1. *USSUMDUM:* A dichotomous seasonal variable for the United States. May through September is designated as summer.

2. *ETOTALL:* The monthly average of weekly earnings for all manufacturing workers in the United States. Source: Bureau of Labor Statistics.

Non-CSD and Common Cost Factors

3. *WKBEARN:* The U.S. average weekly earnings of brewery workers (monthly). Source: Bureau of Labor Statistics.

4. *WKGRDIST:* The U.S. average weekly earnings of grocery distribution workers (monthly). Source: Bureau of Labor Statistics.

5. *PBEERCAN:* The U.S. producer price index (PPI) for beer cans (monthly). Source: Bureau of Labor Statistics.

6. *PFRJCAN:* The U.S. PPI for fruit juice cans (monthly). Source: Bureau of Labor Statistics.

7. *FCOFFEE:* The U.S. futures prices index for coffee beans (monthly). Source: George Gordon Paton & Co., Inc.

8. *AAPPLES:* The U.S. futures price index for apples (monthly). Source: U.S. Department of Agriculture.

9. *PCANESUG:* The U.S. PPI for cane sugar (monthly). Source: Bureau of Labor Statistics.

CSD Cost Factors

10. *WCSDEARN:* The U.S. monthly average weekly earnings of CSD bottling workers. Source: Bureau of Labor Statistics.

11. *PCSDCAN:* The U.S. PPI for CSD cans (monthly). Source: Bureau of Labor Statistics.

12. *PKOLA:* The U.S. PPI for cola concentrate (monthly). Source: Bureau of Labor Statistics.

A priori, the direct demand variables, *ETOTALL* and *USSUMDUM,* are predicted to have positive coefficients. The cost variables are also predicted to have positive coefficients.

Statistical Results. Table 4–3 reports the coefficient estimates for inverse residual demand for all CSDs in the United States.[29] From it we see that the regressors as a group explain a significant amount of the variation in the dependent variable.[30] More importantly, the coefficient for CSD volume is statistically significant.[31] The residual demand elasticity estimated for the United States is − 6.00.[32] The large magnitude of residual demand elasticity

Table 4–3
Regression Coefficient Estimates, All Carbonated Soft Drinks Residual Demand

	Total U.S.
Constant	10.503
	(4.98)
CSD volume	−0.166**
	(−8.24)
USSUMDUM	0.012
	(1.61)
ETOTALL	0.388
	(0.94)
WKBEARN	0.298**
	(3.02)
WKGRDIST	−1.534**
	(−3.26)
PBEERCAN	−0.305
	(−1.61)
PCANESUG	0.263
	(1.04)
AAPPLES	−0.015
	(−1.11)
FCOFFEE	0.018
	(0.28)
PFRJCAN	−0.302
	(−1.02)
rho	0.529
	(4.08)
Adjusted R^2	0.89
Durbin-Watson statistic	1.97
F-statistic	50.86

Note: The dependent variable is price.
**Significant at the 1 percent level in a two-tailed test.

means that CSD suppliers as a group would have to restrict volume substantially to achieve a significant price increase.

Markup Test. Notwithstanding the substantial magnitude of the estimated residual demand elasticities for all carbonated soft drinks, one cannot accurately draw conclusions about market definition without a competitive benchmark. For carbonated soft drink market definition, the appropriate benchmark is the average percentage contribution margin earned by carbonated soft drink firms in the present state of competition. In the absence of precise firm-specific price/cost margins, we implemented the market definition test based on a number of different sources, including information from Coca-Cola's 1988 *Annual Report*. Coca-Cola reported net operating revenues of $2,284.4 million and operating income of $351.9 million for its domestic soft drink operations for 1988—a 15 percent return. Since operating income is net of fixed and certain variable expenses, however, the rate of return understates Coca-Cola's percentage contribution margin (net sales minus variable cost as a percentage of net sales).

If we estimate Coca-Cola's contribution margin by adding selling, general, and administrative (SG&A) back to operating income, we find a 51 percent margin.[33] Given these findings, a better estimate of Coca-Cola's contribution margin is obtained by adding Coca-Cola's 1988 media advertising expenditures ($186.7 million according to *Beverage Marketing*) to its operating income in an attempt to account for some amount of the fixed cost included in SG&A.[34] The resulting estimate of Coca-Cola's percentage contribution margin is 24 percent.[35]

Assuming that an average contribution margin of 24 percent governs the profitability of a price increase, it would be unprofitable for all carbonated soft drink firms to raise price 10 percent in the United States.[36] Specifically CSD suppliers would have to restrict volume 60 percent to raise price 10 percent. The gain from such action would be 10 percent of the average competitive price times the remaining volume sold. The cost would be the contribution margin (24 percent) times the average competitive price, times the output restriction. Based on the average weekly U.S. price and volume in our sample ($3.58 per 192-ounce case and 46.9 million cases per week) and the estimated residual demand elasticity, the gain per week equals $6.7 million and the cost per week equals $24.2 million. (For a 1 percent price increase, the gain per week is $1.6 million and the cost $2.4 million.)

Thus, a relevant product market defined as only carbonated soft drinks is too narrow.[37] Carbonated soft drinks clearly compete with and are affected by other beverages.

Hirschman-Herfindahl Analysis of Relevant Market

In applying the *Justice Department Merger Guidelines,* one must consider both the increased market concentration produced by a merger and the resulting postmerger concentration level. In the case of carbonated soft drinks, both of these factors are affected by the relevant product market definition adopted. In order to illustrate this point, we examine PepsiCo's proposed acquisition of Seven-Up in 1986. The point is not to discuss this proposed merger as such but to show how the concentration statistics look in the context of a beverage market rather than simply a carbonated soft drink market. Basically, we show how the inclusion of additional beverages mitigates the increase in carbonated soft drink concentration brought about by the proposed merger between PepsiCo and Seven-Up.

Table 4–4
Share of Volume, 1986

Beverage Category	PepsiCo	Seven-Up	Increase in HHI
CSD	27.4%	6.3%	345
CSD, BW	24.5	5.6	274
CSD, BW, PSD	21.9	5.0	219
CSD, BW, PSD, tea	19.4	4.5	175
CSD, BW, PSD, tea, juices	17.6	4.1	144
CSD, BW, PSD, tea, juices, coffee	12.8	2.9	74
CSD, BW, PSD, tea, juices, coffee, milk	10.6	2.4	51
CSD, BW, PSD, tea, juices, coffee, milk, beer	8.8	2.0	35
CSD, BW, PSD, tea, juices, coffee, milk, beer, wine	8.6	2.0	34
CSD, BW, PSD, tea, juices, coffee, milk, beer wine, liquor	8.5	2.0	34

Source: *Maxwell Report* (Richmond, VA: First Wheat Securities, 1989).
Note: CSD = carbonated soft drinks; BW = bottled water; PSD = powdered soft drinks.

The analysis of market concentration is summarized in table 4–4. There we show the volume shares of the two merger partners in 1986 and the resulting postmerger increase in the Herfindahl-Hirschman Index (HHI) under alternative relevant product market definitions. Going down the table, we add beverage products sequentially to the market definition. The order of inclusion is arbitrary; a rearrangement of the sequence would not affect our main conclusion.

In the first row of table 4–4, combining the share volumes of PepsiCo and Seven-Up would lead to an increase of 345 in the HHI if the relevant product market is narrowly defined to include only carbonated soft drinks. Adding just bottled water and powdered soft drinks to the market reduces the HHI increase to 219, and so on. Importantly, adding only six beverages to the market definition—bottled water, powdered soft drinks, tea, juice and coffee—brings the postmerger HHI increase to less than 100. Finally, if the market definition is expanded to encompass a number of other beverage products, the HHI increase falls below 50.

Notes

1. Based on Crest data.
2. M. Shanken, "The U.S. Non-Alcoholic Beverage Market," M. Shanken Communications, (New York, NY).

3. *Supermarket News* (February 1989).

4. Ibid.

5. *Wall Street Journal,* December 30, 1986.

6. *Beverage Industry Annual Manual* (Cleveland, OH: Edgell Communications, Inc., 1989/1990), p. 48.

7. "Supermarket Sales Manual," *Progressive Grocer* (July 1989).

8. *Wall Street Journal,* March 19, 1986.

9. "United States of America Coffee Drinking Study," *International Coffee Organization* (London: International Coffee Organization, Winter 1989).

10. *Reuter Business Reprint,* February 11, 1988.

11. *New York Times,* January 20, 1988; and *Los Angeles Times,* December 2, 1987. In an attempt to compete with carbonated soft drinks, Nestle S.A. has developed an iced coffee drink called Nescafe Frappe. The product was launched in Europe in 1989 as a soft drink product. *Wall Street Journal,* March 27, 1989.

12. Speech by George Boecklin, president of the National Coffee Association, before the National Coffee Association of U.S.A., Inc., Annual Convention, February 9, 1988, pp. 1–2.

13. Petition of American Dairy Association to Reopen and Terminate or Modify Consent Order against It, American Dairy Association and Leo Burnett Company v. Federal Trade Commission, Docket No. C–2495, June 24, 1986, p. 13.

14. Roger W. Miller, "Soft Drinks and Six Packs Quench Our National Thirst," *FDA Consumer* (October 1985).

15. United Dairy Industry Association, news release, 1989.

16. *Beverage Industry Annual Manual (1988/1989),* p. 12.

17. *Beverage Industry Annual Manual (1989/1990),* p. 56.

18. *Beverage Industry Annual Manual (1988/1989),* p. 14.

19. "Supermarket Sales Manual," *Progressive Grocer* (July 1989), p. 90.

20. Securities filings of soft drink companies reflect their basic belief that they operate in a market broader than carbonated soft drinks. For example, the 1988 *Annual Report* for Royal Crown stated that "RCC's soft drink products compete with all liquid refreshments." Similarly, Dr Pepper's 1988 10-K report stated that the "company's soft drink products compete generally with all liquid refreshments." The 1988 Coca-Cola 10-K report stated that "other beverages also compete with soft drinks." Bottlers of soft drinks have reached similar conclusions.

- With respect to soft drinks, competition was encountered from other national brands, various private labels and from juices, powdered mixes and other noncarbonated drinks. Universal Foods, Form 10-K (1985).

- Soft drinks produced and marketed by the Beverage Division compete with other national soft drinks (principally Coca-Cola products) and local and regional soft drinks (including private label brands), as well as with other beverages of all kinds, including juice and juice-based drinks. General Cinema, Form 10-K (1985).

- Approximately 40 brands of soft drinks compete with the brands marketed by the Corporation in its principal marketing areas, including national and regional private label soft drink products, as well as noncarbonated refreshment drinks, citrus and non-citrus fruit drinks and powdered drink mixes. Beverage Management, Form 10-K (1982).

- The Company's products also compete with other beverages such as noncarbonated drinks, juices and bottled water. Coca-Cola Bottling of Miami, Form 10-K (1981).

21. Louis and Yazijian, *The Cola Wars,* p. 353.

22. Most people conceive of carbonated soft drink bottlers as exclusively distributing carbonated soft drinks. This is not the case. Hundreds of carbonated soft drink bottlers in virtually every state also distribute iced tea, juice products (HiC, Hawaiian Punch, Lipton Tea, Country Time Lemonade), water, and other beverages. Literally hundreds of beer distributors and wine/spirit distributors handle soft drinks and juices and want to add more diverse products to their line. Food brokers also handle a diverse list of alternative beverage products.

23. These results cast doubt on an FTC position. In a complaint alleging anticompetitive consequences from a combination of two soft drink bottlers, the FTC stated that the relevant market at issue was "branded soft drinks" or a market "no broader than all soft drinks." In the Matter of Harold Honickman, Docket No. 9233, November 3, 1989.

24. In our illustrations of the market definition test, we use a 10 percent price test. In our actual implementation of the profitability criterion, we use alternative levels of 10 percent, 5 percent, and 1 percent.

25. A positive contribution margin may reflect the returns to risk taking in a dynamic setting. Moreover, even in a perfectly competitive market, price exceeds average variable cost because marginal cost rises in the short run and because under normal conditions, capital and overhead must be reimbursed. Therefore, a positive contribution margin is not necessarily an indication that price exceeds marginal cost; instead, it may merely indicate that variable cost does not exhaust total cost.

26. We conduct the product market definition test as if the geographic market were the entire United States. The appropriateness of this geographic market depends on the antitrust matter at issue. For example, a combination of local bottlers may require investigation concerning the possibility of a narrower geographic market, while a merger between concentrate manufacturers would typically entail a regional or national geographic market. Basing our analysis on U.S. demand elasticity is justified even for ostensibly local issues, however, because it is unlikely that the elasticity of demand for all carbonated soft drinks varies significantly across different geographic areas.

27. Nielsen surveys all supermarkets with annual sales at least equal to $2 million. Supermarkets with at least $2 million in annual sales account for 73 percent of all grocery sales. See *Progressive Grocer Marketing Guidebook* (Stamford, CT: Maclean Hunter Media, Inc., 1989).

28. The data used as a basis for estimating the various residual demand models have different observational frequencies. Nielsen Scantrack data provide weekly observations for average price and volume for carbonated soft drink products purchased in supermarkets in the United States. These observations are available for a time series of weeks beginning April 4, 1987, and ending September 2, 1989. In contrast, the

observational frequency for the underlying cost variables and nonprice demand variables is monthly. To retain the variation present in the CSD price and quantity variables, we based our demand estimation on weekly time series, repeating available monthly data for each week in the corresponding month.

29. Since the time period over which residual demands were estimated is approximately two years, we did not normalize volume for population changes or adjust prices and wages for inflation.

The residual demand model whose estimates are reported in table 4–3 was specified in several alternative ways to include different explanatory factors. Various combinations of the variables reported in table 4–3 and several other input price variables were alternatively included as regressors. The other variables include monthly PPIs for (1) high-fructose corn syrups; (2) beer bottles; (3) the monthly price of oranges; (4) the monthly auction price of tea; and (5) the average weekly earnings of beer distribution workers. The estimated residual demand elasticity ranged from -5.6 to -7.6 in these alternative specifications. We also included the monthly all-item CPI in several of the model specifications. When the CPI was included, a serial correlation correction was typically unnecessary. With the CPI, residual demand elasticity estimates ranged from -4.8 to -7.3.

30. Although the regression model itself is statistically significant, only three variables' coefficients are statistically significant. The coefficient of own volume is highly significant and has the correct sign. Among the other regressors, *WKBEARN* and *WGRDIST* are statically significant. Some of the variables whose effects can be predicted a priori enter with the wrong sign. *WGRDIST, AAPPLES, PBEERCAN,* and *PFRJCAN* have negative coefficients; the predicted signs are positive. However, only in the case of *WGRDIST* is the coefficient statistically significant. Our income measure, *ETOTALL,* has a positive effect on CSD demand; however, the coefficient estimate is not statistically significant.

31. All-CSD residual demand was also estimated with logged quantity as the dependent variable. This model fit equally as well as the model in inverse form. With one exception, the same variable coefficients are statistically significant, and their signs are identical. In the direct specification, the seasonal dummy variable also has statistically significant coefficient. The residual demand elasticity estimate is -4.78.

32. It could be alleged that inventory demand by consumers gives rise to spuriously high estimates of demand elasticity. Consider a loyal Pepsi drinker who shops once a week at one supermarket for food and beverages and holds Pepsi inventories that are normally replenished every two weeks. In a given week, if the price of Pepsi were abnormally high (off special in this customer's store), our hypothetical consumer may wait until the next week to make purchases to replenish inventory. If this consumer's demand were estimated using weekly data, it would be highly elastic, and it may not precisely indicate Pepsi's power over price.

The upward bias in the demand elasticity in the example is highly specific to the special circumstances assumed. Specifically, it was assumed that the price and volume data were available by customer and store and that the customer did not readily substitute among beverages. In contrast, the data we used to estimate residual demand aggregates purchases across the United States. These aggregate data would not reflect the behavior described for several reasons. Discount pricing for CSDs is generally specific to brands, stores, and areas of the country, and discounting is not synchronous.

Moreover, consumers generally differ according to their shopping frequencies, days of inventory, and willingness to substitute among alternative beverages, including CSDs. The combination of all these facts suggests that a residual demand elasticity estimate based on weekly aggregate purchases and weighted average price in the United States would not be biased upward.

In circumstances when spurious elasticity estimates may result because observation periods are shorter than inventory holding periods, unbiased estimates may be obtained by lengthening observation periods. To assure ourselves that our residual demand elasticity estimate is not biased, we also obtained estimates using biweekly data. As expected, there is no essential difference between these results and those reported. Specifically residual demand elasticity estimated using biweekly data is greater than our reported elasticity based on weekly observations, and the biweekly elasticity is statistically significant, though less significant than our reported estimate.

33. This is found by using Coca-Cola's consolidated income statement to estimate soft drink SG&A. Total SG&A as a percentage of total net revenue is 36 percent. Adding 36 percent of soft drink net revenue to operating income yields $1,174 million—51 percent of soft drink net revenue.

34. Some of Coca-Cola's annual carbonated soft drink advertising expenditure should most likely be charged as a cost in the current year. Thus, our measure of contribution margin as advertising expenditure plus operating income as a percentage of net sales is too large because some variable advertising cost is included in the numerator. However, on balance, this estimate of contribution margin is likely to be conservative since there are other fixed costs in SG&A not added back in by our procedure.

35. Information from DWG Corporation's 10-K indicates that for fiscal 1989, RC's operating profit (after G&A) is $22.6 million, which is 18.8 percent of net sales ($120.1 million). When RC's $8.8 million of media advertising (according to *Beverage Marketing*) is added back to operating profit, the percentage margin is 26.1 percent, higher than the percentage we conservatively estimated for Coca-Cola. Similarly, Dr Pepper's most recent 10-K reports income and expenses for fiscal 1988 (ending December 31) in some detail. If contribution is defined as net sales less cost of goods sold less marketing operating expenses, the percentage margin for Dr Pepper is 32 percent ($244,355,000 − $48,325,000 − $117,625,000/$244,355,000).

36. Even if the appropriate price test were 1 percent or 5 percent, not 10 percent, it would be unprofitable for all these firms to raise prices when the applicable contribution margin is 24 percent.

37. If the smaller residual demand elasticity, estimated from the quantity-on-the-left model specification, were used to implement the profitability criterion, an all-CSD market is also too narrowly defined, for a 1 percent, 5 percent, and a 10 percent price test.

5
Entry

M odern antitrust analysis puts the conditions of entry in an industry on a virtually even footing with characteristics of market structure such as concentration. In fact, in some respects, conditions of entry take precedence over structure in that ease of entry can promote competition irrespective of underlying concentration statistics.[1] Entry is an important issue in understanding the degree of competition among soft drink and other beverage producers.[2]

As we discuss entry, an important proviso must be kept in mind. Entry has taken place within the carbonated soft drink industry and across the broader span of all beverages. This entry is significant; it curtails the ability of PepsiCo and Coca-Cola to raise prices. On the other hand, no individual firm or brand has entered into carbonated soft drink sales on the scale of PepsiCo or Coca-Cola. The reason lies in the competitive nature of the carbonated soft drink industry.

Entry and Expansion

Past Entry

The soft drink industry has been characterized by frequent and regular entry for many years. During this period, a large number of new soft drink products have been introduced into the market, and their entry has been competitively significant.

Numerous Product Entries. One recent report concluded that "driven by the consumer's thirst for anything new and different, the beverage industry today continues to introduce new flavors, brands, and whole drink categories."[3] A thousand new beverage products were introduced in the United States during 1988 and 1989 alone (table 5–1).[4] This is not a recent trend. Appendix I reviews new product introductions over the 1970–1988 period,[5] and table

Table 5–1
New Product Introductions, January 1988–August 1989

	Number	*Percentage*
Carbonated	503	35.4
Noncarbonated	917	64.6
Total	1,420	100.0
Nonalcohol	1,331	93.7
Alcohol (low alcohol)	89	6.3
Total	1,420	100.0
Nonjuice	685	48.2
Juice based	559	39.4
Juice	176	12.4
Total	1,420	100.0

Source: *New Product News* (Chicago, IL: Gorman Publishing Company, 1988–1989).
Note: Does not include February 1988. That issue of *New Product News* was unavailable.

5–2 lists the number of new carbonated, nonalcoholic beverage products introduced from 1970 to 1988 by PepsiCo, Seven-Up, Coca-Cola, Dr Pepper, and RC. Many of these products have been successful introductions such as Diet Coke and Pepsi Free. Smaller companies have also successfully introduced new products; A&W's Cream Soda is an example. But other products, such as Cherry Seven-Up, have not fared as well. The large number of new products shows that entry is feasible.[6]

Consumer Receptivity to New Products. The entry of such a great number of new beverage products should not be surprising in the light of consumption patterns for beverages. Industry data (SIP, Crest, and others) show that the average consumer drinks a wide array of beverages each day and over time. A recent article concluded that successful "drink makers innovate to satisfy the consumer's never-ending thirst for something new" by introducing "new flavors, brands, and whole drink categories."[7]

Moreover, the industry data suggest that the average consumer seeks variety even within narrow beverage categories. Within carbonated soft drinks the success of products such as "natural" sodas, flavored seltzers, and juice-added soft drinks speaks loudly to this point. Additional data shed more light on this issue. Of households that buy groceries in supermarkets, a significant percentage purchase nondiet colas and nondiet flavored (not cola) soft drinks during some portion of the year (table 5–3). The intersection of these two sets and others (cola versus diet, for example) is substantial. Even within the soft drink category, brand sampling is heavy. Over half of the households that purchased diet cola bought both Coca-Cola and PepsiCo products during the year. Two underlying phenomena are thus observed: (1) consumer trial is relatively inexpensive, and (2) consumers value variety. Both invite and make entry easier.

Table 5–2
New Carbonated, Nonalcoholic Beverages, by Selected Firms, 1970–1988

Year	PepsiCo	Seven-Up	Coca-Cola	Dr Pepper	RC
1970	0	1	1	0	3
1971	0	1	0	1	1
1972	0	0	1	0	0
1973	1	0	1	0	1
1974	0	1	3	0	1
1975	1	0	4	0	0
1976	0	1	0	0	0
1977	1	0	0	0	1
1978	1	1	1	0	2
1979	0	0	2	0	0
1980	0	0	1	0	1
1981	0	0	1	0	0
1982	1	2	1	1	3
1983	0	0	3	1	1
1984	1	9[a]	1	1	0
1985	1	0	3	1	8[b]
1986[c]	0	0	1	0	4
1987[d]	0	0	2	0	10[e]
1988[f]	1	2	0	0	2

Source: Ibid.

[a] The nine products are nine flavors of Howdy Soda, added to the preexisting Howdy Cola.

[b] The eight introductions were RC Cherry Cola, three Nehi Natural flavors (grapefruit, lemon-lime, and mandarin orange), two Nehi chocolate sodas (regular and diet), and two diet RCs (with and without caffeine).

[c] Does not include January, February, and March. These *New Product News* issues were not available.

[d] Does not include January and May. These *New Product News* issues were not available.

[e] The ten introductions were eight Nehi diet flavors (tangerine, lemon-lime, pink grapefruit, black cherry, red raspberry, peach, white grape, and caramel cream) and two Nehi Seltzer flavors (natural and lime).

[f] Does not include February. This *New Product News* issue was not available.

Table 5–3
Overlap Purchasing by Households of Different Types of Carbonated Soft Drinks

	Minimum/Maximum Percentage Also Buying			
Of Households Buying	Cola	Diet Cola	Flavors	Diet Flavors
Cola	100.0	60.6/73.4	89.9/100	55.3/68.1
Diet cola	82.5/100	100.0	86.3/100	39.1/92.8
Flavors	87.5/97.3	61.6/71.4	100.0	56.5/66.3
Diet flavors	81.1/100	42.1/100	85.2/100	100.0

Source: *Marketing Factbook* (January 1985).

The data on price and usage suggest that many consumers (the switchers) value variety and are not wed to the prominent nationally advertised brands. But there is also a group of consumers loyal to certain brand names. Our analysis suggests, however, that the switchers are sufficiently large enough in numbers to influence demand and supply. A bottler of soft drinks in Washington, D.C., recently documented that "there isn't really any brand loyalty here . . . we can only count on about 20% of consumers buying our brand . . . the other 80% look for pricing and availability."[8]

Regional Aspects of Entry. Another phenomenon conducive to entry is the opportunity to enter and operate on a limited geographic scope. Regional brands have long survived and prospered in the beverage industry. The option of regional entry allows an entrant to keep costs and scale down, test the product, and pick an area. Picking the right region to enter can increase an entrant's chances of success. Not only is such entry feasible, it can be significant. The fact that brands with regional strengths can be a significant force in the market was illustrated in table 3–9.

Coca-Cola and PepsiCo sales are vulnerable on a regional basis, as evidenced by the variability in shares across regions. The variance strongly suggests that where PepsiCo and Coca-Cola do hold large shares, it is a result of competitive performance and consumer satisfaction rather than a consequence of dominance and barriers to competition. Moreover, the regional variance suggests the disciplining effect of what some may call the competitive fringe in the industry.

Entry and Strategic Groups

The economic concept of strategic groups is useful in understanding the dynamics of competitive conduct and performance in the soft drink industry and helps to explain why successful entrants and competitors need not necessarily mirror PepsiCo or Coca-Cola in their business organization and competitive strategy.[9] Firms that have made a similar choice with respect to important strategic variables such as advertising or distribution channels constitute a strategic group. The impact of strategic variation on the ability of firms within an industry to collude successfully is similar to that of the impact of the number of firms or the extent of product differentiation.[10]

Entrants, expanders, and competitors must make choices with regard to a lengthy list of strategic elements:

Product characteristics (flavors, degree of carbonation, caffeine content).

Product form (liquid, syrup, powder).

Packaging (cans, bottles, glass, aluminum, plastic).

Package sizes (10 ounce, 12 ounce, 16 ounce, quart, 1 liter, 2 liter).

Length and breadth of product line.

Sales outlets (on premise, vending, fountain).

Internal production versus purchase at various input stages (research and development, flavors, concentrate, marketing, distribution).

Distribution (store door versus warehouse, bottlers, beer distributors).

Advertising (budget size, media).

Pricing (everyday low price, frequency of promotions, coupons).

Recent soft drink product entry reflects the diversity of strategic groupings in the industry. Not only have firms that bear little strategic resemblance to PepsiCo or Coca-Cola introduced new products, the fashion in which they subsequently compete is often different. For example, Canfield's flavor line is often warehouse distributed but sometimes bottler distributed, not heavily advertised, offered primarily in individual serving package sizes, often contract packed, and originated by a small, entrepreneurial enterprise. By contrast, Crystal Light, a powdered soft drink, is warehouse distributed, heavily advertised on television, offered as a powdered mix, centrally manufactured, and marketed by a food conglomerate (Philip Morris/General Foods). Perrier flavored waters are both warehouse and store-door (bottler and beer wholesaler) delivered, occasionally advertised in national media, offered in individual and larger package sizes, and bottled abroad.[11]

Specific examples of entry and expansion illustrate the diversity of entry and expansion strategies. For example, the Stroh Brewery Co., which entered the soft drink business in early 1986, produces Sundance Natural Juice Sparkler, a carbonated juice-based soft drink, at a Stroh plant in Van Nuys, California. The product was introduced on the West Coast and was recently distributed nationally. Stroh also sells All Natural High Five Soda on the West Coast and in the Midwest.[12]

Other examples are Original New York Seltzer, R.J. Corr Naturals, MBC, Snapple, and Hansen. Essentially, each of these represents entry by individuals rather than large corporations like Stroh. Sharon Corr and her husband began R.J. Corr (Corr's brand) Naturals Inc. of Chicago in 1978 with $1,200. R.J. Corr now makes twenty flavors and had revenues of over $10 million in 1988. The distribution of R.J. Corr started with health food stores, but its sales today include grocery stores. R.J. Corr relies primarily on beer distributors for distribution. MBC Beverages sells Sweet 'N Low soda. In 1982 Richard Manney licensed the Sweet 'N Low trademark from Cumberland Packing Corp. and hired a flavor firm to develop twenty syrups (cola, ginger ale, and so forth). MBC sells primarily through food brokers rather than bottlers. In two years, MBC was selling 1.4 million cases in twenty-two states and turning a profit. Says Manney: "We don't have to be Coke or Pepsi to make a nice living." Snapple began producing fruit juices in 1979 and soft drinks in 1981. By 1984 it was selling 2 million cases of juice per year and 1.2 million cases of soft drinks. Snapple had 138 distributors in 1984, many of them beer distributors. Hansen's natural soft drinks are a spinoff from a family-run juice company. Hansen started selling natural soft drinks in 1980 and by 1983 had annual soft drink sales of over $30 million, selling in grocery stores in seventeen western states. Original New York Seltzer began shipping in 1982, and case sales grew from 3,000 to over 13 million in 1988.[13]

There has also been notable private label entry. Kroger has had success with its Big K brand in recent years and purchased an idle Pepsi-Cola bottling plant to produce its own products. Giant Foods, a Washington, D.C., area supermarket chain, built its own bottling plant to produce its in-house private label soft drinks. A large share of Giant's soft drink sales is represented by its own brand.

There are also expanders like Vernors, A&W, and Squirt, now all sold by A&W Brands.[14] Vernors, a ginger ale brand from Detroit, is rapidly expanding its distribution by increasing the number of its franchisees and using the traditional bottler network. Over the 1980s, A&W case sales increased more than 50 percent. Since 1985 case sales have increased by 25 percent. Squirt, a grapefruit soft drink, is also a strong recent expander. Between 1981 and 1988, sales rose from 18 million to 27 million cases.[15]

The existence of different strategic groups facilitates entry by offering the prospective entrant a menu of alternative ways to enter an industry. The greater the number of strategic groups, the greater is the number of paths to entry into the industry. Deterrence of entry into an industry requires the simultaneous deterrence of entry into each of the industry's groups, and deterrence of entry into a strategic group requires that entry into the group be barred to both firms outside the industry and firms in other groups in the same industry.

Requirements for Competitive Entry

This section examines the process of entry from product conception through manufacturing, bottling, distribution, and marketing.

Product Conception and Innovation

Product conception must be related to consumer demand if it is to be meaningful and ultimately profitable. The complexity of product conception prior to entry can be imagined as a continuum ranging from the decision of a retail grocery chain to sell a "me-too" private label product line to extensive new product efforts. Products like PepsiCo's Slice attempt to fulfill certain demands in a new and/or better way. Private label products try to satisfy certain consumers with a product similar to another one but at a lower price. It is not difficult to imagine the process of conceiving of a new private label product. It is less obvious how a sophisticated marketing firm like PepsiCo approaches the problem.

Generally, PepsiCo begins with considerable market and consumer research, as well as laboratory research. It devotes a significant amount of resources to product conception. But a variety of new products have come from less expensive conceptual processes (including Corr, Hansen, SoHo, and Snapple). This is not to say that the products forthcoming from PepsiCo-type processes, such as Slice, could just as easily have come from small-scale budgets. However, it is apparent that small-scale budgets can come up with competitive products.[16]

Concentrate Production

Concentrate is generally shipped from the beverage manufacturer to a local or regional bottler or canner, who adds carbonated or still water and often a sweetener to prepare the beverage for packing and consumption. Transportation of the concentrate to a local bottler or canner is more economical than if the beverage's entire water content is included. Production and/or procurement of concentrate is a requirement of competition and is not difficult to meet. (Moreover, some soft drink production processes do not use concentrate. Some require only extracts and/or flavors, and others, such as seltzer, require none of these.) Some smaller recent entrants produce their own concentrate, but investment in production facilities is not necessary. Concentrate can be purchased rather than produced. In the United States today there are about eighty-two producers of soft drink concentrate.[17]

Concentrate companies include firms such as PepsiCo and Coca-Cola but also a significant number of lesser-known but competitively important firms, among them A-Treat Bottling located in Allentown, Pennsylvania; America '76' Company in Palatine, Illinois; Associated Beverages in Houston; Big Red in Waco, Texas; Bubble-Up in Chicago; Carolina Beverage in Salisbury, North Carolina; Double Cola in Chattanooga, Tennessee; Faygo Beverage in Detroit; Krier Foods in Belgium, Wisconsin; MBC Beverage in New York; Monarch Company in Atlanta; Quench Company in Seattle; Quest Flavors in Owings Mills, Maryland; Shasta Beverage in Hayward, California; Snapple Natural Soda in Ridgewood, New York; Sun Rise in Marshall, Minnesota; and Virginia Dare Extract in Brooklyn. Moreover, certain corporations similar in size to PepsiCo and Coca-Cola also have concentrate facilities, among them Lipton Inc., in Englewood Cliffs, New Jersey; General Foods in White Plains, New York; and Nestle in Purchase, New York.[18]

Numerous private label and proprietary brands compete successfully by utilizing purchased concentrate. For example, C&C Cola is made entirely from purchased concentrate. Faygo, Canfield's, Safeway, and Shasta are examples of firms that make some of their concentrate and purchase some. By contrast, some brands have relied on internally produced concentrate but have not had great commercial success (such as Seven-Up's Like). There is little or no evidence to support the notion that production of or access to concentrate is a nettlesome requirement for entry.[19]

Bottling and Canning

The following discussion is divided into two parts. The first part discusses the availability of bottling and canning capacity. The second part discusses flavor exclusivity and its effect on access to bottling capacity.

Available Capacity. A new entrant or expander can gain access to bottling and/or canning capacity in several ways. Because the capital costs are not prohibitive, a new entrant can construct its own production facility or facilities. General Cinema, a former multifranchise operator (MFO), constructed a state-of-the-art canning and bottling plant in the Tampa, Florida, area in the 1980s for approximately $12 million. MEI, another former MFO, constructed various new bottling facilities in recent years for between $5 million and $10 million each depending upon size and location. Joint venturing in new facilities is common practice and significantly reduces the costs facing an individual firm. A firm has the option of buying into the equity of an already existing plant (co-oping). In fact, co-oping is the most common method of operation for small bottlers today, many of them with no production facilities of their own. Or, a firm can buy and reopen some idled excess capacity, as Kroger Supermarkets did when it purchased an idled Pepsi-Cola bottling plant in Bluefield, West Virginia.

An entrant need not invest in production capacity in order to have its product bottled or canned economically. It can use capacity already in place and available for contract to entrants and expanders. Our investigation, including numerous interviews of existing bottlers, suggests that excess capacity exists and is available to new entrants. This capacity includes not only existing capacity or equipment not being used but the ability of bottlers to increase production quickly by adding to the number of lines or shifts per day.

Entrants seeking to package their products nationwide do not require facilities located in every local geographic area of the country. Faygo competes over a wide portion of the United States principally from a single production facility in Detroit and a handful of contract packers, and Shasta utilizes twelve production facilities nationwide. Although brand, flavor, and package mix, along with sales volume, are important factors in determining the efficient number of production facilities to utilize, clearly an entrant can compete effectively over a multistate area from an individual plant.

An additional issue is whether the production capacity available to entrants is efficient—specifically whether production-scale economies are available. Production-scale economies have motivated a substantial consolidation of U.S. soft drink production facilities. Roughly 6,600 plants were in production in 1950; only about 1,000 are producing today. Despite this drop, there may yet be substantial economies to be reached by further consolidations.

Scale economies are achieved through joint ventures, bottling co-ops, contract bottling, and acquisitions. Coca-Cola and PepsiCo have been active in refranchising their bottler networks in recent years, in part to hasten the achievement of attainable scale economies. Refranchising encompasses a variety of activities on the part of the concentrate company: outright acquisition of bottlers, equity investments, and financial assistance to independent multifranchise operations to assist them in mergers and acquisitions.

Both PepsiCo and Coca-Cola have integrated vertically since the late 1970s by purchasing bottling and franchise rights, suggesting that the two major concentrate producers believe there are in-firm economies from owning bottlers rather than simply contracting with them for various services. Such economies may arise from more efficient levels of local promotional activities, which are in the interest of the integrated producer to devise and enforce.

Antitrust concerns raised concerning these acquisitions advance the idea that vertically integrated producers might be better situated to foreclose nonintegrated competitors from the marketplace and otherwise act in noncompetitive ways (such as by collusion). Our examination of the data suggests, however, that vertical integration in the carbonated soft drink industry has not resulted in any adverse competitive effects (see appendix M).

Flavor Exclusivity. Certain concentrate manufacturers, including PepsiCo and Coca-Cola, enter into contracts with regional bottlers, giving each bottler an exclusive territory in which to bottle, market, and sell the manufacturer's designated products.[20] The manufacturers have sometimes demanded flavor exclusivity from their bottlers; that is, a bottler cannot bottle or distribute another flavor similar to the flavor being bottled and distributed under contract or can bottle or can a directly competing flavor as long as the bottler does not distribute it. Exclusivity may extend to some of the manufacturer's products but not to others. Flavor exclusivity and exclusive territories are designed to provide bottlers with incentives to maximize sales effort on behalf of the manufacturer's products.

Our analysis suggests that flavor exclusivity does not create a true barrier to entry for a number of reasons. First, a new entrant can build new production capacity if required. Second, the existence of such contract provisions has not stemmed the recent tide of new product introductions, and it has not stopped the expansion of numerous fringe firms, regional competitors, and private label companies whose avenues of alternative entry include contract packers and local or regional bottlers without national brand affiliations.

Third, bottlers can drop a manufacturer's brand or flavor with relative ease, usually with only advance notice. A bottler/distributor has an economic incentive to take on new products that will expand sales and profits and will replace a product in its line with a similar one that it believes will be more profitable. Under existing competitive conditions, it is not likely that a bottler will drop the cola brands of Coca-Cola or PepsiCo, although the secondary brands of these companies do not have similar strength. The relevant issue, however, is whether bottlers would consider dropping these brands if they began to behave in a manner that would significantly and adversely affect the bottler's interests (such as raising prices and restricting output). In such an environment, a bottler may well seek out a new cola product offered by, say, Nestle or Campbell Soup.

Distribution

Distribution is the system of transport that conveys beverages from the bottling and canning plants to retail outlets. It can be direct to the retail outlet (store-door delivery), through a retailer's own warehouse, or through a warehouse operated by a wholesale grocer or food service distributor (warehouse delivery). All types of distribution channels are available to new entrants and to fringe firms.

Store-door Delivery. With store-door delivery, beverages are shipped directly from the bottler to the retail outlet by the bottler or an independent shipper.[21] PepsiCo generally relies on a bottler store-door delivery system to sell and deliver its products to all types of retail accounts.[22] Although it uses bottlers for food store deliveries, Coca-Cola relies heavily on a food broker–food service distributor system to service fountain syrup accounts. This method of distribution has served Coca-Cola well; Coca-Cola accounts for significantly more fountain business than PepsiCo.

Other prominent exceptions to bottler store-door delivery include the use of wholesalers (the food broker–food service distribution system) by Seven-Up and Dr Pepper for a portion of their fountain accounts and the successful use of warehouse delivery for foodstore sales by RC in some parts of the country. And the substantial volume of private label soft drinks sales is warehouse delivered.

Store-door delivery is generally available to new entrants in the beverage industry, as well as to expanding fringe firms. The most obvious option is to piggy-back existing bottler and store-door distribution systems. Most bottlers, including those for Coca-Cola and PepsiCo, already distribute brands of more than one concentrate company. The only impediment to piggy-backing existing bottler distribution is a flavor exclusivity clause.

In addition to soft drink bottlers, a number of other food product vendors deliver on a frequent store-door basis to grocery stores, convenience stores, restaurants, and other retail outlets. For example, the predominant method of distribution by beer manufacturers is also store-door delivery. Beer distributors, and many spirit distributors, deliver directly to grocery stores, convenience stores, restaurants, package stores, bars, and taverns, and they commonly distribute soft drinks and other beverages to their accounts along with beer (table 5–4).

As table 5–4 shows, a significant number of beer and wine and spirits distributors are potentially available for store-door delivery of the beverage products of new entrants or expanding fringe firms. Our interviews with such distributors confirm that they are eager to take on or expand their sales of nonalcoholic beverages, explained in part by relatively flat alcohol sales recently.

The similarities between beer wholesaling operations, for instance, and soft drink distribution are striking. In fact, beer wholesalers may present certain advantages for entrants compared to piggy-backing existing bottler distribution. The entrant may receive better service from the beer distributor than from the soft drink bottler since the entrant's product will usually constitute a greater proportion of the beer distributor's nonalcoholic sales. Beer wholesaler penetration of certain types of on-premise and smaller off-premise accounts may be greater than the bottler. Finally, any problem of exclusivity is often minimized or eliminated with beer distributors.

Table 5–4
Combination Distributors, 1988

Current joint distribution	
Beer–soft drink distributors	904
Wine and spirits–soft drink distributors	474
Total	927[a]
Potential for joint distribution	
States with beer–soft drink distributors	51[b]
States with wine and spirits–soft drink distributors	46
All beer distributors in these states	3,793
All wine and spirits distributors in these states	1,688

Source: *National Beverage Marketing Directory* (Mingo Junction, OH: Beverage Marketing Corporation, 1989).
[a]Includes beer distributors that are also wine and spirits distributors.
[b]Includes the District of Columbia.

Warehouse Delivery. Warehouse delivery is the system predominantly used by food manufacturers in the United States to distribute food products to grocery stores, convenience stores, and restaurants. Typically, food products are transported to central warehouses, which then deliver a combination of food products to retail outlets. Warehouses serving grocery stores and convenience stores are called wholesale grocers. (Some grocery chains are large enough to establish their own vertically integrated food distribution centers.) Those serving restaurants, office buildings, hospitals, and other institutional accounts are called food service distributors.

Sales responsibilities are handled directly by employees of the manufacturer or by food brokers, independent sales agents representing manufacturers on a commission basis. The primary role of the food broker is to convince the retail outlet to buy the product from the warehouse. The food broker also has the responsibility for ensuring that the product is adequately stocked and displayed at the retail level.

Manufacturers of all types of beverage products use warehouse delivery. Many food brokers sell soft drinks and other types of beverages on behalf of manufacturers. Many wholesale grocers and food service distributors distribute soft drinks and other types of beverages to grocery stores, convenience stores, and restaurants. Most juice products are sold through warehouses. Currently, Shasta and Faygo are predominantly warehouse delivered, as are most private labels like Cragmont, Giant, and Big K. Furthermore, there are a large number of food brokers, wholesale grocers, and food service distributors scattered throughout the United States potentially available to sell and distribute the beverage products of new entrants or expanding fringe firms.[23] It seems unlikely that there is any area of the United States where food brokers and food service distributors are not available to distribute the products of a carbonated soft drink entrant.

Conclusions. Ultimately, the facts from the marketplace speak to the issue of the viability of different distribution systems. Access to bottler store-door delivery as a barrier to entry is an issue only so long as the product market definition is held narrowly to carbonated soft drinks alone. Any broadening of the product market definition will decrease the percentage of the products distributed by bottler store-door delivery. Even within the narrow carbonated soft drink market definition, it appears that between 20 and 30 percent of the product is distributed outside the bottler store-door delivery system.[24]

Hundreds of beer distributors, in addition to wine and spirit distributors, already distribute carbonated soft drinks and offer entrants an alternative to the traditional carbonated soft drink bottler–store-door distribution system. With respect to food brokers and food service distributors, Coca-Cola's extensive use of that channel speaks eloquently to its effectiveness. Perhaps most importantly, in nearly every (if not all) supermarkets across the country, there are lower-priced carbonated soft drink alternatives to the PepsiCo and Coca-

Cola brands. And these lower-priced alternatives are almost always delivered through warehouses. Coupled with the availability of canning and bottling capacity, it is difficult to argue that warehouse delivery is not effective when these brands can be delivered to the consumer at a lower price than Coca-Cola and PepsiCo products. Private labels' share of 17.6 percent in Buffalo and 13.4 percent in San Francisco, the presence of Safeway's private label, Cragmont, in other grocery chains and convenience stores in northern California, and Shasta's annual sales exceeding one case per American household testify to the viability of the warehouse delivery system—the same system that is the conduit through which most food products and many beverages pass on their way to grocery and convenience store shelves.[25]

The majority of carbonated soft drink sales—50 to 60 percent—are made through retail outlets such as supermarkets and convenience stores. Two other channels, which are often discussed separately, are fountain and vending. The fountain sales channel is not an entry issue. Except for a tiny fraction of its sales, Coca-Cola does not utilize bottlers to service this channel. Since Coca-Cola has the leading share of sales in this channel, clearly alternative distribution is effective in this area.

Access to bottler store-door delivery is not an entry requirement to the vending channel. Many vending companies are not integrated into bottling. For example, Macke and ARA are very large vending companies operating in the Washington, D.C. area. Coca-Cola and PepsiCo bottlers are usually vertically integrated into vending. (Alternatively stated, Coca-Cola and PepsiCo bottlers are coincidentally beverage vending companies.) Many concentrate manufacturers have chosen not to emphasize the vending channel, and many bottlers are not significantly integrated into vending. However, carbonated soft drink producers can enter the vending channel by selling products to vending companies and/or by buying and placing vending machines. Moreover, there is no apparent economic reason that beer distributors could not enter the vending business.

Marketing

The remaining entry issues concern marketing, including advertising, brand loyalty, shelf space, and cooperative marketing agreements (CMAs), each bearing some relationship to the other entry requirements already discussed.

Advertising. A variety of factors, including quantity discounts, the costs of local or regional (so-called spot advertising) versus network television time, the nature of consumers' responses to commercial repetition, and the determinants of brand loyalty are potentially important in determining the effects of advertising on entry.[26] These factors are themselves of some interest, and most have been the subjects of considerable research; however, no single individual factor can determine the effects of advertising on entry since the negative effects of one factor may be offset by the positive effects of another. What is relevant is the overall effect of advertising. Economic theory provides some guidance concerning the overall effect of advertising, but ultimately this question can only be resolved empirically.

In the soft drink industry, a variety of corporate strategies serve as examples of effective or successful competition. Some of these strategies employ little or no advertising (not counting food store newspaper ads). Other strategies make use of network and spot television advertising to varying degrees. The firms responsible for important new product introductions and expansions in recent years illustrate the full range of possible advertising strategies. Given the successes of firms that are not heavy advertisers, it is clear that advertising is not a barrier to entry into the soft drink industry.[27]

Scale Economies. If advertising is to be a barrier to entry, there must be some range of increasing returns to scale in advertising that provides large advertisers with a cost advantage relative to small advertisers. In recent empirical work on returns to scale in advertising, Boyer and Lancaster point out that "a necessary but not sufficient condition for the existence of 'scale economies in advertising' is that, relative to smaller firms, large firms support their market shares with a relatively small share of advertising capital."[28]

To test for the existence of scale economies in advertising, Boyer and Lancaster examined the relationship between firms' advertising expenditures and their market shares to see if advertising per market share point was less for large firms than for small firms. Their regression analysis, which used Leading National Advertisers' (LNA) measures of advertising expenditures by brand for a representative sample of industries, produced "no evidence to support the existence of such an advantage for large firms."[29] If anything, the evidence pointed in the opposite direction: the advertising of small firms was just as effective in generating market share as the advertising of large firms, and possibly more effective.

Consistent with the Boyer and Lancaster approach, we compared sales volume with television advertising expenditures for soft drink companies and brands for 1988. This analysis shows a relationship consistent with the relationship suggested by their regression results (table 5–5).

We would expect that Coca-Cola and PepsiCo would clearly have the lowest advertising expenditure to sales volume ratios if there were significant scale economies in advertising. The data in table 5–5 reflect little relationship between advertising and sales. Firms such as Faygo, Frank's, and Shasta are more efficient than Coca-Cola Classic. Brands such as Diet Coke and Slice do not fare very well under this measure. This analysis is based on only one year, but the results are consistent with the large majority of literature, which supports the position that scale economies in advertising are limited.[30]

Table 5–5
Efficiency of Carbonated Soft Drink Advertising Expenditures, 1988

Brand	Advertising Expenditures ($000)	1988 Sales (million cases)	Advertising Expenditure per Thousand Cases ($)
Faygo	29.8	47.0	0.63
Barq's (regular and diet)	335.4	31.2	10.75
Frank's	248.6	22.5	11.05
Shasta (regular and diet)	1,545.4	120.0	12.88
Sunkist (regular and diet)	1,719.3	55.5	30.98
Vernor's (regular and diet)	460.5	12.4	37.14
Coca-Cola Classic	65,186.1	1,501.0	43.43
Diet Rite (RC's diet brand)	2,344.4	51.2	45.79
Royal Crown Cola	5,635.8	122.0	46.20
Pepsi-Cola	63,835.4	1,370.0	46.60
Seven-Up brand	13,718.6	235.0	58.38
Canada Dry (regular and diet)	6,923.5	102.0	67.88
Dr Pepper (regular and diet)	24,460.0	358.7	68.19
Squirt (regular and diet)	1,958.0	27.1	72.25
Diet Coke (including caffeine free)	55,488.7	760.0	73.01
Sprite (regular and diet)	29,807.1	323.5	92.14
Diet Seven-Up	7,167.8	73.6	97.39
Diet Pepsi (including caffeine free)	48,486.1	470.0	103.16
Slice (regular and diet)	15,001.3	135.0	111.12
Schweppes	4,822.3	41.8	115.37
A&W Soft Drink (regular and diet)	8,847.0	66.5	133.04
Crush and Hires (regular and diet)	10,364.1	72.0	143.95

Sources: *Maxwell* (1989); and *Ad $ Summary* (New York: Leading National Advertisers, 1988).

Network Advertising. Critics of advertising have argued that large companies with nationally promoted brands can procure television advertising at a lower cost than smaller companies with regionally distributed brands. These large firms, it is said, can take advantage of network television advertising, considered a cheaper means of reaching television audiences than spot advertising over local television stations.

Analysis of the actual advertising expenditures of soft drink companies casts considerable doubt on the proposition that Coca-Cola and PepsiCo enjoy any advertising cost advantages over other soft drink firms due to savings associated with network purchases. If network advertising does provide a cost advantage to high-volume products with national distribution, one would expect that this cost advantage would be reflected in higher ratios of network-to-spot advertising expenditures for these high-volume products. The 1988 network and spot advertising expenditures and sales are shown for the principal Coca-Cola and PepsiCo soft drinks in table 5–6. Also shown are the television advertising expenditures and sales for other soft drinks products that had network-to-spot ratios at least as high as the ratios for Pepsi-Cola and Diet Pepsi.

A number of brands with sales volumes much smaller than Pepsi-Cola and Diet Pepsi had considerably higher network-to-spot ratios. While Coca-Cola brands have some of the highest ratios, there are other brands with much smaller sales volumes that have comparable network-to-spot ratios. It is also clear that Coca-Cola and PepsiCo differ considerably in the advertising strategies they employ in promoting their principal brands, with Coca-Cola relying more heavily on network advertising as measured by dollars per case.

Brand Loyalty. The value or strength of a brand name is most often explained by the consistency and quality of the associated product. Brands convey consumer information, and a price premium to a strong trademark is an incentive to producers to continue to deliver consistent quality at competitive prices.[31]

The strength of the PepsiCo and Coca-Cola brands does not seem to impede entry or price competition in this industry. Various measures of brand

Table 5–6
Network and Spot Advertising, 1988

| Brand | Advertising Expenditure | | Ratio, Network /Spot) | Sales (million cases) |
	Network	Spot TV		
Regular				
Minute Maid	$5,751,500	$1,646,600	3.49	53.7
A&W	4,097,600	1,505,400	2.72	52.5
Dr Pepper	9,161,600	4,660,200	1.97	325.6
Sprite	12,545,300	6,468,600	1.94	267.5
Coca-Cola Classic	36,058,000	19,274,500	1.87	1,501.0
Seven-Up	7,583,300	4,876,900	1.55	235.0
Cherry Seven-Up	7,064,400	5,578,000	1.27	34.0
Coca-Cola	3,337,800	3,379,000	0.99	95.0
Pepsi-Cola	21,164,400	39,643,700	0.53	1,370.0
Seven-Up Gold	1,615,400	6,922,700	0.23	5.1
Mountain Dew	319,800	5,407,600	0.06	255.0
Slice	197,800	10,861,800	0.02	122.0
RC	0	5,170,100	0.00	122.0
Canada Dry	0	4,167,700	0.00	102.0
Diet				
Diet Sprite	5,627,700	1,929,300	2.92	56.0
Diet Coke	33,228,000	14,032,300	2.37	612.0
Diet Dr Pepper	5,763,600	3,772,280	1.53	33.1
Diet Seven-Up	3,834,600	3,270,000	1.17	73.6
Diet Pepsi	18,842,900	27,259,100	0.69	390.0
Mountain Dew	0	4,538,900	0.00	30.0

Sources: *Maxwell Report* (1989); and *Beverage Industry* (July 1989).

loyalty (as opposed to strength of brand image) indicate that soft drink consumers purchase a wide variety of brands and frequently switch among them. There is no indication that product loyalty impedes entry. Moreover, all available evidence indicates strong price sensitivity, even for the high-share brands. The strength, vitality, and continued entry of private label brands of soft drinks underscore this last point.

Shelf Space. To be commercially successful, soft drink manufacturers must find retailers willing to sell their products. Shelf space is important at two stages in the product introduction process. First, a firm introducing a new soft drink may desire shelf space in at least a few food stores to test consumer response to the product.[32] Second, if test marketing indicates success is likely, shelf space in a larger number of stores is required to sell the product in commercial quantities on a sustained basis.

Companies that already market one or more soft drinks on a national or regional basis can test market by introducing a prospective new product through their usual distribution networks in limited geographic areas. Coca-Cola, for example, may ask its bottler in a particular area to stock a new product along with the Coca-Cola products the bottler already places on supermarket shelves.[33] If a test suggests a new soft drink has potential, the results of the test can then be used to introduce the product into other areas.

Available data and trade literature show that once a new soft drink has demonstrated its appeal to consumers, manufacturers can rapidly expand distribution to a large number of supermarkets. The case histories of A&W, Snapple, Vernor's, New England Apple, Canfield's, and many others are illustrative.

The apparent ease with which manufacturers of new soft drinks can find supermarkets to stock their products and the rapidity with which distribution can be expanded once a product's commercial potential has been demonstrated are a natural consequence of profit-maximizing behavior on the part of grocery stores. To build and maintain volume, grocery stores constantly adjust their product offerings to create a mix attractive to potential customers. Consumers vary widely in their tastes, and consumer preferences are constantly changing. This is as true for soft drinks as for other food products. For these reasons, food stores stock a variety of brands and flavors and quickly introduce products proved successful elsewhere. If they do not, they will lose customers to other stores that offer opportunities for experimentation.

Shapiro, who examined the motivation for consumer experimentation, points out that experimentation is economically rational, especially for products like soft drinks that are purchased frequently:

> A "mystery" product is well worth a try in case it happens to suit your taste well. If it is a poor product you can always return to the established brand.

So long as consumers believe there to be a reasonable probability that the new product is superior to existing brands, there is a large "information value" to sampling the new brand. This is an inducement, rather than a barrier, to entry.[34]

Some of the concerns expressed about the ability of manufacturers to acquire space for new products reflect the impressions that shelf space is seriously limited in supply and thus cannot be expanded to accommodate new products and the space that is available is allocated to established, high-volume brands, such as those of Coca-Cola and PepsiCo, out of proportion to their contributions to total soft drink sales.

Concerns that the supply of shelf space for soft drinks has not been expanding are unfounded. Estimates of average shelf space allocated to soft drinks from 1973 through 1987 are shown in table 5–7. Over this fifteen-year period, soft drinks' shelf space in the average supermarket increased from 145 feet to 276 feet, a gain of over 65 percent. Clearly the supply of shelf space for soft drinks has been highly elastic. Moreover, many supermarkets are developing separate (and additional) sections for storing soft drinks.[35]

Even if the supply of shelf space were not elastic, new products could still expect access to shelf space if sales of individual brands did not increase in proportion to their shelf space allocations. In such situations, super-

Table 5–7
Shelf Space Allocated to Carbonated Soft Drinks in Supermarkets, 1973–1987

Year	Average Linear Feet	Annual Percentage Change	Cumulative Percentage Change from 1973	Cumulative Percentage Change from 1977
1973	145	————	————	————
1974	155	6.9	6.9	————
1975	169	9.0	15.9	————
1976	182	7.7	23.6	————
1977	193	6.0	29.7	————
1978	195	1.0	30.7	1.0
1979	209	7.2	37.9	8.2
1980	223	6.7	44.6	14.9
1981	221	(0.9)	43.7	14.0
1982	228	3.2	46.8	17.2
1983	239	4.8	51.7	22.0
1984	247	3.3	55.0	25.4
1985	251	1.6	56.6	27.0
1986	258	2.8	59.4	29.8
1987	276	7.0	66.4	36.7

Sources: *Progressive Grocer* (September 1984, 1985, 1986, 1987; November 1988) and *Chain Store Age/Supermarket* (October 1977, 1980, 1981).

markets would have strong incentives to add new soft drink products, even if shelf space allocated to more established products has to be reduced. Mark Albion reviewed the research on the relationship between volume and shelf space and concluded that this "research indicates that the amount of shelf space given to a brand does not increase proportionately with the brand's unit sales at the store."[36] Indeed, Coca-Cola and PepsiCo's products are under-represented on retailers' shelves when comparing percentage of shelf space with sales levels.

Albion's analysis is consistent with the results of statistical studies of the relationship between shelf space and sales volume for retail consumer goods that have shown that for a given brand, sales increase if the brand's shelf space is increased but by a smaller proportion than the increase in shelf space.[37] This means that even if shelf space cannot be expanded, a supermarket offered a new soft drink with demonstrated consumer appeal may increase its total soft drink sales by reducing the space allocated to its current soft drinks to make room for the new product. By adding the new soft drink, total sales per unit of shelf space will be increased.

All evidence points to the conclusion that manufacturers can acquire shelf space for trial or general distribution. This is exactly what economic analysis would predict for supermarkets that try to maximize profits.

Cooperative Merchandising Agreements. A majority of soft drink volume at both retail and wholesale is sold on promotion. The retailer's motivations to promote are a reflection of its profit-maximizing calculus. The retailer makes a decision to promote a product if it believes the costs of promoting will be outweighed by the gains from additional sales. Although the retailer hopes a specific promotion will increase sales of that product, promotion of individual products is often used to build traffic at the retailer's stores. More consumers will enter the store in order to purchase the promoted product, and once in the store, they tend to buy items that are not on sale as well.

When deciding which products to promote, the retailer is concerned with the product's own sales, as well as its ability to draw in customers. Nelson and Hilke found that three characteristics determine whether a specific product receives promotional support: past purchases, availability, and past market share.[38] Past purchases are important because consumers have information about those brands; they know what levels of price and quality to expect. They are thus more likely to recognize a good price on a frequently purchased product and respond favorably to its promotion. Brand availability is also important. Brands that are easily available are more likely to be sold in many stores. Thus, consumers can compare prices across stores and readily recognize the value of the promotion. Finally, market share is important because the inventory costs are lower for products with larger shares. The retailer acquires additional supplies when planning a promotion. Promoting an item with a small share may leave the retailer with a large inventory and is unlikely to build store traffic.

Trade promotion is also important to the manufacturer of the product. Promotion increases sales, which raises market share.[39] Hence, both the retailer and the manufacturer have incentives to participate in product promotion. However, display space and advertising lineage may be limited at a particular time for the retailer. This may mean the retailer does not follow the promotion suggestions of a particular manufacturer interested in increasing sales and the market share of its product. As a result, the promotional efforts of the retailer and the manufacturer may differ with respect to specific products. This difference often necessitates coordinated promotional efforts by the manufacturer and the retailer. One study found that retailers were much more likely to promote particular products when coordinated with manufacturer promotional support.[40]

Among the marketing promotions employed in the carbonated soft drink industry to promote products are cooperative merchandising agreements (CMAs) offered by bottlers to grocery chains. A CMA is a contract between a bottler/distributor and retail outlets to promote particular products cooperatively—a point typically lost in the opposition to CMA agreements. That is, the CMA is an agreement between the bottler/distributor and the retailer. The retailer is free to decide whether to enter into the agreement and, having decided to participate in such an agreement, it is the retailer—not the bottler—that has the final word on contract provisions. Because the control of the contract is in the hands of the retailer, there are almost as many different versions of a CMA as there are retailers.

Typically the distributor offers improved price terms in exchange for marketing assistance from the retailer (for instance, inclusion in feature newspaper ads, in-store displays, temporary promotional exclusivity for a particular brand, package size, or flavor). CMAs are not found at every retail chain or in all local and regional areas, and their terms vary widely. Moreover, many representatives of the grocery trade do not generally consider CMAs to be binding, perhaps reflecting the relative bargaining strength of retailers.[41]

CMAs result in cost savings. One cost saving arises because the typical CMA is between a bottler and several retail outlets combined through the local chain organization. Transaction cost is reduced because one transaction between a bottler and several retail stores in a chain or a co-op is cheaper than several separate transactions, provided the desired feature promotion is relatively uniform. Of course, the latter proviso may not apply in all cases. A supermarket chain may decide that newspaper advertising of specials specific to several store locations is not cost-effective. The upshot of this cost-benefit calculus is that, depending on the circumstances, a more or less inclusive CMA will be efficient. Most importantly, the opportunity to contract with several retail outlets through a chain or a co-op organization reduces the cost of transacting.

CMAs also promote inventory and production scheduling efficiencies for retailers and bottlers. Feature promotion is expected to result in increased sales for the featured products. Anticipation of sales increases leads bottlers to expand production and build inventory and retailers to expand their inventories and perhaps provide additional shelf or floor space. The use of CMAs thus facilitates production and inventory planning.

There are additional scheduling benefits that accrue to retailers. Retailers sell numerous products, many of them featured, and must therefore schedule several different feature promotions in the same time period. CMAs facilitate retailers' plans to accommodate competing demands for shelf and floor space and for advertising space by different types of products. They allow bottlers and retailers to realize greater planning efficiencies than would be available without them.

Some competitors complain that CMAs are a form of unfair competition; the exclusivity provisions of various CMAs, they charge, shut them out of marketing opportunities. The arguments against CMAs presume a degree of exclusivity that may not exist in practice and a much narrower set of marketing options than actually exists. In fact CMAs usually are exclusive with respect to only the newspaper promotion of a particular brand or package size. Therefore retail stores (using its own brands) and competing bottlers remain free to conduct in-store displays and promotions and frequently do so (many times trading on the exclusive promotion and the traffic it generates).

For example, even if a seller locks up twenty-six weeks of a newspaper promotion of a particular brand or package at chain A, that does not foreclose competing sellers from the other twenty-six weeks at chain A. Moreover, competitive products are still displayed in other ways at chain A, and there are other chains in the same area with available slots.[42] Convenience stores, drug chains, and service stations are also receptive to and frequently engage in soft drink promotions. For example, at Basics, a grocery chain in the Washington, D.C., area, the Thorofare brand is always available to compete against Coke and Pepsi promotions. During the week of October 16, 1989, Thorofare soft drinks (cola, orange, grape, root beer, and several other flavors) were available for 78 cents for a 2-liter container. The 3-liter container was featured in an end-aisle display; its sale price was 98 cents. In addition, Basics had other brands, such as Shasta, available for 83 cents per 2-liter container.

Carbonated soft drinks are promoted most heavily on holiday weekends. Washington, D.C., area supermarket ads for the week prior to Memorial Day in 1988 were sampled. Giant had Classic Coke on sale for 99 cents per 2-liter bottle. Safeway was promoting Cragmont Cola 12-ounce cans, twenty-four per case, for $3.99; MacGruder's featured three carbonated soft drink ads:

Canada Dry, Orange Crush, and Hires 2-liter containers for 89 cents and 12-ounce six-pack cans for $1.49, Seven-Up (Regular, Diet, and Gold) 16-ounce six-pack bottles at $1.69 and 2-liter bottles for 99 cents, and Pepsi 16-ounce six-pack bottles at $1.89 and 2-liter bottles for 77 cents. High's Dairy Stores also had a variety of food ads on the same day. Pepsi products were featured in ads: 16-ounce six-packs for $1.89 and 2-liter for 99 cents. Other beverages featured were Canada Dry, Perrier, and Budweiser.[43]

We performed some empirical research on the impact of CMAs on carbonated soft drink volume and price in selected areas of the country. (The results are reported in appendix K.) These results first compared the Chicago area, which does not extensively use CMAs, with geographically proximate areas that do employ CMAs extensively—St. Louis, Indianapolis, and Cleveland— on per capita carbonated soft drink consumption and average carbonated soft drink prices. In all cases, carbonated soft drink prices were higher and volume lower in Chicago.

The second analysis, of the Boston area, ran three separate regressions as a function of CMA intensity. The three dependent variables were brand volume, brand price, and brand displays, with data gathered on Pepsi, Coke, Seven-Up, RC, Dr Pepper, Canada Dry, and private label brands. The results were that Pepsi and Coke volume respond positively to CMA intensity, while their prices responded negatively. The prices and volumes of other brands were unaffected by the intensity of Pepsi and Coke CMAs. Moreover, there was no effect in the data of the Pepsi CMA on Coke, and vice versa. These results suggest that CMAs are additive to market volume and have little affect on other brands. This evidence provides some indication that CMAs play a procompetitive role in the grocery store; they facilitate the expansion of a brand's output at a reduced price.

Complaints about CMAs may simply be a reaction to the tremendous volume effect that promotions have on products with very strong brand images. The data suggest that, despite the advertising and other brand promotion of Coca-Cola and PepsiCo products over the years, Coke and Pepsi drinkers are extremely price sensitive. Pepsi and Coke have strong positive brand images, which means that while consumers on average will not pay relatively higher prices for Coca-Cola and PepsiCo products, they will buy large quantities if those brands are selling at a reduced price. Consequently, competitors may be mistaking the efficacy of CMAs with the strength of the PepsiCo and Coca-Cola brand images. This suggests that CMAs are ultimately a manifestation of a particular competitive strategy. They do not exclude lower-priced brands from the supermarket or from the consumer. Rather, they spur competition and increase consumer welfare.

Albion explains why soft drinks are so heavily promoted. He developed and empirically tested an economic model that explains the large differences observed in the margins grocery stores earn on different types of products.

Grocers typically select certain of their products for intense (low price) promotion in order to draw additional customers into the store. Once they are in the store, the retailer hopes that they will purchase other products, which are not on sale, as well.

The choice of products to promote at low prices is not random. Those most frequently promoted are products the retailer believes will draw large numbers of consumers—typically those frequently purchased by a large percentage of a store's potential customers. Because soft drinks have a household penetration rate of over 89 percent, they fall in the group of products that retailers promote more heavily.[44]

Among the products in categories with high penetration rates, the brands that will be most heavily promoted are the ones that are most visible to consumers. According to Albion's model, manufacturers advertise their products in part because this causes retailers to price their products more competitively, which increases sales. Referring to the grocery market, he explained that "in a retail market so heavily dominated by price competition as a means of differentiation among the stores . . . it is the price competition on advertised brands, which reduces their gross margins and total contributions, that is central to the profit-maximizing mass retailer's strategy."[45] Albion also points out that price competition on highly advertised brands limits the prices of less advertised brands as well. This too may explain the opposition of certain soft drink companies to the use of CMAs by other soft drink companies.

Even without CMAs, where each wholesaler offers deals weekly, retailers will choose to promote the more popular brands a relatively higher proportion of the time. Strength of brand image is built and earned over time on the basis of consistently fulfilling consumer expectations with respect to the price and quality delivered. It can be expected that, if the price and quality package delivered by Coca-Cola and PepsiCo diminished relative to that of their competitors, the proportion of CMAs and promotions accounted for by PepsiCo and Coca-Cola in retail outlets would also fall. Moreover, it should be emphasized again that CMAs do not prevent alternative pricing and promotional activities with respect to competing products by the retailers.

The argument against CMAs can be reduced to the proposition that entry is difficult in the soft drink industry because promotional pricing is too aggressive (low).

Notes

1. Rather than focusing on "barriers to entry," the current *Department of Justice Merger Guidelines,* Fed. Reg. 26,283, June 29, 1984, analyze ease of entry or the likelihood of entry in response to noncompetitive pricing. Analyzing entry in terms of barriers can be misleading in that many so-called barriers are often nothing more than

requirements for entry that entrants with varying degrees of ability can meet. Requirements that may reduce the probability of entry are those with significant (relative to the scale of the business) fixed costs that cannot be substantially recovered through resale in the event of exit. Highly specialized and costly production equipment for which there is no resale market is an example; delivery trucks would not be a good example because they can be readily used in a number of different businesses.

2. Entry for the purposes of our analysis properly includes both de novo entry and expansion by incumbent fringe firms. Expansion by small or fringe sellers is as important as new entry because "collusion is less likely to occur if small or fringe sellers in the market are able profitably to increase output substantially in response to a 'small but significant and nontransitory' increase in price and thus to undermine a cartel." *Department of Justice Merger Guidelines,* secs. 3.3, 3.43.

3. "New Packages Revitalize 'Old' Products," *Packaging* (October 1988).

4. For many years, *New Product News* has reported monthly the introduction of new consumer products ranging from beverages, cereals, canned meat, and specialty foods to household supplies and health and beauty aids. In all, *New Product News* reports on twenty-six categories of consumer goods. The new product introductions include both de novo entry and expansion. If a manufacturer introduces a new product line with multiple flavors, each flavor is counted as a separate product introduction. Separate tabulations of the number of firms introducing products and number of introductory "events" (counting the simultaneous introduction of several flavors in a given month as a single event) are provided in appendix I. The number of new products discussed in this analysis should be a conservative estimate since *New Product News* does not report new products from many local or regional manufacturers or private label brands.

5. Appendix I contains tabulations of the number of entities making introductions in various time periods and the number of introductory events (counting multiple flavor introductions in a given month as a single event). These tabulations make clear that the pattern of persistent and frequent entry is not an artifact of the measure of entry employed.

6. Although a large percentage of the successful new carbonated soft drink products were introduced by PepsiCo and Coca-Cola as measured by volume of product sold as compared to the number of new products, the aggregate amount of new product introductions is important in an entrepreneurial sense: it strongly indicates that sufficient product space is available for new products.

7. "New Packaging Revitalizes 'Old' Products."

8. "Diverse Population Governs District's Distinct Tastes," *Beverage Industry* (February 1988).

9. See Richard Porter, *Cases in Competition Strategy* (New York: Free Press, 1983); and Richard Caves and John Pinter, "From Entry Barriers to Mobility Barriers," *Quarterly Journal of Economics* 91 (1977): 241–261.

10. See *Department of Justice Merger Guidelines,* secs. 3.1, 3.411.

11. The extent to which different groups compete for the same set of customers is an important factor in determining the effect of strategic differences among groups on the intensity of competition. Media advertising utilized by the various soft drink

and beverage groups makes it particularly obvious that firms in different groups are targeting the same sets of customers.

12. "Stroh Sundance Natural, High Five Expanding into New U.S. Markets," *Beverage Industry* (October 1988).

13. "Corr Adding Water to New-Product Flood," *Crain's Chicago Business,* April 7, 1986; "A New Beverage's Ancient Roots," *U.S. Chamber of Commerce* (March 1983); "Now Soft-Drink Makers Brace for the Juice Wars," *New York Times,* June 2, 1985; "New Markets for an Old Brand Name," *Forbes,* December 17, 1984; "Snapple Enters the Mainstream," *AD Week,* October 2, 1989; "Snapple Cracks Tough Pop Market," *Crain's New York Business,* August 14, 1989; and "Sweetened Seltzers Losing Bit of Their '80s Fizz," *Beverage Industry* (April 1989).

14. See "Root Beer Float," *Forbes,* December 11, 1989.

15. Of course, not all brands do as well. Procter & Gamble recently sold the Crush brand to Schweppes because of its failure to generate greater sales.

16. In addition, there are a large number of food marketing firms engaged in significant levels of research and development, such as Nestle and General Foods.

17. Based on *National Beverage Marketing Directory* (Mingo Junction, OH: Beverage Marketing Corporation, 1989).

18. Ibid.

19. Concentrates sold by manufacturers like Coca-Cola and PepsiCo generally carry higher list prices than unbranded concentrate, in large part, because these sellers utilize the concentrate price to charge bottlers for the marketing, research and development, and quality control functions performed by the concentrate seller on behalf of the brand. Subsequently, reductions in the net transaction price of concentrate are given to bottlers in the form of funds for various marketing programs. The mainstream soft drink firms use concentrate production and sales as a marketing vehicle. This is a strategic characteristic that distinguishes these firms from other soft drink firms (such as Faygo, Shasta, Cragmont) and from other competitive beverage firms.

20. In 1980 the Soft Drink Interbrand Competitive Act (15 U.S. Code 3501) was passed. Section 2 provides that "nothing contained in any antitrust law shall render unlawful the inclusion and enforcement in any trademark licensing contract or agreement, pursuant to which the licensee engages in the manufacture (including manufacture by a sublicensee, agent, or subcontractor), distribution, and sale of a trademarked soft drink product, of provisions granting the licensee the sole and exclusive right to manufacture, distribute, and sell such product in a defined geographic area or limiting the licensee, directly or indirectly, to the manufacture, distribution, and sale of such product only for ultimate resale to consumers within a defined geographic area." 15 U.S.C. 3502.

21. Route drivers are often responsible for making sales, although preselling by a separate sales force is becoming more common. Route drivers are also usually responsible for ensuring that shelves are stocked adequately and that the beverage is displayed properly.

22. PepsiCo is increasingly utilizing truck load deliveries to significant chains in combination with preselling.

23. Almost 2,000 food brokers and more than 1,000 wholesale grocers operate

in the United States. In addition, almost 500 candy, tobacco, and other distributors are available to distribute beverages. See appendix J.

24. This includes nearly all of Coca-Cola's fountain syrup sales, much of the fountain sales of Dr Pepper and some of Seven-Up's, most private label sales, sales of brands such as Faygo and Shasta, and portions of RC's grocery store sales.

25. That is not to say that warehouse delivery guarantees success. Procter & Gamble's failure with Crush is an example.

26. Research on these factors has generated a voluminous literature. The most recent work on the topic generally favors the view that advertising facilitates entry and does not represent a special concern to antitrust enforcement agencies. See, for example, Carl Shapiro, "Advertising as a Barrier to Entry," *FTC Working Paper* (June 1982).

27. Advertising can be a barrier to entry only into strategic groups for which heavy advertising is an important element of strategy. Even if advertising does impede entry into a strategic group characterized by heavy advertising, this is potentially a competitive problem only if less advertised brands do not discipline the prices of heavily advertised brands. Otherwise advertising as a barrier to entry into a strategic group of firms with high advertising expenditures reduces to the meaningless proposition that a firm must advertise a lot to be one of the firms with high advertising. That is, for heavy advertising by some firms to be a competitive problem, this advertising must both limit the entry of new firms that also advertise heavily and insulate to some degree the prices of highly advertised brands from competition from less advertised brands.

28. Kenneth Boyer and Kent Lancaster, "Are There Scale Economies in Advertising?" *Journal of Business* 59 (1986): 510.

29. Ibid., p. 523.

30. See, for example, Shapiro, "Advertising as a Barrier to Entry."

31. See Benjamin Klein and Keith Leffler, "The Role of Market Forces in Assuring Contractual Performance," *Journal of Political Economy* 89 (August 1981).

32. While it is apparently typical to test market a new brand or product concept (e.g., PepsiCo's Lemon-Lime Slice), firms frequently omit test marketing for new products that are similar to their own existing products or similar to a competitor's products (e.g., Cherry Cola Slice).

33. A bottler's affiliation with Coca-Cola or PepsiCo does not guarantee additional shelf space for new soft drinks. Firms that already have a shelf space allotment, such as Coca-Cola and PepsiCo bottlers, are frequently required to cannibalize the space of their existing products to test market a new soft drink. Even in this case, the change must still be authorized by the store.

34. Shapiro, "Advertising as a Barrier to Entry," p. 5.

35. "On Safari: Secondary Soft Drink Brands Hunt for New Merchandising Ideas," *Beverage World* (May 1988).

36. Mark Albion, *Advertising's Hidden Effects* (Boston: Auburn House, 1983), p. 115.

37. See, for example, Ronald Curhan "Shelf Space Allocation and Profit Maximization in Mass Retailing," *Journal of Marketing* (July 1973): 54–60.

38. Phillip Nelson and John Hilke, "Retail Featuring as an Entry or Mobility Barrier in Manufacturing," *FTC Working Paper* (September 1986).

39. See "The Dillon Study," *Progressive Grocer* (1960). Michel Chevalier and Ronald Curhan make the same point in "Retail Promotions as a Function of Trade Promotions: A Descriptive Analysis," *Sloan Management Review* 18 (1976).

40. Larry G. Hamm, "Food Distributor Procurement Practices: Their Implications for Food System Structure and Coordination" (Ph.D. diss., Michigan State University, 1981).

41. Some CMAs are annual contracts; others may be arranged quarterly or even monthly. The retailer has a choice of how many weeks it will feature the bottler's product and on which weeks the promotions will occur.

42. Even if chain A has a 25 percent share of grocery sales, twenty-six weeks would represent only a 12.5 percent lock-up of displays.

43. Couponing is yet another marketing approach not restricted by CMAs.

44. Albion, *Advertising's Hidden Effects,* p. 210. Household penetration rate is defined as the fraction of all households that make a purchase from a product class during a one-year period.

45. Ibid., p. 131.

6
Collusion

S oft drink concentrate producers have no history of collusion, and there appear to be a number of fundamental reasons for this fact. Each reason is important in its own right, and when all factors are considered together, they may well explain why this industry performs so well despite high concentration statistics as measured by carbonated drink sales.

Factors That Inhibit Collusion

Competition from Other Beverages

Soft drinks face vigorous competition from such beverages as coffee, tea, powdered soft drinks, juice, bottled water, and milk. This competition has an important implication for the prospect of collusion among concentrate producers. Loss of sales to producers of substitute beverages would reduce the gains from collusion and hence the prospect of collusion in the first place. This basic point is important. If soft drink prices rise, consumers can and will shift to alternative beverages.

The point here is not whether these alternative beverage products should be added together for the purpose of calculating concentration statistics. The issue is whether these alternative products discipline the conduct of PepsiCo, Coca-Cola, and other concentrate producers. The evidence on this issue is overwhelming: marketers of carbonated soft drinks do not stand alone, without competition from other beverages.

Prospects for New Entry and Expansion

Entry is a real threat in the beverage industry; it mitigates strongly against the prospects for collusion by carbonated soft drink producers.[1] The identity of potential entrants is both predictable and unpredictable. The specific identities of entrants like Snapple and R.J. Corr are not predictable because they are de novo entrants in the purest sense. New soft drink product introduction in reaction to profitable opportunities by established food marketing companies that already produce and sell beverages is more predictable. These food marketing companies include firms like Nestle, Beatrice, and Borden, which are every bit as formidable as PepsiCo and Coca-Cola. Table 6–1 lists some food marketing firms and selected brands.[2]

Virtually all beverage firms have the production and distribution capabilities to enter the growing carbonated soft drink business. This new entry is another strong disciplinary force on any attempt at collusion and higher prices by existing soft drink firms.

Competitive Conditions

Number of Concentrate Producers and Strategic Groups. A collusive scheme faces two basic problems.[3] First, sellers must agree on the details of a collusive agreement. How will output be restricted? How will excess returns be shared? Second, once put into place, the scheme must be monitored and enforced. Otherwise individual firms will find it in their interest to cheat on the agreement by secretly cutting prices, thereby leading to the demise of the collusion. On both counts, the number of competitors (actual and potential) is relevant when analyzing the probability of successful collusion.[4]

On this issue, it is clear that there are more than a few soft drink producer-sellers, not to mention competitors in other beverage categories (how feasible is it to think, for example, that a coffee producer and a soft

Table 6–1
Beverage Products, by Firm

Firm	Prominent Brands
Nestle	Nestea, Nescafe, Taster's Choice, Libby, Juicy Juice
Beatrice	Tropicana, Tropi, Meadow Gold, Swiss Miss
General Mills	Nature Valley
McKesson	Sparklett's Alhambra
Borden	Wylers Lite Line, Borden, RealLime, Sippin Pak, Kava
Heinz	Alba 66, Weight Watchers, Heinz
Quaker	Gatorade
Campbell Soup	Juiceworks, Juice Bowl
Stroh Brewery	Stroh, Sundance Natural Sparklers

drink producer will collude?).[5] Moreover, firms that have made a similar choice with respect to important strategic variables constitute a strategic group. Variation among strategic groups is an important dimension of competition, which reduces the likelihood of noncompetitive performance. In industries with two or more strategic groups, firms in one group may have difficulty understanding and responding to the strategies of members in different groups. Furthermore, firms in different groups may have different objectives. Both of these factors reduce the likelihood of successful collusion.

Within the soft drink segment of the beverage market, there is substantial strategic variation, which would make cartel formation and implementation extremely complex and difficult. Some strategic groups or variables include private label brands (Safeway, McDonalds, Kroger, Giant); warehouse brands (Faygo, Shasta); regional brands (Big Red, Cheerwine, Sun-Drop, Franks); brands that rely on non-PepsiCo non–Coca-Cola bottlers (Seven-Up, RC, A&W, Canada Dry); limited line brands (A&W, Squirt, Dr Pepper, Bubble-Up, Vernor's, Seven-Up); cola brands (Coke, Pepsi-Cola, RC, Double Cola); and firms such as Coca-Cola and PepsiCo. PepsiCo and Coca-Cola also differ in their competitive strategies. Coca-Cola, for example, uses food service distributors to sell its product to food service accounts, while PepsiCo uses bottlers. Coca-Cola and PepsiCo, moreover, pursue differing strategies on advertising.

For all the reasons enumerated, it is not likely that PepsiCo and Coca-Cola could profitably maintain a price conspiracy at the concentrate level. Should they take such a course of action, they would be disciplined in the market by other soft drink producers and by consumers, who would switch to alternative beverage products.

Number of Soft Drink Brands and Packages. A basic issue related to the probability of collusion can be summarized with a question: what must the conspirators agree on? As we have seen, there are a large number of soft drink producers and strategic groups and among these producers an incredibly large array of brands. In 1988, for example, over 200 different soft drink brands were identified. Such differentiation compounds the difficulty of reaching a collusive agreement or maintaining one. Not only must prices be agreed upon, but nonprice competition across brands and types of products must be controlled if collusion is to be totally successful. A collusive scheme could be undone by both secret price cutting and/or by nonprice competition.

Moreover, nonprice competition entails many other aspects of soft drink products than simply brands, among them, package sizes, convenience of purchase, and quality of advertising.[6] (Appendix B shows the relative growth of plastic containers as a packaging innovation.) Plastic containers accounted for no soft drink sales in 1973 but 32 percent of packaged gallons by 1988.

Collusion must control all of these factors if it is to succeed. Product differentiation and nonprice competition increase the complexity of collusion, thereby making such behavior less likely.

New Products. A nonprice factor that mitigates against the prospect of collusion is the frequent appearance of new products. There is clearly a great deal of entry of new products in the industry, many of them from smaller firms. Like any other form of entry, these new products make collusion less likely because they take away the gains from collusion. Thus, even in the unlikely event of effective collusion over the price and nonprice dimensions of existing soft drink products, new product innovations would also have to be controlled for collusion to be totally successful. This does not seem feasible in the soft drink category, much less for beverages as a whole.

Pricing. Successful soft drink producers seek to increase their volume of sales to maintain and increase their market shares. The route to increased volume is heavy promotion and price discounting of products. This behavior follows from the nature of the soft drink business, which is characterized by largely fixed marketing organizations. The objective of the firms is to increase the amount of soft drinks sold by the fixed marketing organizations. This is why volume is so important in this business; it spreads the cost of fixed marketing assets and increases returns to the firms. To achieve and maintain volume, firms must aggressively market and price their products. Firms that do not behave in this way do not fare well in this industry (Seven-Up is an example).

This model implies that collusion among concentrate producers would be difficult to sustain. Price increases would lead to volume decreases, inconsistent with the way firms in the industry operate. Collusion implies lost volume, which puts heavy pressure on soft drink firms to lower prices.

One would thus expect to see that successful soft drink firms are volume and price conscious. Pricing in the industry will be intensively competitive, and volume of sales will be quite sensitive to pricing. In the end, it all redounds to the benefit of soft drink consumers in terms of lower prices for products.[7]

The pricing sequence in this industry begins with the pricing of concentrate. Concentrate is sold to bottlers, who mix it with other ingredients to produce the finished soft drink product and deliver it for final sale in retail outlets. Concentrate prices by themselves are very misleading, however, because concentrate producers offer price incentives to bottlers so as to be competitive at the retail level. There are a myriad of incentive accounts maintained between concentrate suppliers and bottlers. The sheer variety of these accounts would make collusion between concentrate producers on soft drink prices difficult to originate or sustain. Secret price cutting could be masked in the maze of accounts between the concentrate suppliers and the bottlers.

To make matters more difficult, the levels of promotional monies provided to bottlers by the same concentrate producer as a percentage of concentrate price vary significantly from year to year and even more significantly from product to product in a year. Also, the level of promotional monies from the same concentrate producer as a percentage of revenues may vary from bottler to bottler, and given the manner in which the local bottler determines its actual transaction prices (the vast majority are based on a variety of promotions), it is very difficult to infer the net transaction price from bottler pricing activity.

In summary, marketing is tied extremely closely to aggressive pricing for the most successful firms like PepsiCo and Coca-Cola. Because true transaction prices for concentrate are complex, highly variable, and largely invisible, the structural environment makes collusive oligopoly pricing difficult between firms such as Coca-Cola and PepsiCo.

Regional and Local Differences in Competition. Another factor mitigating against the prospect of collusion is that major competitive battlegrounds are regional and local. Promotion varies across locales in response to competitive pressures. Such a myriad of market circumstances makes collusion very unlikely by being much more costly to effect and sustain.

The immense variety in the circumstances of local competition was already discussed with the aid of Nielsen data. The incredible array of competitive circumstances across localities and regions significantly retards the possibility of collusion. Under these conditions, collusion by concentrate producers is not likely.

Role of Buyers. Another element limiting the ability of a combination of concentrate producers to raise prices above competitive levels is the role of retailers. Many of the retail chains in this country are of significant size (table 6–2). Each of these chains is devoted to providing value to consumers by providing soft drinks at low prices. Regional chains fulfill the same role in their areas.

In the fountain area, firms such as McDonald's and Burger King provide similar significant discipline to Coca-Cola, PepsiCo, and other concentrate producers.

Company Behavior

The competitive rivalry between PepsiCo and Coca-Cola is inconsistent with collusion among soft drink concentrate producers. Competition between the two rivals can best be described as all-out war and is so well entrenched that it is unlikely to change.

Table 6–2
Size of Retailers

	Number of Stores	Retail Sales (1987) (billions)
Safeway	1,568	$18.3
Kroger	2,176	17.7
American Stores	1,460	14.2
Atlantic & Pacific	1,200	9.7
Winn-Dixie	1,253	8.8
Lucky Stores	483	6.9
Albertson's	465	5.9
Supermarket General	140	5.1

Source: *Marketing Guidebook* (Stamford, CT: Maclean Hunter Media, 1989).

Interfirm Rivalry

Collusive or cooperative behavior refers to situations in which firms recognize their mutual benefit in raising prices and restricting output and are capable of implementing and policing such market outcomes. Certain economic literature also suggests that less than perfectly competitive outcomes can result from noncollusive behavior. Economic models of competition in industries categorized by several large firms and numerous fringe competitors predict less than perfect economic performance under some circumstances.[8] By noncooperative behavior, we mean to suggest situations in which firms respond to reductions in output by their rivals by maintaining or expanding output. Noncooperative behavior results in less than perfectly competitive performance when a reduction in output by one firm is not fully offset by an expansion of output by the remaining firms.

The standard measure of market performance is the Lerner Index, which is the percentage markup of price over marginal cost. It can be calculated based on the HHI for carbonated soft drinks (2,713), the residual demand elasticity for carbonated soft drinks (-6.0), and an assumption about carbonated soft drink firms' responses to their competitors' behavior. For purposes of conservatively estimating the Lerner Index for the carbonated soft drink industry, we assume that in response to a reduction of output, rivals would maintain their output as opposed to expanding output. In these circumstances, the Lerner Index is $2713/6.0$, or 4.5 percent. Thus, even when the highest price-cost margin consistent with competitive interaction among carbonated soft drink firms is assumed, overall industry performance is estimated to be outstanding.

Bottler Price-Fixing Allegations

In the mid-1980s the United States Department of Justice Antitrust Division began to investigate and prosecute allegations of local price fixing by soft drink bottlers. Since 1986 a number of indictments have been handed down against independent bottling companies and their executives. Many of these indictments have resulted in convictions, following individual and corporate pleas. Substantial fines have been levied, and a number of individuals have been sentenced to jail. All of the indictments have been against bottlers owned by independent franchises of PepsiCo, Coca-Cola, and other franchisors.

Naked cartels to fix prices are not in the public interest, and the detection and prosecution of such activities represent one of the most praiseworthy aspects of antitrust law enforcement. Nevertheless, there is something to be learned from a closer look at these bottler price-fixing cases.

First, the alleged price fixing in the carbonated soft drink bottling business is consistent with the literature that suggests that attempts at overt collusion may be a manifestation of the degree of actual competition that exists in an industry. The intensity of competition in the beverage market has been documented in other parts of this study. This point bears on the earlier analysis of residual demand and markups in the industry.

Second, the bottler cases also indicate that tacit collusion (that is, collusion without overt communication) is not likely in the case of bottlers. The dynamic nature of the industry, the diverse and complex methods by which carbonated soft drinks are marketed, and the many bases on which such products compete with other beverages appear to limit the possibility of tacit collusion in this industry.

Third, no company-owned bottlers or personnel have been indicted. This follows from the nature of the industry. Company-owned bottlers are managed and operated by corporate executives of a vertically integrated concentrate producer and hence are driven by the corporate imperative of increasing volume in order to increase profits. Company-owned bottling executives, in addition, do not necessarily stand to gain anything personally from price fixing. They are part of a vertically integrated firm. Independently owned bottling executives, on the other hand, are typically part of a family-owned firm and potential residual claimants to the monopoly rents produced by a price-fixing scheme. For such reasons, vertical integration is consistent with reduced incentives for price fixing in the industry.

Fourth, we suspect that attempts at overt price fixing may not have had a significant impact on consumer welfare in the specific geographic areas where the price fixing allegedly took place given the dynamic nature of the competitive pressures that are likely to mount on such an agreement. Clearly, the total volume affected by this alleged activity represents a very small percentage of total carbonated soft drink volume sold in the 1980s. The industry has continued to perform exceptionally well, with overall prices declining in the 1980s and volume increasing dramatically. This does not mean that price fixing among bottlers should not be policed. Obviously, there is no dilemma here for antitrust enforcement. The prosecution of price fixing with a low social cost can create valuable precedents for use against price fixers in other industries.

The point is not to exonerate price fixing by independent bottlers. It is simply to place such activities in the proper interpretative context. Such activities do not mean that the whole industry should be labeled as uncompetitive. The stellar performance of this industry speaks for itself. Moreover, such activities do not constitute an argument against vertical integration in the industry or against horizontal consolidation of concentrate producers.

Notes

1. See Harold Demsetz, "Why Regulate Utilities?" *Journal of Law and Economics* 11 (April 1968): 55–66; Eugene Fama and Arthur Laffer, "The Number of Firms and Competition," *American Economic Review* 62 (September 1972): 670–674. These works show that in the absence of significant entry barriers, potential competition can discipline the pricing behavior of an industry with a few firms or even one firm. More recently, William Baumol, John Panzar, and Robert Willig offer a contestability theory of market structure that stresses ease of entry and exit, rather than the number of firms, as the critical determinants of competitive outcomes in a market. Baumol, Panzar, and Willig, *Contestable Markets and the Theory of Industry Structure,* 2d ed. (New York: Harcourt Brace Jovanovich, 1987).

2. Size is no guarantee of success; for example, Procter & Gamble did not fare well in selling soft drinks under current competitive conditions. The relevant issue is whether such firms (including Procter & Gamble) could and would sell soft drinks if Coca-Cola and PepsiCo restricted output and raised prices above competitive levels.

3. For a discussion of cartel theory, see George Stocking and Myron Watkins, *Cartels or Competition* (New York: Twentieth Century Fund, 1948); George Stigler, "A Theory of Oligopoly," *Journal of Political Economy* 72 (February 1964): 44–61; Daniel Orr and Paul McAvoy, "Price Strategies to Promote Cartel Stability," *Economica* 32 (May 1965): 186–197; Dale Osborne, "Cartel Problems," *American Economic Review* 66 (December 1976): 835–844; and John Mills and Kenneth Elzinga, "Cartel Problems: Comment," *American Economic Review* 68 (December 1978): 938–941.

4. This is especially true when colluders must avoid detection by antitrust agencies. With the threat of prosecution of collusion, colluding firms many times resort to "tacit" methods. Robert Bork questions the viability of collusion in such an environment. Bork, *The Antitrust Paradox* (New York: Basic Books, 1978).

5. Although the presence of a few firms may be necessary for successful collusion, Asch and Seneca argue that it is not a sufficient condition for collusion. More is involved in successful collusion than simply a small number of firms. Peter Asch and Joseph Seneca, "Is Collusion Profitable?" *Review of Economics and Statistics* 58 (February 1976): 1–12.

6. See Kevin Lancaster, "A New Approach to Consumer Theory," *Journal of Political Economy* 74 (April 1966): 132–157; and Sherwin Rosen, "Hedonic Prices and Implicit Markets: Product Differentiation in Pure Competition," *Journal of Political Economy* (February 1964): 34–55, for a discussion of how nonprice competition represents the responses of firms to the demands of consumers with varying incomes and varying uses for the product.

7. In other words, the demand for soft drinks is price elastic; small changes in price bring about large changes in quantity sold. High demand elasticity reduces the profitability of collusion and therefore the incentive to collude. See Richard Posner, *Economic Analysis of the Law* (Boston: Little, Brown, 1977); and Yale Brozen, *Concentration, Mergers and Public Policy* (New York: Macmillan, 1982).

8. See, for example, Janish Ordover, James Sykes, and Robert Willig, "Herfindahl Concentration, Rivalry and Mergers," *Harvard Law Review* 95 (1981–1982): 1857.

7
Vertical Integration

T his book has focused primarily on issues of horizontal competition among carbonated soft drink producers at the various levels of the business: concentrate production, bottling and distribution, and retail. Since the mid-1960s, there has been a significant amount of consolidation among bottlers, with the number of bottling plants falling from 6,662 in 1950, to 2,398 in 1975, and approximately 1,000 in 1988.[1] Moreover, the industry has been increasingly characterized by vertical integration. In the late 1970s, PepsiCo and Coca-Cola began buying back bottling and franchise rights from their independent bottlers. Appendix L lists the more significant vertical acquisitions by PepsiCo and Coca-Cola between 1979 and 1989. Our purpose in this section is to review this bottler consolidation and vertical integration, albeit briefly, and also to review some recent evidence concerning the economic effects of these trends.

Bottler Consolidation and Economies

We believe there should be little, if any, debate about whether bottler consolidations have reduced production and other related costs. In many instances, the exclusive territories granted to bottlers by PepsiCo, Coca-Cola, and other concentrate producers were delineated many years ago and are highly inefficient in the light of current technologies in production, packaging, distribution, and promotion. Increased economies of scale in bottling and canning, the development of bulk distribution, and the consolidation of local media markets have increased the optimal size of franchise territories.

The large majority of bottler consolidations have included the closing of small, relatively inefficient bottling operations and the consolidation of operations into larger, more efficient firms. The general competitive pressures in the industry and the larger number of products now marketed make it difficult for many small bottling plants to exist because they cannot efficiently handle the large, multifilling lines dedicated to specific products and package types necessary to produce products at the lowest cost.[2] One recent study concluded that bottler consolidations resulted in the combination of "several smaller production operations into a large, single high-tech production site" and that plant consolidation "has proven to be an efficient and cost saving method of improving scale economies in an industry whose production costs tend to be high."[3]

The magnitude of the changing economies of scale in this industry can be estimated with a simple example. According to the 1989 *Beverage Marketing Report,* there were 2,398 bottling plants in 1975. Total packaged volume that year was 4.561 billion gallons. Thus, each plant produced, on average, 1,902,012 gallons. In 1988 roughly 860 bottling plants produced 9,317,500,000 packaged gallons, or 10,834,302 per bottling plant, according to this source.[4] As a result, average per plant production increased 469 percent—from 1.9 million gallons to almost 11 million gallons. As output has increased for the average size bottling plant, costs have not increased at the same rate, and therefore cost per unit of production (gallons or case) has decreased. The per unit costs that tend to decline as output increases include direct labor costs and factory expenses (equipment, maintenance costs, and so forth). Increased plant volume also allows for purchasing cost savings as a result of volume discounts, longer-term contracts, and more sophisticated procurement techniques.[5] Undoubtedly these dramatic decreases in unit costs of production explain to some degree the fact that the real price of carbonated soft drinks has fallen significantly over roughly this same period.

In addition to production efficiencies, warehousing, distribution, marketing, and overhead economies are associated with bottler consolidation.[6] Many of these efficiencies result from the combination of contiguous bottlers and the elimination of inefficient or duplicate operations. For example, recently through the consolidation of warehouses and sales routes in the Minneapolis area, along with the cost savings associated with purchasing, PepsiCo was able to decrease costs by roughly $.35 per case.[7] Similarly, reports suggest that in 1990 and 1991, PepsiCo expects cost savings of $20 million per year more than the substantial savings originally associated with its acquisition of General Cinema's bottling operations.[8] Coca-Cola Enterprises reports savings of more than $100 million in manufacturing and raw material expenses associated with the consolidation of acquired bottlers.[9]

The changing nature of the retail trade has also contributed to the efficiencies associated with bottler consolidation. Historically, retail grocery stores were largely independent organizations with chains mostly limited to a particular city or local area. Today, large retail chains cover vast geographic areas and seek to coordinate their purchasing and promotional activities over these areas. This development has similarly led to an increased demand on bottlers to be larger in size and to cover larger geographic areas.

Vertical Integration and Economies

Much of the bottler consolidation in this industry has been faciliated by PepsiCo and Coca-Cola as they vertically integrate into the bottling business.[10] Vertical integration can obviously increase economic efficiency.[11] The *Department of Justice Merger Guidelines* prescribe that potential efficiencies merit considerable weight in vertical merger analysis: "An extensive pattern of vertical integration may constitute evidence that substantial economies are afforded by vertical integration."[12]

If one looks strictly at scale economies in production, it may not be clear why PepsiCo and Coca-Cola have been leading the vertical integration movement in the industry. These same scale economies could, in principle, be realized through the horizontal consolidation of the independent bottlers into a system of larger bottlers as has happened in certain situations. However, the number of such opportunities for an independent bottler may be more limited than that available to PepsiCo or Coca-Cola. A particular bottler, such as General Bottlers, may have bottling plants at locations dispersed throughout the country. An independent bottler may have contiguous facilities in only a small number of geographic locations, thereby limiting the magnitude of the potential efficiencies. PepsiCo or Coca-Cola, however, is likely, on average, to enjoy greater potential for production consolidation and other related efficiencies.

Moreover, a bottler can realize economies of scale from bottling anything. This situation would put PepsiCo and Coca-Cola in an anomalous situation. They maximize the effectiveness of their brand names in the long run through promotions and price discounting. A bottler will not necessarily have the same incentives. Such an entity can replace reduced volume of PepsiCo products with other carbonated soft drink or beverage products and hence in general may not promote and price its PepsiCo products as aggressively as PepsiCo.

Vertical integration solves this problem effectively for PepsiCo and Coca-Cola by leading to increased volume, lower prices, and more local promotion of their products in the affected franchise areas. And despite significant vertical integration in the 1980s by both PepsiCo and Coca-Cola, the real prices of carbonated soft drinks have declined, discounting has increased, and volume has grown at a record pace.

There are, of course, other cost savings associated with vertical integration: lower transaction costs associated with the interaction between two independent organizations, more efficient coordination of regional and national marketing strategies, more efficient coordination between marketing programs and production plans, and more opportunities to introduce new products or marketing concepts, among others. The economic logic of these and other factors is that vertical integration solves problems arising from the interrelatedness of activities where independent decision making leads to potentially inefficient results.[13] Arrangements such as vertical integration arise to maximize the joint value of successive activities.[14]

One should also not fail to account for some practical business reasons that PepsiCo and Coca-Cola are pursuing a strategy of vertical integration. The argument, for example, that economies of scale in bottling could be achieved by a horizontal consolidation of bottlers fails on such grounds. Why would PepsiCo or Coca-Cola wish to place their destiny in the hands of five or six large bottlers when they own the asset around which the business is built? Moreover, changes occurring now in the soft drink business have already taken place in the marketing of other food products. Soft drinks are virtually the last major food product distributed through franchised dealers. The soft drink industry is mimicking the natural economic development of the marketing of other food products.

Critics of vertical integration in the carbonated soft drink industry raise such issues as possible foreclosure of competitors and facilitation of collusive practices, a concern fueled, in part, by the fact that when PepsiCo or Coca-Cola purchases a bottler, it may inherit the franchise rights to the products of other concentrate companies. In effect, PepsiCo or Coca-Cola may become the bottler for a competitive product. This concern has also been engendered in part by recent work in economics that falls under the heading of "raising rivals' costs," in which vertical acquisitions are hypothesized to have horizontal anticompetitive effects.[15] Various methods of vertical foreclosure have been discussed in the literature, including control of vital inputs. In the case of the bottler acquisitions, for example, rival products would not be promoted by the acquiring concentrate firm or ultimately be excluded from the bottling operation. But such a result depends on critical factors such as the ability of a rival to procure alternative bottling facilities and the degree of competition in the final product market.

There is thus a potential trade-off in the antitrust analysis of vertical acquisitions in the carbonated soft-drink industry between various types of efficiencies and gains from in-firm coordination and scale economies versus possible problems of access by nonintegrated producers to bottling and other business arrangements.

Vertical Foreclosure

To test the applicability of the vertical foreclosure theory to the carbonated soft drink industry, we examined PepsiCo's 1986 acquisition of MEI's seventeen bottling franchises to determine the effect of vertical integration on carbonated soft drink performance. The results are reported in appendix M. Pre-

and postacquisition total carbonated soft drink volumes in the MEI areas were compared to determine if vertical integration decreased volume relative to U.S. total carbonated soft drink volume. In addition, the frequency and value of advertising promotions were similarly examined, as were total carbonated soft drink performance and the effect of vertical integration on the volume and promotion of MEI's non-PepsiCo brands. For example, in Minneapolis/St. Paul, MEI also bottled Seven-Up, Dr Pepper, A&W, Hires, Vernor's, and Squirt. In Omaha, the MEI bottler bottled Hires. The St. Louis bottler produced A&W in addition to its PepsiCo products.

The results indicate that the total volume of carbonated soft drinks in the MEI areas increased as a result of PepsiCo's acquisition of MEI. In Minneapolis/St. Paul, vertical integration resulted in a statistically significant increase in total carbonated soft drink volume. These results also indicate that the relative volume of non-PepsiCo carbonated soft drinks produced by these bottlers increased since PepsiCo acquired these franchises from MEI in 1986. In Minneapolis/St. Paul, the acquisition resulted in a statistically significant increase in non-PepsiCo volume. These results support the position that vertical integration has not resulted in a restriction of output as predicted by the vertical foreclosure theory.[16] On the contrary, the MEI acquisition was at worst competitively neutral and in many instances was procompetitive.

Before moving ahead, it would be useful to briefly discuss PepsiCo's promotion of non-PepsiCo products at the bottling level. The finding that PepsiCo-owned bottlers effectively promote non-PepsiCo products is primarily based on two considerations. First, the cost of producing soft drinks at the bottling level is significantly dependent on volume. Volume increases allow for reduction in direct labor, factory, procurement, and other expenses. Such cost reductions are critical in this industry because of the intense competition among beverage products at the retail level. Second, in many instances, the products PepsiCo inherited as a result of a bottler acquisition generally are of a different flavor than that offered by PepsiCo or the non-PepsiCo product is a more successful product than that offered by PepsiCo. PepsiCo's success with brands such as A&W is a good example of such a situation.

Collusion

An examination of the relative effects of competition in symmetric versus asymmetric franchise areas was used to test whether vertical symmetry facilitates collusion. Output and advertising frequency were examined for evidence of restricted output. (These results are also reported in appendix M.) Geographic franchise areas were chosen where PepsiCo operated a bottler and where Coca-Cola Enterprises (CCE) purchased the independently owned Coca-Cola bottler, thus transforming the geographic area from an asymmetric to a symmetric franchise area. Structuring the statistical analysis in this manner allowed testing for the significance of the CCE ownership transfer as the relevant event. Evidence that relative volume increased or remained the same would support the hypothesis that direct competition between vertically integrated PepsiCo and Coca-Cola bottling operations benefits consumers.

The results indicated that the relative volume of carbonated soft drinks has not changed in a statistically significant sense since PepsiCo began competing against the CCE-owned bottlers in Los Angeles, Phoenix, Houston, Detroit, and Orlando. In three of the five areas, relative volume was higher when PepsiCo and CCE bottlers competed than when there was asymmetric competition—that is, when a PepsiCo-owned bottler competed against an independently owned Coca-Cola bottler. Only in Houston was the measured positive effect nearly statistically significant, however. In the areas with measured relative volume decreases, the declines were not statistically different from zero. The statistical analysis of the relative volume effects provides no basis for the hypothesis that symmetry in the vertical franchise ownerships of PepsiCo and CCE bottlers is more likely to result in collusion than in asymmetric PepsiCo and Coca-Cola franchise ownership organizations.[17]

Based on the statistical analysis performed, there is no credible evidence that output or feature/price advertising was adversely affected by direct competition between CCE and PepsiCo-owned bottlers following the acquisition of the independently owned Coca-Cola bottler by CCE. The statistical analysis fails to support the theory that symmetry in vertical organizational structure facilitates collusion within the carbonated soft drink industry.

Summary

Our results are based on the examination of a limited number of episodes of vertical integration in the carbonated soft drink industry. Yet, they make sense when viewed from the perspective of the overall healthy performance of the industry in the 1980s, despite significant vertical integration, and the results are consistent with the theoretical literature that argues for the efficiency-increasing effects of vertical integration.

These results are also consistent with enforcement programs. For example, the FTC interposed no objection to PepsiCo's vertical acquisition of MEI in 1986, following a review of voluminous materials submitted in response to a second request and the depositions of key PepsiCo personnel. The record developed in the MEI transaction demonstrated the efficiencies PepsiCo hoped to achieve through vertical integration. These projected efficiencies have been realized as the MEI bottlers have been integrated into PepsiCo's corporate distribution system. Nor did the FTC object to PepsiCo's acquisition of Grand Metropolitan and General Cinema's soft drink bottling operations in recent years[18] or to Coca-Cola's vertical acquisitions.

One would not expect vertical acquisitions of bottling operations to dampen horizontal competition, and they appear not to do so. In fact, by reducing costs in the vertically integrated firm, such acquisitions serve to increase horizontal competition at all levels in the industry.[19]

Notes

1. "U.S. Soft Drink Market and Packaging Report, 1989," *Beverage Marketing* (August 1989): 195; and *Beverage Industry Annual Manual* (Cleveland, OH: Edgell Communications, Inc., 1989–1990), p. 22.

2. Certain "bottlers," in fact, neither bottle nor can carbonated soft drinks. Rather, they purchase bottled or canned products from other bottlers or cooperatives and then distribute the product in their respective territories from warehouse facilities.

3. *Beverage Marketing,* p. 195.

4. Other sources put the number of existing bottling plants at roughly 1,000, which would place average volume per bottling plant at 9,317,500 gallons. *Beverage Industry Annual Manual (1989/1990),* p. 22.

5. For a more detailed review of bottler size and costs, see "The Future of the Soft Drink Industry, 1985–1990," prepared by the Boston Consulting Group for the National Soft Drink Association (1985).

6. Also, consider media areas or markets. One of the reasons for assigning exclusive territories to franchise bottlers is to encourage efficient promotion through feature advertising. Without exclusive territories, franchise bottlers would tend to free ride on each other's feature promotions, resulting in too little feature promotion. The optimal size of a franchise territory is determined in part by the breadth of local media areas. When the breadth of local media areas widens, larger territorial assignments are necessary to maintain proper incentives for bottlers to promote products through feature advertising.

7. PepsiCo., Inc., *Annual Report* (1988).

8. "Promising Pepsi Pace," *Beverage World* (November 1989).

9. "Bottling Is Hardly a Classic for Coke," *Business Week,* December 11, 1989.

10. Coca-Cola, through Coca-Cola Enterprises and other equity interests, reportedly has an equity interest in bottlers that represent 70 percent of its U.S. volume. PepsiCo reportedly has an equity interest in bottles representing 65 percent of its U.S. volume.

11. Certain antitrust scholarship suggests that vertical integration in general and vertical mergers in particular generally increase economic efficiency. Jan Tirole, *The Theory of Industrial Organization* (Cambridge: MIT Press, 1988); and Roger Blair and David Kaserman, *Law and Economics of Vertical Integration and Control* (New York: Academic Press, 1983).

12. *Department of Justice Merger Guidelines,* Federal Register 26,823, June 29, 1984, sec. 4.24.

13. See Benjamin Klein, "Vertical Integration as Organizational Ownership: The Fisher Body—General Motors Relationship Revisited," *Journal of Law, Economics and Organization* (Spring 1988): 199.

14. Other potential solutions such as long-term contracting may sometimes create "hold-up" problems. See Ronald Coase, *The Firm, the Market and the Law* (University of Chicago, 1988); and Benjamin Klein, Robert Crawford, and Armen Alchian, "Vertical Integration. Appropriable Rents, and the Competitive Contracting Process," *Journal of Law and Economics* (October 1978): 21,297.

15. Thomas Krattemaker and Steven Salop, "Anticompetitive Exclusion: Raising Rivals' Costs to Achieve Power over Price," *Yale Law Journal* 96 (1986): 209.

16. A similar analysis was performed using the frequency and raw weighted value of feature advertising as the dependent variable. Feature advertising data were available for Hires Root Beer in Omaha and A&W Root Beer in St. Louis. Both the frequency and value of feature advertisement increased or remained unchanged as a result of PepsiCo's acquisition of MEI.

17. We also performed an analysis to test the null hypothesis that the relative number and raw weighted value of feature advertising for carbonated soft drinks have not declined following direct competition between the PepsiCo-owned and the CCE-owned bottlers in the five geographic areas examined. Neither the average relative number of feature advertisements nor the average relative raw weighted value of feature advertisements was statistically affected by the change in franchise ownership of the Coca-Cola bottler to a CCE-owned bottler in Phoenix, Houston, and Orlando. In Los Angeles, the difference in average relative number of feature advertisements increased significantly (in a statistical sense) as a result of symmetric franchise ownership between the PepsiCo and CCE bottlers. However, the ownership change did not result in a statistically significant change in the relative raw weighted value of the feature advertisements. In Detroit, both the relative number and raw weighted value of feature advertisements increased as a result of symmetry in the PepsiCo and CCE franchise ownership organizations.

18. In General Cinema, the FTC raised concerns about horizontal overlaps where, as a result of the acquisition, PepsiCo would compete as the franchised bottler of another concentrate company in the same geographic area as an independent bottler of PepsiCo products. In the Matter of PepsiCo, Inc., FTC Docket No. C–3256, June 29, 1989.

19. Further evidence that vertical integration is procompetitive is found in recent action by Royal Crown. According to the *Wall Street Journal,* December 12, 1989, Royal Crown asked the FTC to force Coca-Cola and PepsiCo to sell franchise companies that they have purchased. This action, taken by a direct competitor that would suffer if competition increased but would benefit if prices increased as a result of collusion, is strong evidence that vertical integration increases competition.

8
Seven-Up

I n 1986, PepsiCo attempted to acquire the domestic rights to the Seven-Up brand. We believed in 1986 that the combination of PepsiCo and Seven-Up would not result in anticompetitive effects, in large part because of the overall state of competition and performance in the industry. Another important part of the story, however, was the state of health of the Seven-Up brand:

- Seven-Up's share of overall sales declined from 7.2 percent in 1983 to 5.9 percent in 1985 and to 4.7 percent in 1988. A recent report placed Seven-Up's 1989 share at 4.3 percent.[1]

- The regular Seven-Up brand represented only 3.1 percent of sales in 1988, down from almost 5 percent in 1983. Reports are that the regular Seven-Up brand fell to 2.9 percent in 1989.[2]

- Seven-Up's share of grocery store sales has been falling in most major metropolitan areas reviewed by Nielsen.

- On an individual brand basis, Seven-Up has also been losing ground. Regular Seven-Up sales grew from 242 million cases in 1983 to 260 million cases in 1985 and then fell to 235 million cases in 1988. Sprite sales grew from 166 million cases to 268 million over the same period, an increase of 61 percent.

Seven-Up's inability to compete with other soft drink products is most dramatically illustrated by table 8–1, which compares its performance (both regular and diet) with that of Coca-Cola's Sprite brand. Moreover, other lemon-lime drinks, such as Squirt and Bubble-Up, have also outperformed Seven-Up.

Seven-Up has trouble competing for three reasons: (1) its prices are higher than Pepsi-Cola, Coca-Cola, and Sprite (figure 8–1); (2) it relies too much on national advertising and too little on promotional activity at the trade level; and (3) it has not introduced and promoted new brands successfully.

Table 8–1
Sales of Seven-Up and Sprite, 1981–1988
(millions of cases)

Year	Seven-Up	Sprite
1981	317.6	165.7
1982	348.6	181.8
1983	372.1	184.9
1984	385.0	232.9
1985	363.3	285.1
1986	330.9	290.8
1987	312.5	305.0
1988	308.6	323.5

Source: *Nielsen Audit Data* (Chicago, IL: Nielsen, 1981–1988).

The Like episode at Seven-Up is perhaps best illustrative of Seven-Up's problems with new products. This cola product never was able to interest any significant number of consumers. Seven-Up introduced Cherry Seven-Up, and although 1987 sales reached 58 million cases, they declined dramatically to 34 million cases in 1988—a drop of 41 percent in just one year. In 1988 Seven-Up introduced Seven-Up Gold, but it was able to garner only 5 million case sales in that year. Apparently, Seven-Up fared no better in 1989: "All in all, 1989 will probably be remembered as the year of discontent for 7UP bottlers, who this year witnessed the demise of Gold, watched the Cherry gravy train come to a screeching halt, and saw their flagship diet recede further from the limelight."[3] The Seven-Up Company's share of carbonated soft drink sales fell to 4.3 percent in 1989 while the Seven-Up brand itself fell to 2.9 percent.

Seven-Up has been a financial failure as well. During the approximately eight years the company was owned by Philip Morris (1978–1986), it was only marginally profitable and subsequent to the 1986 acquisition by Hicks & Haas, matters have gone from bad to worse:

> Squaring off against a colossus such as Coca-Cola would be tough enough for a well-financed marketer—but Dr Pepper/Seven-Up hardly has cash to spare. The company was created in 1986 by the merger of Seven-Up, which had been spun off from Philip Morris Cos., and Dr Pepper, which had been taken private in a leveraged buyout. *The combined company, now private, is saddled with $1 billion in debt, and it has a negative net worth.*

> Last year, operating income rose 9%, to an estimated $109 million, on sales of $504 million, but the gains mainly reflect improvements at Dr Pepper: Income from Seven-Up brands was flat. For now, Dr Pepper/Seven-Up can cover its annual cash interest expense of $75 million, but in 1993 it must make an additional $84 million payment on a zero-coupon bond issue. Partly to contain costs last year, the company cut its marketing budget for Seven-Up by 14%.[4]

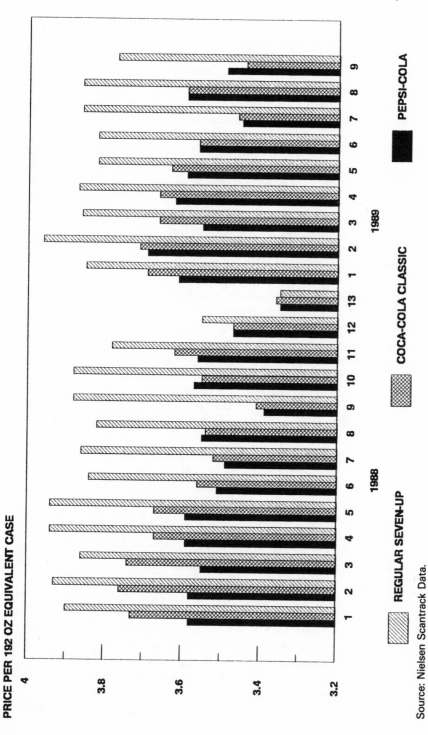

Figure 8–1. Prices of Pepsi-Cola, Coca-Cola Classic, and Seven-Up, Total U.S.

Source: Nielsen Scantrack Data.

According to a prospectus issued in 1989, there is serious question as to whether Dr Pepper/Seven-Up can make its 1993 payment: "Management does not anticipate that the company and its subsidiaries will generate cash flow from operations to repay the entire principal amount of the discount rates at maturity."[5] Many of Dr Pepper/Seven-Up's problems relate to the Seven-Up Company. Indeed, recently Seven-Up "sold" IBC Root Beer to Dr Pepper for $28 million in an apparent attempt to infuse the troubled Seven-Up with capital.[6]

The procompetitive logic of the PepsiCo/Seven-Up merger was inescapable. Seven-Up had been losing ground in the soft drink industry because it had not been operated efficiently. PepsiCo perceived an entrepreneurial opportunity in the acquisition of Seven-Up; it planned to reduce the retail price of Seven-Up to "grow the brand." Clearly, there had to be an efficiency somewhere in this equation. PepsiCo wanted to buy a firm in trouble in order to lower the retail prices of its products. Where else can the ability to do this come from except through more efficient management of the Seven-Up franchise rights?

This point applies to all channels of distribution for Seven-Up. PepsiCo would have made Seven-Up more competitive in grocery stores by the use of more price-related incentives. Seven-Up is overpriced in grocery stores; PepsiCo would have changed this in order to sell more product. Seven-Up has not done well in the vending channel either. PepsiCo would have changed this by offering financial incentives to bottlers to develop the sales of Seven-Up through vending machines. Finally, the PepsiCo/Seven-Up combination would have been a natural for the food service channel. The acquisition would have allowed PepsiCo to market both PepsiCo and Seven-Up brands aggressively in fountain outlets.

PepsiCo did acquire the international rights (including Canada) to Seven-Up in a separate transaction in 1986, and since that time, while domestic sales of Seven-Up have declined, international sales have increased. In Canada, PepsiCo has been particularly successful with Diet Seven-Up, with sales up 37 percent in 1989 after PepsiCo reformulated the product and its advertising.[7] Seven-Up reportedly plans to introduce this new and improved PepsiCo-generated product in the United States during 1990.

The achievement of efficiencies from a merger is not a narrow, technical exercise. It is not simply the fact that some costs go down as a result of a merger. Seven-Up was, for example, vastly overstaffed. The more important efficiencies occurring from a merger such as PepsiCo/Seven-Up derive from the fact that assets that have been poorly managed (Seven-Up) will be placed in the hands of a company that could have managed them more effectively (PepsiCo). The mere transfer of these assets from a lower-valued to a higher-valued use creates value and wealth in the economy. By allowing the capital market to work in this way, the economy becomes more efficient as those firms with the best abilities and expertise come to manage more of the economy's assets. Over time, innovations, product improvements, better service, and lower prices flow from such mergers.

The most obvious explanation for why the FTC turned down PepsiCo's bid for Seven-Up was Coca-Cola's simultaneous bid for Dr Pepper. The FTC may have reasoned that the two acquisitions were too large a step to take at one time. Even in the face of the two deals, there were signs of understanding emitting from the Bureau of Economics and from the chairman's (Daniel Oliver) office, who seemed at least receptive to the idea that the industry was in fact competitive. Nevertheless, the soft drink acquisitions were swept away by the mind-set that only concentration matters. The same fate awaited Coca-Cola in federal court.

Time will tell whether the FTC made the right decision concerning PepsiCo/Seven-Up. Seven-Up has not fared well since it joined with Dr Pepper as part of Hicks & Haas. Given the declining position of Seven-Up, it is unclear if the brand will ultimately be anything more than a niche player in the carbonated soft dink industry.

Notes

1. *Beverage Digest,* December 8, 1989.

2. Ibid.

3. "Frustrating Year Puts Seven-Up on the 'Spot,' " *Beverage World,* October 31, 1989.

4. "Seven-Up: Where Have All the Bubbles Gone?" *Business Week* January 29, 1990, p. 95 (emphasis added).

5. *Grants,* August 4, 1989.

6. *Beverage Digest,* March 2, 1990. An additional indication of possible future problems for Seven-Up concerns the status of its bottling system. Certain reports suggest that bottlers representing some 40 percent of Seven-Up's volume are apparently up for sale, including significant bottlers such as Westinghouse, Kemmerer, and Imbesi. Ibid., February 2, 1990.

7. Ibid., September 22, 1989. In addition to sales increases, PepsiCo has introduced the Seven-Up brand in a large number of other countries, including Belgium, China, Egypt, Greece, Spain, New Zealand, Finland, and Venezuela.

9
Conclusion

The carbonated soft drink industry is quite competitive in almost any way one chooses to analyze it. By the conventional standards of industry concentration, an industry populated by two large firms, such as PepsiCo and Coca-Cola, should not exhibit such intense competition on all fronts. Competition between the soft drink giants inheres in the dynamic logic of how to succeed in this business. Both companies have invested heavily in their brand-names, and these investments have centered on product quality and the availability of products at competitive prices in all channels of distribution. That is, the brand-names imply something about price and quality. In a world where most consumers are switchers among soft drink brands and among beverages in general, soft drink companies are driven to price competitively. Moreover, the brand-name capital of these companies must be maintained over time with continued product quality and price performance in the marketplace.

The consequences of upsetting the precarious relationship that exists between the brand-names of PepsiCo and Coca-Cola and their customers would be disastrous. Consumers (switchers) might never again believe that the PepsiCo and Coca-Cola brand-names implied competitive prices, and hence they would shop for alternative soft drinks at competitive prices or for alternative beverage products. The door to significant new entry into the business would be wide open under these conditions. There would be nothing to deter the entry of other large food and beverage producers into the soft drink business under these circumstances. For such reasons, the industry has remained intensely competitive.

Our analysis carries another message: that contemporaneous developments in the industry, such as the trend toward vertical integration and the earlier interest by PepsiCo and Coca-Cola in acquiring Seven-Up and Dr Pepper, do not threaten the continuation of extremely competitive behavior in the industry. Indeed, a good case can be made that at least Seven-Up will go the way of the horse and buggy unless it is acquired by one of the major firms.

The job that PepsiCo has done with Seven-Up's international rights attests to what it could have done with its domestic rights.

We hope that this study will alter the general perception of the state of competition in the carbonated soft drink industry or at least elevate the quality of the dialogue on this important subject. We need to push beyond the tired rhetoric about this industry if we are to understand it. As we write, however, FTC staff continue to pursue an administrative action against the Coca-Cola Company some four years after Coca-Cola lost (and terminated) its bid for Dr Pepper.[1] What is most interesting (and distressing) from our point of view is the nature of the case that has been presented against Coca-Cola. Two examples suffice to illustrate.

First, consider the complaint counsel's proposed definition of the relevant market: "The relevant product market in the nation taken as a whole will be found to be composed of those firms that manufacture concentrate and syrup used to produce franchised, branded, carbonated soft drinks, sold by direct-store-door delivery, in vending, and through fountain."[2] In this view, Coca-Cola does not compete with, say, Shasta, a warehouse-delivered soft drink product, or with private label brand soft drinks, much less with other beverage products, such as juice and bottled water. But as we have shown, the facts of competition in this industry will not support such a narrow conception of this competition.

Consider also complaint counsel's view of entry conditions in the soft drink industry: "The entry barriers, lag and risk factors associated with effective entry into the manufacture, sale and distribution of concentrate are many and substantial."[3] Our analysis probed this issue extensively, and we encountered numerous ways that entry could (and has) occur(red). These alternative routes include such factors as warehousing, using beer wholesalers, the availability of bottling capacity, and access to advertising. Again, the facts do not support the contention that entry is barred in this industry.

Rather than trying to come to grips with the dynamic nature of competition in the carbonated soft drink industry, complaint counsel in this case has created a rigidly segmented industry in which structure reigns supreme and competition is all but ignored. We have no way of knowing how this case will be decided, but we are looking at the same facts and coming to radically different conclusions. We think we are right and that public policy toward this industry will be better served by a more informed appreciation of the nature of the competition in the industry.

There is an economist's joke that goes as follows: Being an economic historian is like looking for a black cat in a dark room; being an economic theorist is like looking for a black cat in a dark room when it's not there; being an econometrician is like looking for a black cat in a dark room when it's not there and saying you found it. Competition in a modern industrial society is a complex and not completely understood process. In Ronald Coase's words, economists have often labeled industries and business practices as monopolistic when they did not understand them. Maybe we are committing the opposite fallacy and labeling things as competitive when we really do not understand them. We think not. We think we have found the black cat.

Notes

1. The FTC's apparent purpose in this action is to obtain an order requiring Coca-Cola to seek its prior approval before acquiring any other concentrate company. For an overview of the FTC's position in this action, see, generally *In the Matter of Coca-Cola Company,* Docket No. 9207, Complaint Counsel's Pretrial Brief, March 2, 1990.

2. Ibid., p. 10.

3. Ibid., p. 19.

Appendix A:
Carbonated Soft Drink Franchise Companies and Their Brands

A-Treat Bottling Company
  A-Treat

American "76" Company
  Cola Light
  Cream-O-Chocolate-Soda
  Cream-O'Choc Slush
  Exact Match Chocolate
  Exact Match Cola
  Exact Match Lemon Lime
  Exact Match Orange
  Exact Match Root Beer
  Exact Match Strawberry
  Lemon-Lime Light
  Plymouth Rock
  76 Lemon Lime
  76 Flavors

Associated Beverages, Inc.
  Weber's Root Beer
  Weber's Various Flavors

Austin, Nichols & Co., Inc.
  Orangina Sparkling Citrus
    Beverages
  Chocolate Cow
  KoKoBlanco Coconut
  YooHoo Chocolate
  YooHoo Coconut

YooHoo Chocolate Syrup
YooHoo Strawberry

A&W Brands, Inc.
  A&W Diet Root Beer
  A&W Root Beer
  A&W Cream Soda
  A&W Diet Cream Soda
  Country Time
  Squirt/Diet Squirt
  Vernor's/Diet Vernor's
  Rochester Flavors

Barq's, Inc.
  Barq's
  Diet Barq's
  Red Creme/Diet Red Creme

Big Red, Inc.
  Big Red
  Caffeine-Free Big Red
  Diet Big Red
  Caffeine-free Diet Big Red

Bireley's Division
  Bireley's

Borden, Inc.
  Lite Line

"U.S. Soft Drink Market and Packaging Report, 1989," *Beverage Marketing* (August 1989): 321–328.

Bottlers International LTD
  Chips
  Cruzan Punch
  Deri Del
  Glow
  Ho Ko
  Moonshine
  NRG Plus
  Tasty
  Tastywine

Bubble-Up Company
  Bubble-Up
  Diet Bubble-Up

C&C Cola Company
  C&C Cola
  C&C Diet Cola
  Private labels

Cadbury Schweppes
  Barrelhead Root Beer
  Canada Dry
  Cott
  Hi-Spot
  No Cal
  Tahitian Treat
  Wink
  Sunkist
  Diet Sunkist
  Crush
  Hires
  Diet Crush
  Diet Hires
  Diet Sun Drop
  Sun Drop
  Cadbury Schweppes

Caprio Beverage Corporation
  Caprio
  Diet Caprio

Carolina Beverage Corporation
  Caravan Dry
  Cheerwine
  Cool Moon
  Diet Cheerwine

Lite Cheerwine
Carolina Gold

Coca-Cola Company
  Cherry Coke
  New Coke
  Coca-Cola Classic (Regular/
    Caffeine Free)
  Diet Cherry Coke
  Diet Coke (Regular/Caffeine
    Free)
  Diet Sprite
  Fanta
  Fresca
  Mellow Yellow
  Minute Maid Juices
  Mr. Pibb
  Ramblin Root Beer
  Sprite
  Diet Ramblin Root Beer
  Tab (Regular/Caffeine Free)

Corr's Natural Beverages
  Barleycorn Grain Beverages
  Corr's Natural Soda
  Gear Up Vitamin Juice
  Ginseng Rush
  Glase's Pure Water
  Grain Beverage
  Nature's Flavors

Cosco International
  Apple Sidra
  Cosco
  Yes Cola

Dad's Root Beer Company
  Dad's Root Beer
  Diet Dad's Root Beer

Delaware Punch Company
  Delaware Punch

Eastern Brewing Corporation
  Doc Soda

Europa Distributors
  Chapelle

Faygo Beverages
Faygo

The Four Percent Company
Four Percent
Old Red

General Food Corporation
Country Time
Crystal Light
Kool-Aid
Tang

Ginseng Up Corporation
Ginseng Up
Fruitzer

Golden Gate Beverage Co.
Golden Gate Seltzer

Grapette International
Grapette
Lemonette
Mr. Cola
Orangette
Sun Burst

Green River Corporation
Green River
Diet Green River

Green Spot Company
Action Ade
Breakfast Time
Green Spot

Harper's Enterprises
Spana

Hicks & Haas
Dr Pepper Company
Diet Dr Pepper
Dr Pepper
Pepper Free
Salute
Diet Pepper Free
Welch's

Seven-Up Company
Diet 7-Up
I.B.C. Root Beer
Like Cola
Diet I.B.C. Root Beer
Diet Like Cola
7-Up

Jolt Company
Jolt Cola

Krier Foods, Inc.
All American Cola
Fruitland
Jolly Good

A.J. Lehman Company
Lemmy Lemonade
Tom Collins, Jr.

Logret Import & Export
Old Chicago Seltzer

London Dry Ltd.
London Dry

MBC Beverage, Inc.
Sweet N'Low Diet Soda

Ma's Old Fashion Bottling, Inc.
Ma's Diet Beverages
Ma's Flavors
Ma's Old-Fashioned
Stayund Diet Flavors

The Monarch Company
Big Apple Soda
Dr. Wells
Flavette
Frostie
Mason's Root Beer
Moxie
Nesbitt's
Nu Grape
Sun Crest

National Fruit Flavor Company
National Mauna Lei

Ole'
Zodiac

Old Tyme Soft Drinks
Brockdale Beverages
Old Tyme Ginger Beer
Old Tyme N.Y. Style
Sunrisa

Original New York Seltzer Co.
Original N.Y. Seltzer (Regular
and Diet)

PA Dutch Birch Beer
Ju'cy Orange
PA Dutch Birch Beer

Pepsi-Cola Company
Diet Slice
Diet Pepsi
Diet Pepsi Free
Mountain Dew
Patio
Pepsi Free
Pepsi Light
Pepsi-Cola
Slice
Teem
Mug Root Beer
Wild Cherry/Diet Wild Cherry

Premier Beverages, Inc.
Welch's Apple
Welch's Grape
Welch's Orange
Welch's Peach
Welch's Strawberry

Presto-Tek Corporation
Crystal Flavors

The Quench Company
Diet Quench
HoneyDew Flavors
Quench
Lemon Quench

Reggae Imports
Brix 15

Richardson Foods Corporation
Mrs. Richardson
Nance's
Richardson's
Scoopy's

Royal Crown Cola Company
Cherry RC
Diet RC
Diet Rite
Nehi
RC Cola
RC 100

Sarsaparilla Company
Kiwi Soda
Natcher'ly
Ol'Bob Miller
Sarsaparilla

Seagram Company
Soho Natural Soda

Shasta Beverages, Inc.
Shasta
Spree

Snake River Brewing Company
Idaho Sparkling Natural Soda
Idaho Sparkling Spring Water

Snapple Natural Soda
Private labels
Purity
Rich Harvest
Snapple

Sun Rise, Inc.
Sun Rise
White Light-nin'

Sunglo Cooperative
Sunglo Plus

Triple XXX Corporation

Diet Triple XXX
Triple XXX Root Beer

Uptown Beverage Corporation
Uptown

Vess Beverages, Inc.
Dr. Schnee
Generics
Old Dutch
Diet Vess
Ticket
Vess Flavors

Whistle Orange
Ever Vess Seltzers

Virginia Dare Extract Company
Korker
South Seas
Virginia Dare

White Rock Products
Famous Amos
White Rock

Appendix B:
U.S. Carbonated Soft Drink Sales

Table B–1
Total Gallonage, by Flavor, 1985–1988

Year	Cola	Lemon-Lime	Pepper Type	Juice Added	Root Beer	Orange	All Others
1985	67.5%	12.2%	4.9%	3.9%	2.7%	5.1%	3.7%
1986	68.8	11.3	4.6	4.9	2.6	2.4	5.4
1987	69.0	10.6	4.7	4.5	3.0	2.2	6.0
1988	69.5	10.5	5.1	3.8	3.3	2.0	5.8

Source: Beverage Industry/Annual Manual (Cleveland, OH: Edgell Communications, Inc., 1989–1990), p. 34.

Table B–2
Total Gallonage, Regular versus Diet, 1985–1988

Year	Regular	Diet
1985	74.7%	25.3%
1986	74.0	26.0
1987	73.6	26.4
1988	72.3	27.7

Source: "U.S. Soft Drink Market and Packaging Report, 1989," *Beverage Marketing* (August 1989): 38.

Table B–3
Total Gallonage by Package Type, 1973–1988

Year	Cans	Returnable Glass	One-Way Glass	Plastic	Aseptic	All Other
1973	29.0%	54.0%	17.0%			
1974	29.0	53.0	18.0			
1975	32.0	47.0	21.0			
1976	34.5	44.0	21.5			
1977	38.2	40.3	21.5			
1978	43.8	37.8	10.8	7.6%		
1979	42.5	33.8	9.1	14.6		
1980	37.2	30.7	14.2	17.9		
1981	35.8	28.2	15.9	20.1		
1982	35.4	27.9	15.7	21.0		
1983	36.2	23.8	15.2	24.0	0.1%	0.7%
1984	37.8	20.1	14.8	26.5	0.3	0.5
1985	39.3	16.3	14.1	29.4	0.3	0.6
1986	39.9	14.2	13.9	31.4	0.5	0.1
1987	41.8	12.4	13.7	31.5	0.5	0.1
1988	43.7	10.2	13.7	31.8	0.5	0.1

Source: Ibid., p. 209.

Appendix C:
Selected Carbonated Soft Drink Brand Sales

Table C–1
Case Sales

Year	Coca-Cola[a]	Pepsi-Cola	Seven-Up	Dr Pepper	Royal Crown Cola	Crush and Hires	Canada Dry Ginger Ale	A&W Root Beer	Squirt
1981	1,341.6	1,104.0	242.0	219.2	117.7	59.1	36.9	34.4	18.4
1982	1,355.5	1,120.0	259.5	209.7	122.5	65.0	39.8	35.4	20.3
1983	1,335.2	1,095.0	282.6	210.8	117.7	68.0	44.5	38.8	21.7
1984	1,379.3	1,170.0	282.9	230.9	110.5	75.4	47.1	40.4	23.8
1985	1,370.1	1,230.0	260.3	253.9	111.8	80.7	47.7	41.8	25.0
1986	1,459.4	1,260.0	233.7	263.5	109.7	81.5	49.4	42.7	25.7
1987	1,535.0	1,331.0	240.0	284.6	118.5	75.0	50.0	47.5	23.3
1988[b]	1,596.0	1,370.0	235.0	325.6	122.0	72.0	53.8	52.5	27.1

Source: *Maxwell Report* (Richmond, VA: First Wheat Securities, 1989).
Note: According to John Maxwell, case sales included in the *Maxwell Report* represent all sales of soft drinks: at the grocery level, convenience stores, fountain, and vending.
[a]Includes New Coke and Classic Coke after 1985.
[b]Estimated.

Table C–2
Index of Case Sales

Year	Coca-Cola[a]	Pepsi-Cola	Seven-Up	Dr Pepper	Royal Crown Cola	Crush and Hires	Canada Dry Ginger Ale	A&W Root Beer	Squirt
1981	100.0	100.0	100.0	100.0	100.0	100.0	100.0	100.0	100.0
1982	101.0	101.4	107.2	95.7	104.1	110.0	107.9	102.9	110.3
1983	99.5	99.2	116.8	96.2	100.0	115.1	120.6	112.8	117.9
1984	102.8	106.0	116.9	105.3	93.9	127.6	127.6	117.4	129.3
1985	102.1	111.4	107.6	115.8	95.0	136.5	129.3	121.5	135.9
1986	108.8	114.1	96.6	120.2	93.2	137.9	133.9	124.1	139.7
1987	114.4	120.6	99.2	129.8	100.7	126.9	135.5	138.1	126.6
1988[b]	119.0	124.1	97.1	148.5	103.7	121.8	145.8	152.6	147.3

Source: Ibid.
Note: According to John Maxwell, case sales included in the *Maxwell Report* represent all sales of soft drinks, including sales at the grocery level, convenience stores, fountain, and vending.
[a]Includes New Coke and Classic Coke after 1985.
[b]Estimated.

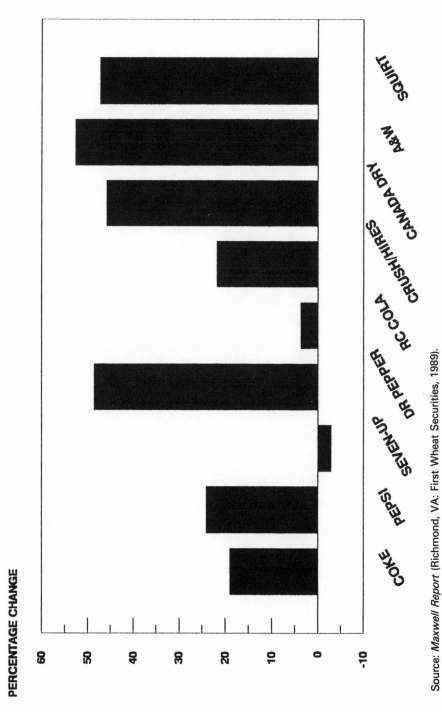

Source: *Maxwell Report* (Richmond, VA: First Wheat Securities, 1989).

Figure C–1. Percentage Change in Case Sales, 1981–1988

Appendix D:
Changes in Regional Share of Sales

Table D–1
Percentage Change in Share of Sales, Atlanta

	PepsiCo	Coca-Cola	Seven-Up	Dr Pepper	RC	Private Label
February–March 1985	0.26%	-6.73%	-17.60%	21.58%	60.53%	10.97%
April–May 1985	-7.76	7.87	-1.98	2.23	-32.41	-5.95
June–July 1985	22.50	-12.84	-2.68	-12.62	3.01	26.64
August–September 1985	-2.90	6.39	-2.78	0.17	-10.26	-20.97
October–November 1985	3.17	-2.66	6.85	-11.44	18.41	5.98
December 1985–January 1986	-5.81	5.21	16.35	-10.22	1.26	-6.44
February–March 1986	5.34	-4.08	-10.66	8.82	6.12	3.82
April–May 1986	-11.37	6.99	-15.33	9.67	-22.57	-6.33
June–July 1986	-1.61	0.18	-2.35	0.35	-7.10	-0.47
August–September 1986	7.30	-2.91	-8.81	30.13	11.02	-17.49
October–November 1986	12.24	-2.35	6.59	-7.21	-9.64	7.27
December 1986–January 1987	-2.75	5.27	5.09	-3.70	-13.47	-0.02
February–March 1987	-4.42	-3.10	5.49	15.88	8.93	15.19
April–May 1987	-1.48	-1.10	0.84	-11.03	3.91	12.93
June–July 1987	2.09	-1.33	-3.97	9.31	-17.30	-2.02
August–September 1987	6.81	-0.88	7.19	-2.74	0.49	0.03
October–November 1987	1.93	-4.47	12.19	-15.74	29.17	20.06
December 1987–January 1988	-3.11	4.03	3.14	-10.77	-1.40	3.61
February–March 1988	-1.10	-3.65	-8.62	6.67	6.37	5.01
April–May 1988	-7.07	5.31	-13.44	4.61	-9.65	-2.02
June–July 1988	-1.09	0.69	-12.49	28.61	-19.23	-3.27
August–September 1988	8.71	-4.27	2.67	9.30	0.06	-14.89
October–November 1988	4.88	-2.90	3.21	1.30	24.23	12.18
December 1988–January 1989	-8.91	9.37	11.69	-18.22	-6.41	-18.92
February–March 1989	7.73	-9.64	-12.51	13.90	6.88	37.47
April–May 1989	5.39	-1.74	4.64	-0.12	-9.84	-31.36
June–July 1989	-4.15	4.99	-15.03	7.33	-5.59	2.75

Source: Nielsen, *Nielsen Audit Data* (Chicago, IL: Nielsen, 1985–1989).

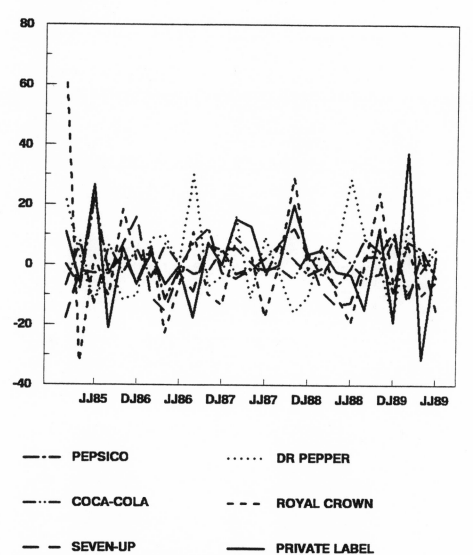

PERCENTAGE CHANGE

Source: Nielsen, *Nielsen Audit Data* (Chicago, IL: Nielsen, 1985–1989).

Figure D–1. Percentage Change in Share of Sales, Atlanta

Table D-2
Percentage Change in Share of Sales, Charlotte

	PepsiCo	Coca-Cola	Seven-Up	Dr Pepper	RC	Private Label
February–March 1985	6.59%	-2.87%	-20.48%	9.01%	-1.09%	13.33%
April–May 1985	-8.42	7.03	-4.67	2.30	-10.87	2.88
June–July 1985	2.53	-8.76	-11.48	-10.29	34.42	11.71
August–September 1985	-0.57	4.42	-5.10	5.46	4.40	-1.83
October–November 1985	-2.36	0.61	8.93	-1.81	7.49	-7.48
December 1985–January 1986	0.27	6.36	-0.12	-6.02	-1.87	-6.54
February–March 1986	-2.18	-6.74	-7.22	0.45	26.65	26.89
April–May 1986	2.71	2.68	-12.68	1.38	-20.82	1.27
June–July 1986	-3.18	4.73	-5.05	-1.57	-12.62	-5.90
August–September 1986	0.11	-4.07	0.98	8.62	11.11	-4.06
October–November 1986	6.95	-4.78	-0.69	-6.13	20.62	2.07
December 1986–January 1987	2.76	-0.57	39.27	-10.89	-9.64	-3.59
February–March 1987	5.40	-3.76	-21.83	12.48	-27.51	24.28
April–May 1987	1.00	-7.98	17.23	6.37	28.72	-13.25
June–July 1987	-2.68	5.18	-10.87	7.10	-13.85	18.96
August–September 1987	0.73	0.37	-0.88	10.07	-9.15	-18.04
October–November 1987	-5.79	-0.67	21.69	-15.27	51.09	7.09
December 1987–January 1988	-4.29	11.32	-7.00	-6.79	-8.41	-8.64
February–March 1988	0.23	-5.49	1.17	-3.03	13.73	44.50
April–May 1988	4.97	-1.82	-2.03	24.98	-26.95	5.11
June–July 1988	-9.77	2.04	-6.89	-13.35	33.07	1.18
August–September 1988	1.42	-0.23	-10.67	-6.15	1.45	-11.52
October–November 1988	7.35	-6.61	7.06	6.03	5.75	-14.20
December 1988–January 1989	-1.05	7.70	-4.66	-6.99	3.29	7.22
February–March 1989	-3.75	-0.13	-11.89	3.84	7.26	15.38
April–May 1989	3.52	-1.34	-6.29	9.04	-23.53	-9.70
June–July 1989	0.90	1.09	1.77	-4.90	-8.03	-12.00

Source: Ibid.

PERCENTAGE CHANGE

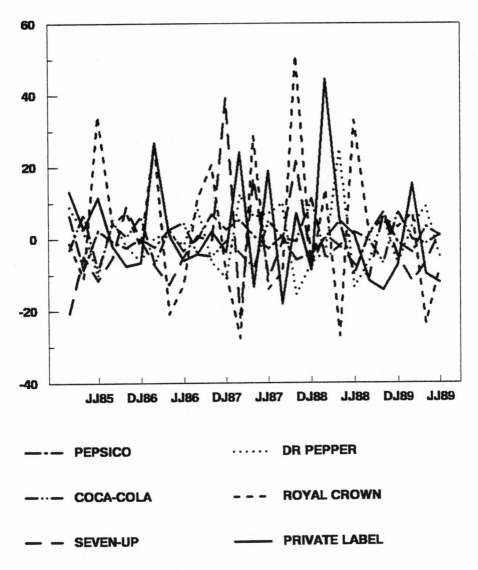

Figure D–2. Percentage Change in Share of Sales, Charlotte

Table D-3
Percentage Change in Share of Sales, Cincinnati

	PepsiCo	Coca-Cola	Seven-Up	Dr Pepper	RC	Private Label
February–March 1985	5.37	0.47	-17.95	12.91	-0.74	5.77
April–May 1985	-2.94	-1.55	-0.15	0.61	-2.75	13.98
June–July 1985	1.09	-2.35	-12.12	4.79	-6.46	14.68
August–September 1985	3.19	2.76	-5.01	-2.87	8.06	-25.95
October–November 1985	-1.56	-1.04	14.06	5.87	39.79	-14.79
December 1985–January 1986	-0.29	2.61	19.99	-26.21	-12.09	-9.38
February–March 1986	-5.78	-1.35	-16.17	13.95	22.42	34.95
April–May 1986	4.60	-2.25	-10.63	-3.40	-18.67	10.77
June–July 1986	-2.53	2.17	2.98	-5.67	-11.10	7.49
August–September 1986	6.88	-1.93	-7.76	3.02	-3.88	-5.36
October–November 1986	-3.08	1.67	6.67	12.36	11.00	-14.71
December 1986–January 1987	0.15	3.25	27.74	-17.01	-4.52	-11.33
February–March 1987	4.80	-6.84	-22.03	21.43	6.14	16.09
April–May 1987	-2.13	1.88	2.53	4.51	-13.41	8.49
June–July 1987	0.23	-0.33	3.57	9.22	-5.77	4.95
August–September 1987	-0.07	2.61	1.44	-5.91	-2.62	-11.31
October–November 1987	-1.46	-0.87	-1.92	8.81	20.04	-3.16
December 1987–January 1988	1.46	1.48	26.59	-14.33	0.22	-26.43
February–March 1988	-0.76	-1.66	-21.87	16.45	14.71	29.02
April–May 1988	-7.76	9.84	-0.70	12.92	-11.27	9.16
June–July 1988	5.90	-2.31	-7.82	-9.04	-14.48	-6.51
August–September 1988	2.63	-8.78	-5.15	15.50	6.67	35.39
October–November 1988	-5.80	12.38	-1.39	-3.36	8.73	-19.07
December 1988–January 1989	5.59	-2.00	27.50	-17.57	-7.75	-19.52
February–March 1989	2.21	-8.35	-13.61	14.05	6.01	15.61
April–May 1989	0.77	2.45	-12.00	-8.66	7.06	2.71
June–July 1989	-0.51	5.28	-10.50	7.95	-11.33	-0.24

Source: Ibid.

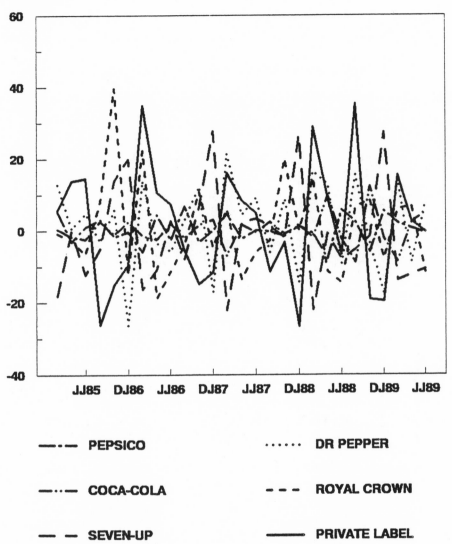

Source: Ibid.

Figure D–3. Percentage Change in Share of Sales, Cincinnati

Table D–4
Percentage Change in Share of Sales, Out-State Michigan

	PepsiCo	Coca-Cola	Seven-Up	Dr Pepper	RC	Private Label
February–March 1985	30.51	0.22	-37.76	-2.90	-22.02	-12.25
April–May 1985	-24.52	9.91	6.71	36.12	34.43	49.20
June–July 1985	11.10	-9.97	-7.89	-15.61	-27.08	47.69
August–September 1985	-14.96	16.54	-9.51	9.59	20.42	-8.01
October–November 1985	5.39	1.10	9.17	0.55	21.89	-23.94
December 1985–January 1986	5.20	-4.20	26.23	-30.28	-22.32	-22.90
February–March 1986	-4.41	-2.90	-1.87	47.30	13.84	78.30
April–May 1986	9.93	-2.90	-22.86	9.70	4.01	-18.26
June–July 1986	-17.86	4.71	-2.05	-6.68	6.43	46.42
August–September 1986	10.34	0.28	-16.31	-8.20	-26.55	-23.29
October–November 1986	-1.24	4.79	42.29	17.11	12.19	-30.39
December 1986–January 1987	11.39	-6.57	11.30	-32.00	-19.70	30.51
February–March 1987	9.22	-3.86	-20.47	49.02	14.09	-30.24
April–May 1987	-7.04	-2.71	4.44	-17.55	15.77	24.78
June–July 1987	-7.17	12.77	20.17	-4.00	-27.42	47.30
August–September 1987	5.59	-7.56	-4.79	15.49	1.26	-29.06
October–November 1987	8.92	12.69	-21.38	-34.75	19.87	-6.37
December 1987–January 1988	-16.36	-16.42	98.02	68.45	38.49	22.50
February–March 1988	12.49	14.57	-41.47	-25.99	-23.37	-0.81
April–May 1988	2.11	-3.58	6.95	22.45	11.25	-36.01
June–July 1988	-17.76	-12.27	-4.00	7.85	14.99	225.78
August–September 1988	3.17	10.37	-7.13	-8.35	-8.59	-26.65
October–November 1988	14.02	5.03	-9.93	-22.71	-21.60	-36.13
December 1988–January 1989	-10.86	11.62	49.70	8.48	-0.48	-23.43
February–March 1989	10.86	-2.29	-34.57	0.92	-13.49	24.06
April–May 1989	1.77	-7.36	-0.70	-5.91	22.96	-12.59
June–July 1989	-6.72	-14.40	15.59	68.79	90.97	107.90

Source: Ibid.

PERCENTAGE
CHANGE

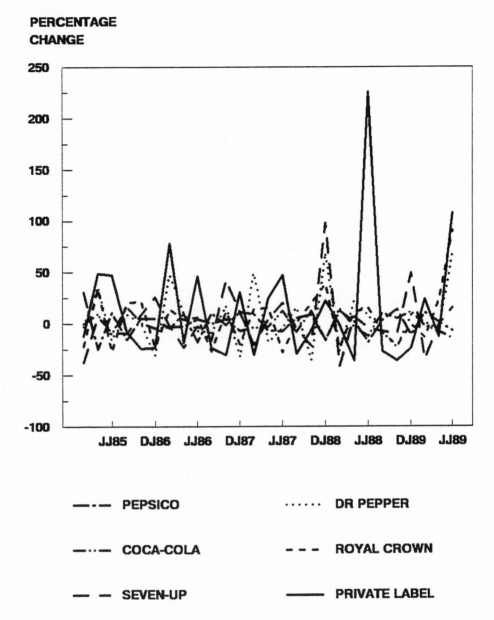

Source: Ibid.

Figure D–4. Percentage Change in Share of Sales, Out-State Michigan

Appendix E:
Rates of Return on Various Food and Beverage Categories, 1987–1988

Table E–1

SIC	Name	Median After-Tax Return on		
		Sales	*Assets*	*Net Worth*
2011	Meat packaging plants	0.9	5.4	11.0
2013	Sausages and prepared meat	1.7	5.2	12.0
2016	Poultry dressing plan	3.3	8.3	26.6
2017	Poultry and egg process	2.3	3.7	17.3
2021	Creamery butter	0.7	3.9	8.6
2022	Cheese natural, processed	1.3	6.2	12.5
2023	Condensed, evaporated milk	2.6	8.1	17.5
2024	Ice cream, frozen dessert	1.7	3.7	5.7
2026	Fluid milk	1.3	4.5	9.7
2032	Canned specialties	3.6	5.9	14.2
2033	Canned fruits, vegetable	2.2	4.2	11.3
2034	Dried dehydrated fruits and vegetables	5.3	10.6	17.5
2035	Pickles, sauce, salad dressing	2.9	5.9	7.6
2037	Frozen fruits and vegetables	0.9	2.1	5.0
2038	Frozen specialties	4.5	11.2	22.4
2041	Flour, grain mill products	2.4	5.4	13.4
2044	Rice milling	2.1	5.3	9.9
2045	Blend, prepared flour	2.8	4.2	10.7
2047	Dog, cat and pet food	2.7	5.5	13.3
2048	Prepared feeds nec	1.6	4.7	8.9
2051	Bread, cake ready products	2.9	7.2	17.6
2052	Cookies, crackers	4.0	7.0	15.5
2065	Candy confectionary products	2.4	4.1	11.8
2066	Chocolate and cocoa products	6.7	7.7	18.7
2074	Cottonseed oil mills	− 0.1	2.7	30.6
2077	Animal and sea fats/oil	0.1	0.4	2.9
2082	Malt liquors	− 0.1	− 0.2	− 0.5
2084	Wine, Brand, Br Spirits	2.4	1.2	13.1
2086	Bottled, can soft drinks	3.0	4.7	7.8
2087	Fluid extract sirup nec	4.3	5.7	10.0
2091	Canned and cured seafood	1.4	6.3	14.6
2092	Fresh/frozen fish	2.1	7.3	14.9
2095	Roasted coffee	2.6	5.7	18.9
2097	Manufactured ice	5.0	8.0	11.8
2098	Macaroni, Spaghetti	2.7	5.0	15.4
2099	Food preparation nec	3.7	6.4	12.4

Source: *Industry Norms and Key Business Ratios* (Murray Hill, NJ: Dun & Bradstreet Credit Services, 1987, 1988).

Appendix F:
Total Beverage Consumption

Table F–1
Total Beverage Volume Consumed by Occasion, 1988

Beverage Category	Before Breakfast	At Breakfast	Between Breakfast and Lunch	At Lunch	Between Lunch and Dinner	At Dinner	After Dinner	Late Night
Carbonated soft drink	6.8%	3.1%	25.7%	37.3%	39.7%	28.3%	35.6%	33.6%
Powdered soft drink	0.6	0.7	3.1	5.2	5.4	6.2	4.4	2.6
Iced tea	1.6	1.7	5.7	14.5	8.2	19.1	8.4	4.7
Fruit drink	1.8	2.6	3.5	3.8	3.6	2.2	3.0	1.8
Fruit juice	10.6	18.4	5.6	4.0	4.4	2.7	3.8	3.5
Bottled water	1.6	0.5	3.1	1.2	3.4	1.6	1.9	2.2
Coffee	63.8	42.7	40.8	9.1	11.4	7.1	9.9	9.0
Hot tea	5.8	5.0	4.0	2.1	2.3	2.5	2.9	2.6
Milk	4.8	21.7	4.2	18.3	4.4	22.2	8.4	10.7
Beer	0.3	a	1.2	1.4	11.5	3.8	14.9	21.5
Wine	0.1	a	0.1	0.3	1.0	1.5	1.0	1.6

Source: *Share of Intake Panel* (Greenwich, CT: Share of Intake Panel, 1988).
[a]Less than 0.05 percent.

Appendix G:
Beverage Consumption Over Time

Table G–1
Percentage Change of Total Beverage Consumption, 1985–1988

Beverage	Change, 1985–1988 Percentage Points
Carbonated soft drinks	2.7
Bottled water	0.8
Beer	0.5
Fruit drink	0.0
Cocoa	0.0
Alcohol/liqueurs	0.0
Coffee	0.0
Fruit juice	−0.1
Powdered soft drinks	−0.1
Breakfast drinks	−0.1
All other beverages	−0.2
Wine	−0.3
Milk	−1.3
Hot tea	−2.0

Source: *Share of Intake Panel, Beverage Consumption Trends—Topline Report* (Greenwich, CT: Share of Intake Panel, 1985–1988).

Appendix H:
Direct Comparative Advertising

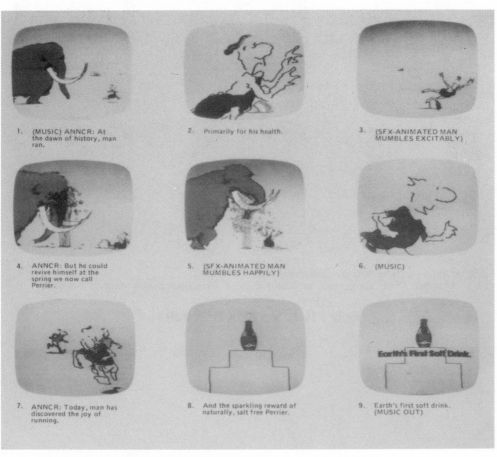

Note: Strategy: Position as carbonated soft drink.
Message: "The earth's first soft drink."

Figure H–1. Perrier Mineral Water

Note: Strategy: Substitute for carbonated soft drink.
Message: Direct comparison to Coke and Pepsi shows competing vending machines.

Figure H–2. Veryfine Fruit Juice

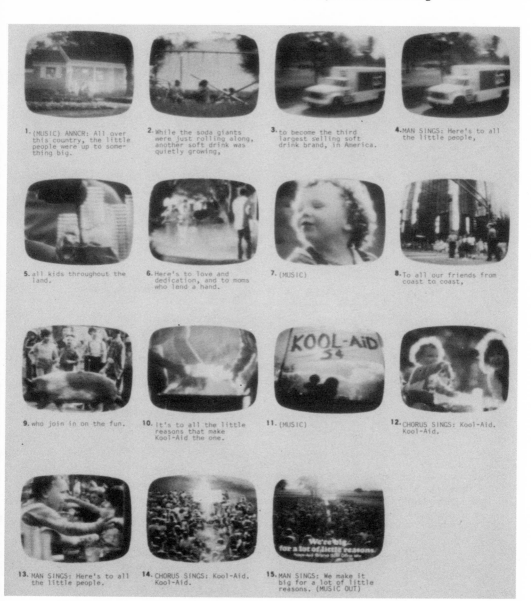

1. (MUSIC) ANNCR: All over this country, the little people were up to something big.

2. While the soda giants were just rolling along, another soft drink was quietly growing,

3. to become the third largest selling soft drink brand, in America.

4. MAN SINGS: Here's to all the little people,

5. all kids throughout the land.

6. Here's to love and dedication, and to moms who lend a hand.

7. (MUSIC)

8. To all our friends from coast to coast,

9. who join in on the fun.

10. It's to all the little reasons that make Kool-Aid the one.

11. (MUSIC)

12. CHORUS SINGS: Kool-Aid. Kool-Aid.

13. MAN SINGS: Here's to all the little people.

14. CHORUS SINGS: Kool-Aid. Kool-Aid.

15. MAN SINGS: We make it big for a lot of little reasons. (MUSIC OUT)

Note: Strategy: Position as the third largest-selling soft drink brand.
Message: Shows Pepsi and Coke delivery trucks in direct comparison.

Figure H–3. Kool-Aid Powdered Soft Drink

1. (SFX-THUNDER)

2. 1st CHILD: No camping today. WOMAN: Wanna bet?

3. MEN SING: Everyday is kid's day...WOMAN: Follow me.

4. MEN SING: ...when any mother tries to do those little extra things that light up little eyes...

5. WOMAN: It's not kid's day without Kool-Aid. 2nd CHILD: Oh boy...

6. WOMAN: I could pop open a soda,

7. but they wouldn't get those fruit flavors or vitamin C.

8. And soda's about twice the price.

9. MEN SING: Moms and Kool-Aid can make it

10. kid's day, any day at all.

11. ANNCR: Kool-Aid Brand Soft Drink Mix. (MUSIC OUT)

Note: Strategy: Position directly against carbonated soft drinks.

Message: Mother says "I could pop open a soda, but they wouldn't get those fruity flavors and vitamin C"

Mother says "Soda is about twice the price"

Emphasis on vitamin C, price, and taste.

Figure H–4. Kool-Aid Powdered Soft Drink.

1. (SFX-BALL BOUNCING ON FLOOR) ANNCR: Here comes a diet soft drink you've been thirsting for.

2. (MUSIC) MAN SINGS: I believe in reaching out to do my best. I believe in a taste different from the rest.

3. ANNCR: The taste they're reaching for, is Crystal Light Diet Soft Drink Mix. The lighter, refreshing taste... (MUSIC OUT)

4. WOMAN: Wait a minute. ANNCR: Hey, what are you doing?

5. WOMAN: Go on. MAN: Telling everyone the news.

6. ANNCR: You mean that Crystal has that lighter, refreshing taste?

7. MAN: Right. In fact, it even outsold Tab and Diet 7Up. ANNCR: Really?

8. MAN: Uh, huh. And now Crystal Light is offering, a delicious free sample.

9. Just grab a pencil and send your name and address to Crystal Light, P.O. Box 1986, Irwin, Illinois 60912.

10. ANNCR: Now back to the commercial.

11. MAN: How did I do? WOMAN: Okay.

12. (MUSIC) ANNCR: Crystal Light. The lighter, refreshing taste that goes down easy, doesn't fill you up.

13. CHORUS SINGS: I believe in Crystal Light because I believe in you.

14. ANNCR: 100% NutraSweet. All these natural flavors, and just four calories.

15. CHORUS SINGS: I believe in Crystal Light because I believe in me. (MUSIC OUT)

Note: Strategy: Position directly against carbonated soft drinks.

Message: Shows cans of Diet Coke and Diet Pepsi. Claims it outsells Diet Seven-Up and Tab.

Figure H–5. Crystal Light Powdered Soft Drink

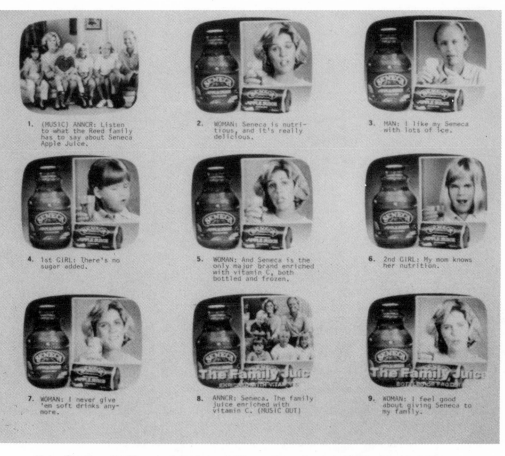

1. (MUSIC) ANNCR: Listen to what the Reed family has to say about Seneca Apple Juice.

2. WOMAN: Seneca is nutritious, and it's really delicious.

3. MAN: I like my Seneca with lots of ice.

4. 1st GIRL: There's no sugar added.

5. WOMAN: And Seneca is the only major brand enriched with vitamin C, both bottled and frozen.

6. 2nd GIRL: My mom knows her nutrition.

7. WOMAN: I never give 'em soft drinks anymore.

8. ANNCR: Seneca. The family juice enriched with vitamin C. (MUSIC OUT)

9. WOMAN: I feel good about giving Seneca to my family.

Note: Strategy: Position as the more nutritious alternative to carbonated soft drinks. Message: "I never give them soft drinks anymore."

Figure H–6. Seneca Fruit Juice

1. MAN: You've never heard of it; you've never experienced it,

2. but you already like it. I'll bet the suspense is killing you.

3. It's Steidl's. It's a wine cooler.

4. I know you'll like it, because you like soft drinks,

5. and Steidl's is the only wine cooler that's part soft drink

6. and part wine. And sometimes, soft drink lovers like us

7. want something a little more grownup. Where's the ice?

8. (SFX-ICE FALLS)

9. ANNCR: Steidl's, in Concord red or crisp white. The wine cooler with a soft drink twist.

Note: Strategy: Position as an adult soft drink.
Message: "Soft drink lovers want something more Grown-up."

Figure H–7. Steidl's Wine Cooler

Appendix I:
Beverage Product Introductions

Table I–1
New Carbonated Nonalcoholic Beverage Product Introductions, 1970–1988

	1970	1971	1972	1973	1974	1975	1976	1977	1978	1979
New product introductions, all manufacturers	24	16	26	20	25	30	18	19	25	28
Percentage of total, 1970–1988 (*N* = 1,264)	1.9	1.3	2.1	1.6	2.0	2.4	1.4	1.5	2.0	2.2
New product introductions by leading manufacturers										
PepsiCo	0	0	0	1	0	1	0	1	1	0
Seven-Up	1	1	0	0	1	0	1	0	1	0
Coca-Cola	1	0	1	1	3	4	0	0	1	2
Dr Pepper	0	1	0	0	0	0	0	0	0	0
RC	3	1	0	1	1	0	0	1	2	0
Total by leading manufacturers	5	3	1	3	5	5	1	2	5	2

Source: *New Product News* (Chicago, IL: German Publishing Co., 1970–1988).
[a]Does not include January, February, and March. These *New Product News* issues were not available.
[b]Does not include January and May. These *New Product News* issues were not available.
[c]Does not include February. This *New Product News* issue was not available.

Table I–2
New Carbonated Nonalcoholic Beverage Product Introductions and Events,

	1970	1971	1972	1973	1974	1975	1976	1977	1978
New product introductions by all manufacturers	24	16	26	20	25	30	18	19	25
New product introduction events by all manufacturers	12	13	10	13	12	14	6	12	20
Percentage of events to new products	50.0	81.3	38.5	65.0	48.0	46.7	33.3	63.2	80.0

Source: Ibid.
Note: An event is defined as a new product line introduction in a given month. Flavors within a product line is introduced over two (or more) months, then it would count as two (or more) events.
[a]Does not include January, February, and March. These *New Product News* issues were not available.
[b]Does not include January and May. These *New Product News* issues were not available.
[c]Does not include February. This *New Product News* issue was not available.

1980	1981	1982	1983	1984	1985	1986[a]	1987[b]	1988[c]	Total 1970 1988	Percentage of New Product Introductions by Manufacturer
27	23	95	46	124	145	91	235	247	1,264	100.0
2.1	1.8	7.5	3.6	9.8	11.5	7.2	18.6	19.5	100.0	
0	0	1	0	1	1	0	0	1	8	0.6
0	0	2	0	9	0	0	0	2	18	1.4
1	1	1	3	1	3	1	2	0	26	2.1
0	0	1	1	1	1	0	0	0	5	0.4
1	0	3	1	0	8	4	10	2	38	3.0
2	1	8	5	12	13	5	12	5	95	7.5

1970–1988

1979	1980	1981	1982	1983	1984	1985	1986[a]	1987[b]	1988[c]	Total 1970 1988
28	27	23	95	46	124	145	91	235	247	1,264
25	13	16	38	25	47	73	38	74	81	542
89.3	48.1	69.6	40.0	54.3	37.9	50.3	41.8	31.5	32.8	42.9

product line are not counted separately as they are for new product introductions. If a

Table I–3
New Noncarbonated Nonalcoholic Beverage Product Introductions, 1970–1988

	1970	1971	1972	1973	1974	1975	1976	1977	1978	1979
New product introductions, all manufacturers	63	53	78	63	60	89	114	112	144	145
Percentage of total, 1970–1988 (N = 3,609)	1.7	1.5	2.2	1.7	1.7	2.5	3.2	3.1	4.0	4.0
New product introductions by leading manufacturers										
PepsiCo	0	0	0	0	0	0	0	4	0	0
Seven-Up	0	0	5	0	0	0	0	4	2	0
Coca-Cola	1	3	7	2	7	9	8	6	8	3
Dr Pepper	0	0	0	0	0	0	0	0	0	0
RC	0	0	0	0	0	0	0	0	0	0
Total by leading manufacturers	1	3	12	2	7	9	8	14	10	3

Source: Ibid.

[a]Does not include January, February, and March. These *New Product News* issues were not available.
[b]Does not include January and May. These *New Product News* issues were not available.
[c]Does not include February. This *New Product News* issue was not available.

Table I–4
New Noncarbonated Nonalcoholic Beverage Product Introductions and Events,

	1970	1971	1972	1973	1974	1975	1976	1977	1978	1979
New product introductions by all manufacturers	63	53	78	63	60	89	114	112	144	145
New product introduction events by all manufacturers	41	39	53	34	36	46	53	56	69	66
Percentage of events by new products	65.1	73.6	67.9	54.0	60.0	51.7	46.5	50.0	47.9	45.5

Source: Ibid.
Note: An event is defined as a new product line introduction in a given month. Flavors within a product line is introduced over two (or more) months, then it would count as two (or more) events.

[a]Does not include January, February, and March. These *New Product News* issues were not available.
[b]Does not include January and May. These *New Product News* issues were not available.
[c]Does not include February. This *New Product News* issue was not available.

1980	1981	1982	1983	1984	1985	1986[a]	1987[b]	1988[c]	Total 1970 1988	Percentage of New Product Introductions by Manufacturer
127	103	198	337	448	368	105	452	550	3,609	100.0
3.5	2.9	5.5	9.3	12.4	10.2	2.9	12.5	15.2	100.0	
0	0	0	0	0	0	0	0	0	4	0.1
0	0	0	0	2	4	0	0	0	17	0.5
10	7	8	6	14	13	1	5	11	129	3.6
0	0	0	0	0	0	0	0	0	0	0.0
0	0	0	2	0	4	0	0	0	6	0.2
10	7	8	8	16	21	1	5	11	156	4.3

1970–1988

1980	1981	1982	1983	1984	1985	1986[a]	1987[b]	1988[c]	Total 1970 1988
127	103	198	337	448	368	105	452	550	3,609
70	68	103	158	177	173	49	187	205	1,683
55.1	66.0	52.0	46.9	39.5	47.0	46.7	41.4	37.3	46.6

product line are not counted separately as they are for new product introductions. If a

Appendix J:
Brokers, Wholesale Grocers, and Other Distributors

Table J–1
Wholesale Grocers in the United States, Sorted by
Number Distributing Soft Drinks

Rank[a]	State	Number Wholesale Grocers	Number Distributing Soft Drinks
2	New York	64	33
3	Texas	61	26
5	Pennsylvania	48	26
4	North Carolina	49	25
9	Alabama	30	21
14	Missouri	26	20
8	Georgia	35	19
15	Mississippi	24	19
7	Ohio	37	18
10	Tennessee	29	17
13	Kentucky	26	17
17	Arkansas	21	16
11	Virginia	29	15
12	Illinois	27	13
19	Wisconsin	21	13
21	Indiana	17	11
22	Minnesota	17	11
18	Massachusetts	21	11
20	Louisiana	20	11
6	Michigan	39	11
1	California	144	10
28	Oklahoma	13	9
24	South Carolina	17	9
25	Washington	17	7
26	West Virginia	16	7
16	Florida	22	7
23	New Jersey	17	6
27	North Dakota	13	5
29	Maryland	12	5
34	Iowa	8	5
37	Colorado	7	5
35	Montana	8	4
45	Vermont	5	4

Table J–1 (continued)

Rank[a]	State	Number Wholesale Grocers	Number Distributing Soft Drinks
36	New Hampshire	8	4
38	Nebraska	7	4
32	Connecticut	10	4
33	Maine	10	4
41	Rhode Island	6	3
40	Kansas	6	3
31	Hawaii	11	2
47	Alaska	3	2
39	Oregon	7	2
30	Arizona	11	2
43	Idaho	5	2
42	Utah	6	2
44	Nevada	5	1
51	District of Columbia	1	1
48	New Mexico	3	1
46	South Dakota	4	1
49	Wyoming	2	1
50	Delaware	1	0

Source: *Directory of Retailer-Owned Cooperatives, Wholesaler Sponsored Voluntaries and Wholesale Grocers, Including Service Merchandisers* (New York: NY: Chain Store Guide Information Services, Lebhan Friedman, Inc., 1989).
[a]Rank by number of wholesale grocers.

Table J–2
Wholesale Grocers in the United States, Sorted by State

Rank[a]	State	Number Wholesale Grocers	Number Distributing Soft Drinks
9	Alabama	30	21
47	Alaska	3	2
30	Arizona	11	2
17	Arkansas	21	16
1	California	144	10
37	Colorado	7	5
32	Connecticut	10	4
50	Delaware	1	0
51	District of Columbia	1	1
16	Florida	22	7
8	Georgia	35	19
31	Hawaii	11	2
43	Idaho	5	2
12	Illinois	27	13
21	Indiana	17	11
34	Iowa	8	5
40	Kansas	6	3
13	Kentucky	26	17
20	Louisiana	20	11
33	Maine	10	4

29	Maryland	12	5
18	Massachusetts	21	11
6	Michigan	39	11
22	Minnesota	17	11
15	Mississippi	24	19
14	Missouri	26	20
35	Montana	8	4
38	Nebraska	7	4
44	Nevada	5	1
36	New Hampshire	8	4
23	New Jersey	17	6
48	New Mexico	3	1
2	New York	64	33
4	North Carolina	49	25
27	North Dakota	13	5
7	Ohio	37	18
28	Oklahoma	13	9
39	Oregon	7	2
5	Pennsylvania	48	26
41	Rhode Island	6	3
24	South Carolina	17	9
46	South Dakota	4	1
10	Tennessee	29	17
3	Texas	61	26
42	Utah	6	2
45	Vermont	5	4
11	Virginia	29	15
25	Washington	17	7
26	West Virginia	16	7
19	Wisconsin	21	13
49	Wyoming	2	1
	Total	1,046	475

Source: Ibid.

[a]Rank by number of wholesale grocers.

Table J–3
Wholesale Grocers in the United States, Sorted by Number of Wholesale Grocers

Rank[a]	State	Number Wholesale Grocers	Number Distributing Soft Drinks
1	California	144	10
2	New York	64	33
3	Texas	61	26
4	North Carolina	49	25
5	Pennsylvania	48	26
6	Michigan	39	11
7	Ohio	37	18
8	Georgia	35	19
9	Alabama	30	21
10	Tennessee	29	17
11	Virginia	29	15

Table J–3 (continued)

Rank[a]	State	Number Wholesale Grocers	Number Distributing Soft Drinks
12	Illinois	27	13
14	Missouri	26	20
13	Kentucky	26	17
15	Mississippi	24	19
16	Florida	22	7
18	Massachusetts	21	11
17	Arkansas	21	16
19	Wisconsin	21	13
20	Louisiana	20	11
23	New Jersey	17	6
24	South Carolina	17	9
25	Washington	17	7
22	Minnesota	17	11
21	Indiana	17	11
26	West Virginia	16	7
27	North Dakota	13	5
28	Oklahoma	13	9
29	Maryland	12	5
31	Hawaii	11	2
30	Arizona	11	2
33	Maine	10	4
32	Connecticut	10	4
34	Iowa	8	5
36	New Hampshire	8	4
35	Montana	8	4
39	Oregon	7	2
38	Nebraska	7	4
37	Colorado	7	5
40	Kansas	6	3
41	Rhode Island	6	3
42	Utah	6	2
43	Idaho	5	2
44	Nevada	5	1
45	Vermont	5	4
46	South Dakota	4	1
48	New Mexico	3	1
47	Alaska	3	2
49	Wyoming	2	1
51	District of Columbia	1	1
50	Delaware	1	0
	Total	1,046	475

Source: Ibid.

[a]Rank by number of wholesale grocers.

Table J–4
Share of Population, Food Store Sales, and Number of Brokers in
Top Fifty-three Areas, Sorted by Food Store Sales

Rank[a]	Area	Number of Brokers	Number of Candy, Tobacco and Media Distributors	Population	Food Store Sales	Cumulative Food Store Sales
1	Los Angeles	80	11	7.3%	6.6%	
2	New York	102	24	7.3	6.3	12.9%
3	Baltimore/ Washington	57	16	3.8	3.6	16.5
4	San Francisco	49	10	3.6	3.6	20.1
5	Boston	98	32	3.6	3.5	23.6
6	Charlotte	38	12	3.1	3.4	27.0
7	Dallas	52	9	2.8	3.3	30.3
8	Chicago	90	21	3.9	3.3	33.6
9	Tampa	39	11	2.4	2.8	36.4
10	Memphis	47	21	2.5	2.6	39.0
11	Philadelphia	77	13	3.0	2.5	41.5
12	Cincinnati	68	17	2.7	2.5	44.0
13	St. Louis	58	20	2.4	2.3	46.3
14	Birmingham	36	10	2.1	2.3	48.6
15	Atlanta	36	10	2.0	2.3	50.9
16	Columbia, South Carolina	35	7	1.8	2.1	53.0
17	Detroit	39	10	2.5	2.1	55.1
18	Houston	23	3	2.0	2.0	57.1
19	Milwaukee	27	9	2.0	2.0	59.1
20	Denver	39	9	1.5	2.0	61.1
21	San Antonio	19	1	1.8	1.9	63.0
22	Cleveland	48	17	2.0	1.9	64.9
23	Nashville	34	6	1.6	1.7	66.6
24	Miami	27	8	1.8	1.7	68.3
25	Albuquerque	22	2	1.4	1.6	69.9
26	New Orleans	16	6	1.5	1.6	71.5
27	Minneapolis	41	13	1.7	1.6	73.1
28	Albany	46	14	1.6	1.6	74.7
29	Indianapolis	52	11	1.6	1.5	76.2
30	Richmond	27	4	1.3	1.5	77.7
31	Pittsburgh	49	12	1.6	1.5	79.2
32	Phoenix	34	4	1.4	1.5	80.7
33	Oklahoma City	27	7	1.3	1.4	82.1
34	Seattle	23	7	1.4	1.4	83.5
35	Portland, Oregon	24	5	1.3	1.3	84.8
36	Salt Lake City	22	8	1.1	1.3	86.1
37	Kansas City	19	6	1.2	1.3	87.4
38	Hartford	18	7	1.2	1.2	88.6
39	Buffalo	43	10	1.2	1.2	89.8
40	Des Moines	17	11	1.0	1.1	90.9
41	Grand Rapids	28	7	1.1	1.0	91.9
42	Louisville	22	7	1.0	1.0	92.9

Table J–4 (continued)

Rank[a]	Area	Number of Food Brokers	Number of Candy, Tobacco and Media Distributors	Population	Food Store Sales	Cumulative Food Store Sales
43	Omaha	19	11	0.8	1.0	93.9
44	Jacksonville	33	2	0.8	0.9	94.8
45	Fresno	1	1	1.0	0.9	95.7
46	Springfield	12	7	0.8	0.8	96.5
47	Charleston/ Roanoke	26	7	0.8	0.8	97.3
48	Spokane	18	4	0.5	0.6	97.9
49	Wichita	9	2	0.5	0.5	98.4
50	Fargo	12	6	0.5	0.5	98.9
51	Billings	12	4	0.3	0.4	99.3
52	Hawaii	17	2	0.4	0.4	99.7
53	Alaska	13	0	0.2	0.3	
	Total	1,920	494	100.0%	100.0%	100.0%

Source: *Progressive Grocer's 1989 Marketing Guidebook* (Stamford, CT: Maclean Hunter Media, Inc., 1989).
[a]Rank in food store sales.

Table J–5
Share of Population, Food Store Sales, and Number of Brokers in Fifty-three Areas, Sorted by Population

Rank[a]	Area	Number of Food Brokers	Number of Candy, Tobacco and Media Distributors	Population	Cumulative Population	Food Store Sales
1	Los Angeles	80	11	7.3%		6.6%
2	New York	102	24	7.3	14.6%	6.3
8	Chicago	90	21	3.9	18.5	3.3
3	Baltimore/ Washington	57	16	3.8	22.3	3.6
4	San Francisco	49	10	3.6	25.9	3.6
5	Boston	98	32	3.6	29.5	3.5
6	Charlotte	38	12	3.1	32.6	3.4
11	Philadelphia	77	13	3.0	35.6	2.5
7	Dallas	52	9	2.8	38.4	3.3
12	Cincinnati	68	17	2.7	41.1	2.5
17	Detroit	39	10	2.5	43.6	2.1
10	Memphis	47	21	2.5	46.1	2.6
9	Tampa	39	11	2.4	48.5	2.8
13	St. Louis	58	20	2.4	50.9	2.3
14	Birmingham	36	10	2.1	53.0	2.3
18	Houston	23	3	2.0	55.0	2.0
15	Atlanta	36	10	2.0	57.0	2.3
22	Cleveland	48	17	2.0	59.0	1.9
19	Milwaukee	27	9	2.0	61.0	2.0

21	San Antonio	19	1	1.8	62.8	1.9
24	Miami	27	8	1.8	64.6	1.7
16	Columbia, South Carolina	35	7	1.8	66.4	2.1
27	Minneapolis	41	13	1.7	68.1	1.6
29	Indianapolis	52	11	1.6	69.7	1.5
28	Albany	46	14	1.6	71.3	1.6
23	Nashville	34	6	1.6	72.9	1.7
31	Pittsburgh	49	12	1.6	74.5	1.5
20	Denver	39	9	1.5	76.0	2.0
26	New Orleans	16	6	1.5	77.5	1.6
34	Seattle	23	7	1.4	78.9	1.4
25	Albuquerque	22	2	1.4	80.3	1.6
32	Phoenix	34	4	1.4	81.7	1.5
30	Richmond	27	4	1.3	83.0	1.5
33	Oklahoma City	27	7	1.3	84.3	1.4
35	Portland, Oregon	24	5	1.3	85.6	1.3
39	Buffalo	43	10	1.2	86.8	1.2
37	Kansas City	19	6	1.2	88.0	1.3
38	Hartford	18	7	1.2	89.2	1.2
36	Salt Lake City	22	8	1.1	90.3	1.3
41	Grand Rapids	28	7	1.1	91.4	1.0
45	Fresno	1	1	1.0	92.4	0.9
40	Des Moines	17	11	1.0	93.4	1.1
42	Louisville	22	7	1.0	94.4	1.0
46	Springfield	12	7	0.8	95.2	0.8
44	Jacksonville	33	2	0.8	96.0	0.9
43	Omaha	19	11	0.8	96.8	1.0
47	Charleston/ Roanoke	26	7	0.8	97.6	0.8
48	Spokane	18	4	0.5	98.1	0.6
49	Wichita	9	2	0.5	98.6	0.5
50	Fargo	12	6	0.5	99.1	0.5
52	Hawaii	17	2	0.4	99.5	0.4
51	Billings	12	4	0.3	99.8	0.4
53	Alaska	13	0	0.2		0.3
	Total	1,920	494	100.0%	100.0%	100.0%

Source: Ibid.

[a]Rank in food store sales.

Table J–6
Share of Population, Food Store Sales, and Number of Brokers in Top Fifty-three Areas, in Alphabetic Order

Rank[a]	Area	Number of Food Brokers	Number of Candy, Tobacco and Media Distributors	Population	Food Store Sales
53	Alaska	13	0	0.2%	0.3%
28	Albany	46	14	1.6	1.6
25	Albuquerque	22	2	1.4	1.6
15	Atlanta	36	10	2.0	2.3

Table J–6 (continued)

Rank[a]	Area	Number of Food Brokers	Number of Candy, Tobacco and Media Distributors	Population	Food Store Sales
3	Baltimore/ Washington	57	16	3.8	3.6
51	Billings	12	4	0.3	0.4
14	Birmingham	36	10	2.1	2.3
5	Boston	98	32	3.6	3.5
39	Buffalo	43	10	1.2	1.2
47	Charleston/ Roanoke	26	7	0.8	0.8
6	Charlotte	38	12	3.1	3.4
8	Chicago	90	21	3.9	3.3
12	Cincinnati	68	17	2.7	2.5
22	Cleveland	48	17	2.0	1.9
16	Columbia, South Carolina	35	7	1.8	2.1
7	Dallas	52	9	2.8	3.3
20	Denver	39	9	1.5	2.0
40	Des Moines	17	11	1.0	1.1
17	Detroit	39	10	2.5	2.1
50	Fargo	12	6	0.5	0.5
45	Fresno	1	1	1.0	0.9
41	Grand Rapids	28	7	1.1	1.0
38	Hartford	18	7	1.2	1.2
52	Hawaii	17	2	0.4	0.4
18	Houston	23	3	2.0	2.0
29	Indianapolis	52	11	1.6	1.5
44	Jacksonville	33	2	0.8	0.9
37	Kansas City	19	6	1.2	1.3
1	Los Angeles	80	11	7.3	6.6
42	Louisville	22	7	1.0	1.0
10	Memphis	47	21	2.5	2.6
24	Miami	27	8	1.8	1.7
19	Milwaukee	27	9	2.0	2.0
27	Minneapolis	41	13	1.7	1.6
23	Nashville	34	6	1.6	1.7
26	New Orleans	16	6	1.5	1.6
2	New York	102	24	7.3	6.3
33	Oklahoma City	27	7	1.3	1.4
43	Omaha	19	11	0.8	1.0
11	Philadelphia	77	13	3.0	2.5
32	Phoenix	34	4	1.4	1.5
31	Pittsburgh	49	12	1.6	1.5
35	Portland, Oregon	24	5	1.3	1.3
30	Richmond	27	4	1.3	1.5
36	Salt Lake City	22	8	1.1	1.3
21	San Antonio	19	1	1.8	1.9
4	San Francisco	49	10	3.6	3.6
34	Seattle	23	7	1.4	1.4
48	Spokane	18	4	0.5	0.6

46	Springfield	12	7	0.8	0.8
13	St. Louis	58	20	2.4	2.3
9	Tampa	39	11	2.4	2.8
49	Wichita	9	2	0.5	0.5
	Total	1,920	494	100.0%	100.0%

Source: Ibid.

[a]Rank in food store sales.

Appendix K:
Statistical Evidence on Cooperative
Merchandising Agreements

Comparisons of Carbonated
Soft Drink Performance

The theoretical mechanism by which cooperative merchandising agreements (CMAs) are allegedly used to promote anticompetitive exclusion is subtle and complex relative to the straightforward theory of CMA efficiencies; substantial evidence casts doubt on the factual predicates of anticompetitive CMAs. Notwithstanding these caveats, we sought to evaluate the welfare implications of CMA use by measuring its actual effects. We conducted two empirical tests. First, we compared carbonated soft drink performance in several geographic areas where CMAs are used to a particular area noted for the absence of CMAs. Measured differences in industry performance between areas with and without CMAs can reasonably be attributed to CMA use if there are no other important differences between the areas. Second, we tested whether the intensity of CMA use in a particular area significantly explains both relative and aggregate carbonated soft drink performance. Based on various carbonated soft drink performance measures for the Boston metropolitan area and on information about CMA use by PepsiCo and Coca-Cola bottlers, we estimated the competitive effects of CMA intensity.

In both the cross-section and the time-series analyses, Nielsen Scantrack data are used as the basis for measuring carbonated soft drink industry performance. Nielsen's Scantrack service provides actual volume equivalent purchases and dollar sales, by week, for a sample of supermarkets in numerous metropolitan areas.[1] Since Nielsen Scantrack data are compiled from checkout scanners, the ratio of dollars to volume (in case equivalents) provides a reasonably accurate measure of the weekly average price of carbonated soft drinks.

Cross-Section Comparison

One significant metropolitan area in the United States where CMAs are not used extensively is Chicago. Thus, a comparison of carbonated soft drink performance in Chicago with that in other metropolitan areas provides a basis for assessing the competitive effects of CMAs.

Methodology

Differences between carbonated soft drink performance in Chicago and in other metropolitan areas may be explained by factors besides CMA use. Ideally, one would test for the significance of CMA use by comparing carbonated soft drink performance in otherwise identical areas. Obviously, ideal test conditions are never achieved; they are only approximated.

We sought to achieve experimental conditions in two ways. First, for comparison purposes, we chose metropolitan areas similar to Chicago in location and size. Specifically, we compared carbonated soft drink performance in St. Louis, Indianapolis, and Cleveland, respectively, to performance in Chicago. Second, in our volume comparisons, we normalized for population differences.

For each comparison area, we charted monthly carbonated soft drink performance for Chicago and the corresponding area. No statistical tests were conducted since area performance differences were obvious from the graphical time-series plots.

Measuring Carbonated Soft Drink Performance

We measured carbonated soft drink performance in two ways in our cross-section comparisons. First, we compared monthly time series of per capita total carbonated soft drink volume by dividing monthly volumes by population for the corresponding month. Monthly population was derived by interpolating between annual population figures. We believe that volume per capita is one available measure of carbonated soft drink industry performance.[2] Second, we measured performance in terms of the average price paid for carbonated soft drinks. In general, consumers benefit from higher volume and lower prices.

Data

Weekly Nielsen Scantrack data for carbonated soft drink case equivalent volume and dollar sales were used to construct monthly time series of volume and weighted average price. Available data enabled us to construct monthly time series from April 1987 through August 1989 for the four areas: Chicago,

Indianapolis, St. Louis, and Cleveland. Annual population statistics were obtained from the Bureau of the Census.

Results

The volume and price comparisons are depicted graphically by the monthly time-series plots in figures K–1 through K–6. In terms of per capita consumption, volume is lower in Chicago in every month than the corresponding volume in each of the three comparison areas. Similarly, in terms of price, the average price of all carbonated soft drinks is higher in Chicago than in each of the comparison areas for every month.

Uniformly, the cross-section comparisons of carbonated soft drink performance support the view that CMAs are an efficient means of promotion. Although these comparisons lack statistical sophistication, they shift the burden of proof to those who would allege CMAs are anticompetitive, exclusionary practices.

Per Person Consumption

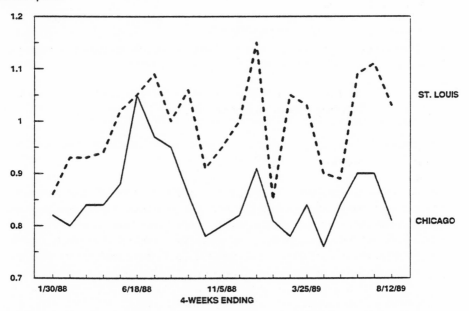

Note: Per person consumption is measured in 192-ounce case equivalent per four-week period.

Figure K–1. Per Person Consumption of All Carbonated Soft Drinks, Chicago versus St. Louis

**Per Person
Consumption**

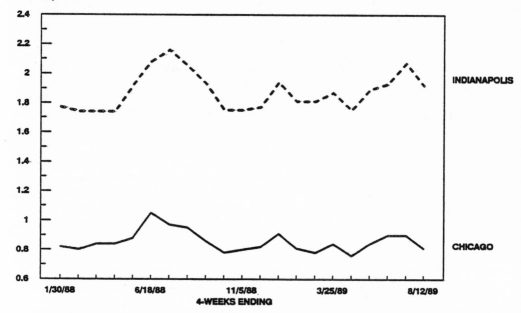

Note: Per person consumption is measured in 192-ounce case equivalent per four-week period.

Figure K–2. Per Person Consumption of All Carbonated Soft Drinks, Chicago versus Indianapolis

Time-Series Analysis

In our time-series analysis, we sought to explain relative and aggregate carbonated soft drink industry performance in a particular area in terms of the intensity of CMA use to promote PepsiCo and Coca-Cola brands. Based on multiple linear regression analysis, we estimated the extent of weekly variation in various performance measures that could be explained by contemporaneous variation in fundamental factors, including intensity of CMA use. This type of analysis enables us to assess the magnitude and significance of changes in CMA intensity on industry performance.

CMA Intensity

We chose the Boston metropolitan area for study because summary information about the use of CMAs in marketing PepsiCo and Coca-Cola brands by

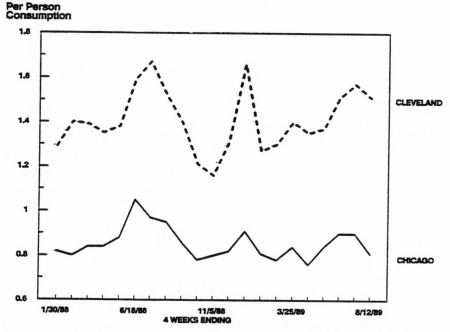

Per Person
Consumption

Note: Per person consumption is measured in 192-ounce case equivalent per four-week period.

Figure K–3. Per Person Consumption of All Carbonated Soft Drinks, Chicago versus Cleveland

the PepsiCo and Coca-Cola bottlers was available. We were able to identify four supermarket chains that concurrently promoted either PepsiCo or Coca-Cola brands pursuant to a CMA agreement with the local PepsiCo and Coca-Cola bottlers. Although these four supermarket chains were not the only ones to use CMAs, these four combined accounted for approximately 61 percent of grocery volume in the Boston metropolitan area over the time period studied.[3]

Based on this information and on statistics concerning the number of stores in each of these chains, we constructed a CMA intensity variable for both the PepsiCo and the Coca-Cola bottlers.[4] CMA intensity is alternatively defined for the PepsiCo and the Coca-Cola bottler as the number of stores in the four subject supermarket chains promoting PepsiCo brand or Coca-Cola brand soft drinks as a proportion of all supermarket outlets in Boston.[5]

The two CMA intensity variables vary week to week for each of the PepsiCo and Coca-Cola brands and range from 0 to 61 percent. The measures are 0 in a week when none of the four supermarket chains promoted PepsiCo

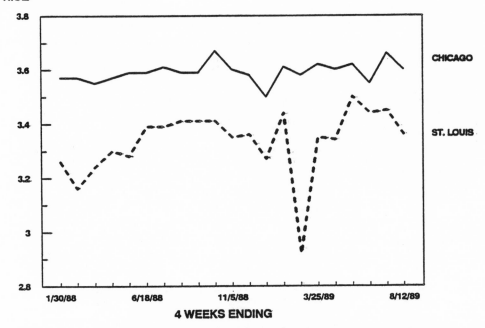

PRICE

Figure K–4. Price per 192-Ounce Case, All Carbonated Soft Drinks, Chicago versus St. Louis

or Coca-Cola brands pursuant to a CMA, and the measures are 61 percent when all four did.

Finally, it is important to note that our two measures of CMA intensity refer only to CMA use by the PepsiCo and Coca-Cola bottlers to promote PepsiCo and Coca-Cola brands in the 2-liter package size.[6] Information about CMA use by non-PepsiCo and non-Coca-Cola bottlers-distributors was not available. Also, our measure of CMA intensity does not capture CMA use in nongrocery retail channels.

Measuring Carbonated Soft Drink Performance

We measured industry performance in the Boston area in several ways. For specific brands and for all brands combined, we constructed weekly time-series data for volume and price.[7] Weekly time series of volume and price were constructed for six brands and for private label products.[8] Each series was constructed for one package size: 2-liter bottles.[9] The PepsiCo and Coca-Cola series included the diet and regular cola brands but not the

PRICE

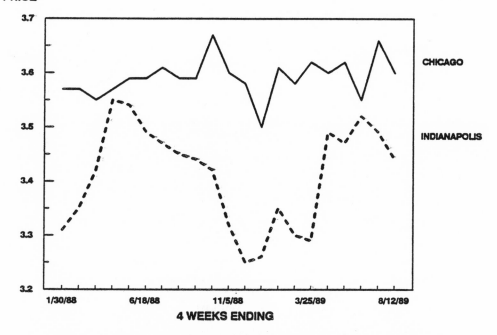

Figure K–5. Price per 192-Ounce Case, All Carbonated Soft Drinks, Chicago versus Indianapolis

caffeine-free products. The other brands were Seven-Up, Dr Pepper, Canada Dry, and Royal Crown, which represent national brands that are frequently distributed by a non-PepsiCo, non-Coca-Cola bottler.[10]

Measuring the Effect of CMA Intensity on Carbonated Soft Drink Performance

For each of the brand categories and for all carbonated soft drinks combined and for volume and price, respectively, we estimated the following regression model:

$$Y = a + bCOOL + cPCMA + dCCMA$$

where

Y is alternatively volume or price for the various brand categories, including all carbonated soft drinks, for the 2-liter package size,

PRICE

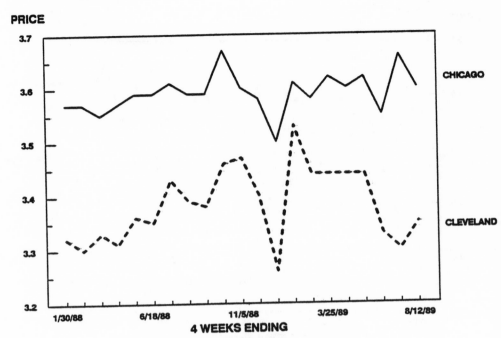

Figure K–6. Price Per 192-Ounce Case, All Carbonated Soft Drinks, Chicago versus Cleveland

COOL is weekly average cooling degree days, which is included to account for seasonal changes in demand for carbonated soft drinks,[11]

PCMA is the intensity of CMA use in promoting Pepsi-brand 2-liter bottles,

CCMA is the intensity of CMA use in promoting Coca-Cola brand 2-liter bottles.

Ordinary least-squares methods were used to estimate the coefficients, *c* and *d,* of the PepsiCo and Coca-Cola CMA variables, respectively.[12] These coefficients represent the measured effects of PCMA and CCMA, respectively, on the various measures of carbonated soft drink performance. For example, both the anti- and procompetitive hypotheses about CMAs would predict that an increase in Pepsi-brand CMA use would have a positive impact (*c* is predicted to be positive) on Pepsi-brand volume, holding CMA use by the Coca-Cola bottler constant. In other instances, the anti- and procompetitive hypotheses about CMA use differ. For example, the anticompetitive hypothesis predicts that an increase in the PepsiCo bottler's use of CMAs, holding the Coca-Cola bottler's CMA activity constant, would negatively affect total carbonated soft drink volume. In contrast, the hypothesis that

CMAs are procompetitive would predict just the opposite aggregate volume effect.

Results

The statistical results are presented in tables K–1 and K–2. In the volume regressions, significant autocorrelation was found in most of the cases. Upon correcting for first-order autocorrelation, the linear models are statistically significant for every brand category. (The critical value of the F-statistic at the 5 percent level is approximately 2.60.) The measured effects of PCMA and CCMA on their respective bottler's sales are as predicted: the PepsiCo bottler's Pepsi-brand CMAs increase Pepsi-brand volume, and the Coca-Cola bottler's Coca-Cola brand CMAs increase Coca-Cola brand volume. Moreover, in each instance the coefficients are statistically significant. Most importantly, however, the effects of PCMA and CCMA on total carbonated soft drink consumption (on total 2-liter carbonated soft drink consumption) are positive and statistically significant in the case of CCMA and nearly statistically significant for PCMA.

The effects of PCMA and CCMA on non-PepsiCo and non-Coca-Cola brand sales are typically negative, but the negative effects are not statistically significant except in one instance. Specifically, an increase in Pepsi-brand CMA use by the PepsiCo bottler is found to have lowered Seven-Up volume. Regardless of any negative effects of the PepsiCo and the Coca-Cola bottlers' use of Pepsi- and Coca-Cola-brand CMAs on competing brand sales, these CMAs are found to be procompetitive here since overall volume increases with CMA intensity. The major implication of the volume regressions is that CMA use by the PepsiCo bottler raises Pepsi-brand sales and CMA use by the Coca-Cola bottler raises Coca-Cola brand sales, partly by marginally reducing all other brands' sales but more significantly by expanding overall sales.

The price regression estimates are reported in table K–2. For each brand category the specified linear model is statistically significant judging by the F-statistic. As in the volume regressions, corrections for serial correlation were typically necessary. Unlike the volume regressions, we twice had to correct for second-order as well as first-order autocorrelation.

It is useful to interpret the price regression results with an illustration. The Pepsi-brand price regression indicates that, on average, the weekly price of Pepsi-brand was $3.05 (per 192-ounce case), ignoring the effect of *PCMA, CCMA,* and *COOL.* The coefficient of *PCMA,* − 0.0056, indicates that the per case price of Pepsi-brand is reduced 56 cents for each percentage point increase in our PepsiCo bottler CMA intensity measure. Thus, by implication, if PepsiCo bottler CMA intensity increased from 0 to 100 percentage points between two weeks, the price per case is predicted to fall 56 cents, from $3.05 to $2.49.

Table K–1
Quantity Regressions

Dependent Variable	Pepsi	Coke	Seven-Up	RC	Dr Pepper	Canada Dry	All Others	Total
INTERCEPT	123,359	171,378	15,162	2,339	3,270	15,632	37,565	331,040
	(17.60)*	(16.87)*	(12.64)*	(5.16)*	(11.73)*	(15.30)*	(17.65)*	(21.76)*
BSCOOL	35.2	22.6	1.1	−1.3	2.1	−10.1	−8.2	68.0
	(1.20)	(0.43)	(0.16)	(−0.63)	(1.36)	(−1.93)**	(−0.73)	(0.92)
BSPCMA	738.5	−76.6	−52.8	−2.6	−3.3	−1.0	−65.3	545.5
	(3.76)*	(−0.34)	(−2.43)*	(−0.56)	(−0.67)	(−0.04)	(−1.55)	(1.50)
BSCCMA	15.8	1036.7	−21.2	−0.9	−1.7	4.7	−19.1	1041.6
	(0.07)	(4.28)*	(−0.91)	(−0.18)	(−0.32)	(0.20)	(−0.43)	(2.63)*
AR(1)	——	0.35	0.52	0.75	0.53	0.38	0.45	0.26
		(2.46)*	(4.32)*	(7.92)*	(4.06)*	(2.80)*	(3.56)*	(1.84)**
AR(2)	——							
DW	1.85	2.01	1.77	1.93	2.20	1.91	1.89	1.89
Adjusted R^2	.19	.32	.25	.57	.36	.21	.16	.20
F-statistic	4.95	7.00	5.20	18.04	8.13	4.33	3.50	4.24

Note: T-statistics are in parentheses.
* significant at 1 percent level.
** significant at 5 percent level.

Table K-2
Price Regressions

Dependent Variable	Pepsi	Coke	Seven-Up	RC	Dr Pepper	Canada Dry	All Others	Total
INTERCEPT	3.0549 (53.12)*	2.7838 (51.41)*	2.9725 (66.39)*	2.9262 (59.00)*	3.1095 (55.43)*	3.1926 (33.80)*	3.0233 (79.70)*	2.9089 (65.39)*
BSCOOL	-0.0004 (-1.57)	-0.0004 (-1.52)	0.0002 (0.80)	0.0002 (0.93)	0.0004 (1.34)	0.0006 (1.60)	0.0005 (2.56)*	-0.0003 (-1.55)
BSPCMA	-0.0056 (-3.47)*	0.0020 (1.66)	0.0017 (2.06)**	-0.0004 (-0.58)	0.0004 (0.54)	-0.0009 (-1.38)	0.0004 (0.90)	-0.0012 (-1.18)
BSCCMA	-0.0005 (-0.28)	-0.0036 (-2.83)*	0.0008 (0.93)	0.0003 (0.32)	0.0002 (0.27)	0.0003 (0.44)	0.0006 (1.26)	-0.0020 (-1.77)**
AR(1)	—	0.3622 (2.52)*	0.4825 (3.82)*	0.6082 (5.65)*	0.6936 (6.23)*	1.1220 (8.50)*	0.8685 (6.38)*	0.2794 (1.92)**
AR(2)	—	—	—	—	—	-0.3280 (-2.49)*	-0.2123 (-1.58)	—
DW	1.67	1.80	1.85	2.07	1.78	2.17	2.06	1.80
Adjusted R^2	.17	.26	.17	.41	.51	.77	.56	.18
F-statistic	4.55	5.40	3.56	9.95	14.43	33.95	13.84	3.84

Note: T-statistics are in parentheses.
* significant at 1 percent level.
** significant at 5 percent level.

The price regression results are consistent overall with the volume regression results. Specifically, a negative and statistically significant effect of CMA intensity on the average price of a brand category corresponds to a positive and statistically significant effect of CMA intensity on volume. Consistent with the volume results, the estimated effect of PepsiCo and Coca-Cola bottlers' CMAs on the average price of all carbonated soft drinks is negative, though the estimated effect is statistically significant only for the Coca-Cola bottler CMA.[13]

Overall, our findings about the impact of the intensity of CMA use on carbonated soft drink volume or price do not support the anticompetitive foreclosure hypothesis. Instead, our regression analysis of volume and price time series supports our a priori hypothesis that CMAs reduce the costs of promotional transactions between bottlers/distributors and grocery retailers.

Notes

1. Nielsen surveys supermarkets with annual sales of at least $2 million. Supermarkets with at least $2 million in annual sales account for 73 percent of all grocery sales. Progressive Grocer, *Marketing Guidebook* (Stamford, CT: Maclean Hunter Media, Inc., 1988).

2. Richard Posner, "The Rule of Reason and the Economic Approach: Reflections on the *Sylvania* Decision," *University of Chicago Law Review* (1977); and Frank H. Easterbrook, "The Limits of Antitrust," *Texas Law Review* (1984).

3. This represents an estimate.

4. The number of food stores in the four chains in the Boston metropolitan area was obtained from the Progressive Grocer's *Marketing Guidebook* (1989).

5. Since the four subject chains uniformly promoted carbonated soft drinks throughout their stores pursuant to CMAs, the numerator is merely the number of chains implementing a CMA weighted by its corresponding number of outlets.

6. Information about the bottlers' promotion of other brands and other package sizes pursuant to CMAs was not available. Notably the PepsiCo and Coca-Cola brands were occasionally promoted in identical weeks with the same supermarket chain.

7. Nielsen Scantrack data provided the basis for constructing these performance measures.

8. Only diet private label information was available.

9. We were able to obtain information about CMA use for only this one package size. The 2-liter size is one of the most frequently featured sizes; thus, our measure of CMA intensity reasonably represents CMA use to promote carbonated soft drinks. Since our CMA variable is based on 2-liter promotions, we chose performance measures corresponding to this size. By using just 2-liter volume and price to measure performance, we would be more likely to find anticompetitive effects than by measuring performance based on volume and price for all package sizes. This is because a negative impact on competing brands' 2-liter sales could be offset by feature promotion of other sizes for the brands. Thus, basing our competitive assessment of CMAs on per-

formance measured only in terms of 2-liter volume and price favors rejection of the procompetitive hypothesis and is therefore conservative.

10. In Boston, these brands are not distributed by the PepsiCo bottler; Dr Pepper is bottled by a Coca-Cola bottler.

11. Cooling degree days are calculatead by subtracting 65 degrees from the average daily temperature. If the average temperature is less than 65 degrees, then zero is recorded for that day. The average daily degrees over 65 are then aggregated for the week.

12. Because our CMA intensity measure understates the extent of CMA use in promoting the PepsiCo and Coca-Cola brands, the coefficient estimates are biased upward on this account. Since our intensity measures also contain measurement errors, there is a counter tendency for the coefficient estimates to be biased downward. A priori, we cannot predict the net direction of this bias.

13. More precisely, the average price is the average price of 2-liter bottles for the following brands: Pepsi, Coca-Cola, Seven-Up, Dr Pepper, Royal Crown, and Canada Dry.

Appendix L:
Selected Vertical Acquisitions
by Carbonated Soft Drink Firms

Bottler Acquired	Acquirer	Date
Atlanta Coca-Cola Bottling Co.	CCUSA	1979
Bryant Beverages	PepsiCo	May 1982
Associated Coca-Cola Bottling Co.	CCUSA	June 1982
Surfside Beverage Corp.	PepsiCo	June 1983
Mid-Atlantic Bottling Co.	CCUSA	August 1984
Wometco Bottling Co.	CCUSA	October 1984
Louisiana Coca-Cola Bottling Co., Ltd.	CCUSA	December 1984
Central States Coca-Cola Bottling Co.	CCUSA	March 1985
Allegheny Pepsi-Cola Bottling Co. (sold by PepsiCo in September 1988).	PepsiCo	May 1985
Franklin Bottling Co.	PepsiCo	July 1985
Athens Coca-Cola Bottling Co.	CCUSA	October 1985
Louisiana Coca-Cola Bottling Co., Ltd.	CCUSA	February 1986
Pepsi-Cola Bottling Company of Perry, Inc.	PepsiCo	February 1986
MEI Corp.	PepsiCo	May 1986
Beatrice Company's Coca-Cola Bottling Operations	CCUSA	June 1986
Pepsi-Cola Bottling Company of Gallup	PepsiCo	March 1986
JTL Corp.	CCUSA	July 1986
Coca-Cola Bottling Co. of New York	CCUSA	November 1986

Bottler Acquired	Acquirer	Date
Coca-Cola Bottling Co. of South Florida, Inc.	CCUSA	December 1986
New Century Beverage Co.	PepsiCo	December 1986
TJF Beverages, Inc.	PepsiCo	December 1986
Pepsi-Cola Bottling Company of Bloomington, Inc.	PepsiCo	October 1987
IC Industries, Inc. —(joint venture) Pepsi-Cola General Bottlers, Inc. (20 percent interest)	PepsiCo	December 1987
Rogers Beverages	PepsiCo	November 1987
Coca-Cola Bottling Co., of Miami; Coca-Cola Bottling Co. of Delaware; Coca-Cola Bottling Co. of Memphis, Tennessee	CCUSA	February 1988
Pepsi-Cola Bottling Company of Tampa	PepsiCo	February 1988
Coca Cola USA	CCE	February 1988
Coca-Cola Bottlers: Jacksonville, Texas, and Wauchula, Florida	CCE	March 1988
Grand Metropolitan, Inc.: Atlantic Soft Drink Co. of South Carolina, and Pepsi-Cola San Joaquin Bottling Co.	PepsiCo	August 1988
Pepsi-Cola Bottling Company of Annapolis, Inc.	PepsiCo	July 1988
Pepsi-Cola Bottling Company of Denver; Pepsi-Cola Bottling Company of Greeley; Astro Canners, Inc.	PepsiCo	August 1988
Confair Bottling Co., Inc.	PepsiCo	September 1988
Laurel Group Limited	PepsiCo	October 1988
Erie Bottling Corporation	PepsiCo	October 1988
Unibev, Inc.	PepsiCo	October 1988
Wilchart, Ltd	PepsiCo	October 1988

Pepsi-Cola Bottling Company of Wilmington, Inc. (formerly known as Carolina Bottlers, Inc.)	PepsiCo	October 1988
Southwest Beverage Corp.	PepsiCo	February 1989
General Cinema Beverages Corp.	PepsiCo	March 1989
Pepsi-Cola Bottling of Reading	PepsiCo	April 1989
Rice Bottling Enterprises, Inc.	PepsiCo	May 1989

Note: CCUSA represents Coca-Cola United States of America and CCE represents Coca-Cola Enterprises.

Appendix M:
Statistical Evidence on
Vertical Integration

Two theories of anticompetitive effect arising from vertical integration have been discussed: vertical foreclosure and collusion facilitated by symmetrical vertical integration. In both cases, the anticompetitive effects result from a reduction in overall output, which increases prices and leads to a decline in consumer welfare. The recent history of vertical integration in the carbonated soft drink industry is a natural setting to test the applicability of these theories. If the vertical foreclosure and collusion theories have merit and if the anticompetitive effects of vertical foreclosure and/or collusion outweigh the cost-reducing efficiencies arising from PepsiCo's and Coca-Cola's vertical integration into the bottling business, the net anticompetitive effect could be detected in carbonated soft drink performance in local areas.

Empirical Tests of the
Vertical Foreclosure Hypothesis

Applicability of Vertical Foreclosure in the
Carbonated Soft Drink Industry

Three conditions are necessary for an upstream concentrate producer's acquisition of a downstream soft drink bottler to result in anticompetitive foreclosure: (1) the upstream producer must significantly raise the cost of supplying a competitive carbonated soft drink, (2) the competitive carbonated soft drink must be unable to avoid the higher input cost, and (3) the upstream producer's "foreclosure" must result in a reduction of output in a relevant market.

The first precondition is the act of foreclosure itself. Foreclosure does not necessarily mean that a competitive carbonated soft drink is denied use of an input altogether; it merely requires a rival carbonated soft drink to pay a higher price for an input. In Salop's terms, the integrated firm hypothetically raises a rival's costs. Hypothetically, after an acquisition, a PepsiCo-owned bottler might charge a noncorporate brand more for bottling services— promotion, bottling, distribution—than it internally charges PepsiCo.

Implicit in the first precondition is that a competitor's cost is raised significantly. For example, if the input whose cost is raised is relatively insignificant
among other inputs, its cost would have to be raised substantially to have a
significant effect on a competitor's cost of business. Alternatively, if the cost
of the input made up a large percentage of overall operating cost, its price
would not have to be raised substantially to have a significant effect on a
rival's unit cost.

The second precondition, which is related to the first, is also necessary
for the integrated firm's hypothetical foreclosure actions to affect rivals' costs
significantly. For example, suppose that PepsiCo's hypothetical foreclosure
entailed denying a carbonated soft drink competitor access to the PepsiCo-
owned bottling facility. Under many circumstances, the competitor would
have access to other bottlers in the area, including a Coca-Cola bottler. If
alternative access were readily available at competitive prices, PepsiCo's hypothetical foreclosure would not have a significant effect on a rival's costs.
Related to the second precondition is the issue of entry. In our hypothetical
example, if there were no barriers or impediments to entry in bottling and distribution, PepsiCo's rivals would have access to good substitutes.

With respect to the third precondition, the integrated firm's actions would
not reduce output significantly if competition is substantial from other carbonated soft drinks, whose costs are hypothetically increased through the integrated firm's foreclosure, and from competing beverages. The intensity of the
competition depends on the substitution in demand between the hypothetical
rival's product(s) and the integrated firm's product(s) and the rival's prod-
uct(s) and other competing brands, as well as substitution among carbonated
soft drinks and other beverages.

Efficiencies of vertical integration are also important in determining
whether output declines overall. If vertical integration results in market efficiencies, then overall carbonated soft drink output may increase even if the
vertically integrated firm were able to raise rivals' costs and prices significantly. In such cases, vertical mergers would result in both anti- and procompetitive effects, with procompetitive effects dominating. A vertical merger
would raise consumer welfare, notwithstanding the accompanying hypothetical vertical foreclosure. In these circumstances, the vertical merger would be
considered competitive, provided the efficiencies from vertical integration
could not be attained as easily without merger.

Measurement and Evaluation of
Carbonated Soft Drink Performance

If the vertical foreclosure hypothesis were applicable and the anticompetitive
effects of vertical foreclosure outweighed the cost-reducing efficiencies associ-

ated with vertical integration, the net anticompetitive effect could be detected in a reduction in carbonated soft drink volume performance in local areas.

To test the applicability of the vertical foreclosure theory in the carbonated soft drink industry, we examined PepsiCo's 1986 acquisition of MEI's bottling franchises to determine the effect of vertical integration on carbonated soft drink market performance. Pre- and postacquisition total carbonated soft drink volume in the MEI areas was compared to determine if vertical integration decreased volume relative to total U.S. carbonated soft drink volume.

In addition, effects on the frequency of advertising promotions were similarly examined. Nielsen Audit and Nielsen MAJERS bimonthly data on volume and feature advertising were analyzed for three geographic areas—Omaha, St. Louis, and Minneapolis/St. Paul—and for the overall United States for the period December 1984–January 1985 to October–November 1988.[1] Nielsen MAJERS data provide various measures of feature advertising intensity. We used both the volume of (Best Food Day) feature advertisements and (Best Food Day) raw weighted value of feature advertisements to measure promotional performance.[2] Nielsen Audit data provide volume and dollar sales data. Only the volume data are analyzed to provide evidence of the effects of PepsiCo's bottling acquisitions, however. Nielsen Audit data generally provide no reliable basis for computing average price in a bimonthly period for our present purposes.[3]

To deal directly with the concern that PepsiCo bottlers may fail to promote allied brands as aggressively as do independently owned Pepsi bottlers, we examined the effect of vertical integration on the volume and promotion of non-PepsiCo brands bottled by the MEI bottler acquired by PepsiCo.[4] However, a reduction in non–Pepsi brand volume following a bottling acquisition is not alone a sufficient condition for anticompetitive vertical foreclosure. Reduced performance of non-Pepsi brands might present preliminary cause for concern since this effect is a necessary component of vertical foreclosure.

The theoretical basis for evaluating carbonated soft drink industry performance in terms of volume and promotion effects is straightforward. Volume and promotional activities, as well as price, are jointly determined by demand, cost, and competitive conditions. More specifically, the demand for carbonated soft drinks in a local area is influenced by consumers' tastes and income, by the number and age distribution of potential consumers, by the prices of competing and complementary products, and by the average price of carbonated soft drinks. The quantity and sales price net of trade deals of carbonated soft drinks depend on the costs of ingredients, bottling, and distribution and on competitive conditions in the area at issue. The interaction of demand and supply results in equilibrium values for carbonated soft drink volume, price, and promotion. Variation in these performance measures occurs over time as the underlying demand and cost determinants change. These latter relationships, called reduced-form functions, are the fundamental derivations of the economic theory of price determination.

Ideally, measurement of the effects of PepsiCo's bottling acquisitions on performance would be based on statistical estimation of these reduced-form relations. Specifically, any change in performance before and after the MEI acquisition not attributable to the underlying demand and supply influences would be assigned to the acquisition itself. Unfortunately, measures of these myriad factors on a bimonthly basis for specific local areas are unavailable. Thus, it appears that the difference between average carbonated soft drink performance in local areas before and after a change in franchise ownership could alternatively be attributable to several unmeasurable influences. For example, if carbonated soft drink consumption were trending upward for reasons unrelated to changes in franchise ownership, the postacquisition average volume would exceed the preacquisition average, yet this finding would not conclusively reject the vertical foreclosure hypothesis.

To control for trends in unmeasured factors that would possibly affect carbonated soft drink consumption and promotion, these performance measures for a specific geographic area were normalized based on performance in the total United States. Specifically the analysis examines area consumption relative to U.S. consumption, area feature advertising frequency relative to U.S. advertising frequency, and area raw weighted value of feature advertising relative to U.S. raw weighted value of advertising.

Ultimately, we tested for possible anticompetitive effects of PepsiCo's MEI bottling acquisition by comparing relative area volume and relative area feature advertising before and after the acquisition. If the statistical analysis indicates that relative area volume and feature advertising remained unchanged or increased following the MEI acquisition, our procompetitive hypothesis must be favored over the vertical foreclosure hypothesis.

Statistical Methodology

Linear regression models were specified to test for differences in average bimonthly relative volume and relative feature advertising before and after MEI. For both the volume and the promotion regressions, a binary (dummy) variable was defined to capture the seasonal increase in demand for carbonated soft drinks in the summer. The variable S equals 1 for the bimonthly periods April/May through August/September and is 0 otherwise. Also, in both models, the binary variable, X, distinguishes the periods before and after the MEI acquisition. Thus, before May 1986 in the geographic areas examined, the PepsiCo bottler was owned by MEI ($X = 0$), and after May 1986, the bottler became a PepsiCo-owned bottler ($X = 1$).

Results

Volume Effects. Two volume regression models were estimated. One measured the effect of MEI on total volume, and one measured the effect of MEI on non-Pepsi brand volume. In the volume regressions, observations from the three MEI areas in the sample were pooled in estimating mean differences before and after MEI. The regression model was specified to allow for area-specific averages in relative volume performance before MEI and area-specific effects of the MEI acquisition.

Alternately, for overall carbonated soft drink volume and for non–Pepsi brand volume, the equation estimated is,

$$CDS\ volume = f\ (C,\ XDOM,\ XDSTL,\ S,\ X,\ DOM,\ DSTL)$$

where

C = constant term,

$XDOM$ = interaction term between X and DOM,

$XDSTL$ = interaction term between X and $DSTL$,

S = seasonal dummy variable (0 if October to March, 1 if April to September),

X = dummy variable for change in franchise ownership (0 before May 1986, 1 after May 1986),

DOM = intercept dummy variable for Omaha relative volume,

$DSTL$ = intercept dummy variable for St. Louis relative volume.

Table M–1 presents the results of this analysis with relevant test statistics, and table M–2 presents the results in terms of the difference in average relative volume for each area. The results indicate that the total volume of carbonated soft drinks in these areas has not decreased in a statistically significant sense as a result of PepsiCo's acquisition of the MEI bottler. On the contrary, in each area relative volume increased following the MEI acquisition, and in the case of Minneapolis/St. Paul, the measured increase is statistically significant. Based on these results, vertical integration did not result in a reduction in output as the vertical foreclosure theory would predict.

The same equation was estimated using total non-PepsiCo volume bottled by the MEI bottler as the dependent variable. Tables M–3 and M–4 present the results of this analysis.

These results also indicate that following the MEI acquisition, relative volume of non-PepsiCo carbonated soft drinks was higher than it was before

Table M–1
Relative Volume of Total Carbonated Soft Drink Sales in the MEI Areas

Variable	Parameter Estimate	Standard Error	T-Statistic
C	0.014184	0.00024894	56.977
XDOM	− 0.001087	0.00043192	− 2.517
XDSTL	− 0.000255	0.00043192	− 0.589
X	0.001277	0.00030541	4.180
S	− 0.000285	0.00017386	− 1.639
DOM	− 0.010609	0.00032988	− 32.159
DSTL	− 0.001449	0.00032988	− 4.393
Adjusted R^2	0.9789		
F-statistic	549.246		

Table M–2
Difference in Average Relative Volume of Total Carbonated Soft Drink Sales in the MEI Areas
(number of 192-ounce cases per million of 192-ounce cases sold in the United States)

Area	Mean Difference	T-Statistic[a]
Omaha	+ 190	0.359
St. Louis	+ 1,022	1.658
Minneapolis/St. Paul	+ 1,277	4.180

[a]The t-statistic for each area except Minneapolis/St. Paul is the square root of the estimated variance of the sum of the coefficients of X and the corresponding interaction term.

Table M–3
Relative Volume of Non-PepsiCo Brands Bottled by the MEI Bottler

Variable	Parameter Estimate	Standard Error	T-Statistic
C	0.016048	0.00057039	28.134
XDOM	− 0.002013	0.00098967	− 2.034
XDSTL	− 0.000484	0.00098967	− 0.489
X	0.002817	0.00069980	4.026
S	− 0.000691	0.00039838	1.736
DOM	− 0.014759	0.00075587	− 19.525
DSTL	− 0.010815	0.00075587	− 14.308
Adjusted R^2	0.9417		
F-statistic	192.146		

Table M–4

Difference in Average Relative Volume of Non-PepsiCo Brand Carbonated Soft Drinks Bottled by the MEI Bottler

(number of 192-ounce cases per million of 192-ounce cases sold in the United States)

Area	Mean Difference	T-Statistic[a]
Omaha	+804	0.663
St. Louis	+2,333	0.766
Minneapolis/St. Paul	+2,817	4.026

[a]The t-statistic for each area except Minneapolis/St. Paul is the square root of the estimated variance of the sum of the coefficients of X and the corresponding interaction term.

Table M–5

Difference in Average Relative Frequency of Advertising for Non-PepsiCo Brands Bottled by MEI Bottler

(ads per thousand national ads)

Area	Mean Difference	T-Statistic
Omaha		
Hires Diet	+54.0	1.85
Hires Regular	+39.9	2.31
St. Louis		
A&W Root Beer Diet	−1.9	−0.96
A&W Root Beer Regular	+1.0	0.81
A&W Megabrand[a]	−0.8	−0.87

[a]Root beer and cream soda products.

the acquisition. And in Minneapolis/St. Paul, the acquisition resulted in a statistically significant increase in non-PepsiCo volume. These results lend further support to the conclusion that vertical integration did not result in a reduction in output as predicted by the vertical foreclosure theory.

Promotion Effects. A similar analysis was performed using the frequency and raw weighted value of feature advertising as the dependent variable. Feature advertising data were available only for Hires Root Beer in Omaha and for A&W Root Beer in St. Louis. The results, presented in tables M–5 and M–6, indicate that advertising promotions, in terms of both frequency and value of feature advertisements, increased following PepsiCo's acquisition of the Omaha MEI bottler. Therefore, contrary to the vertical foreclosure hypothesis, the acquisition was procompetitive. In St. Louis, measured effects are negative in two instances, but in neither is the effect statistically significant. In all other instances, the measured effects in St. Louis are positive, and in the

Table M–6
Difference in Average Relative Raw Weighted Value of Advertising for
Non-PepsiCo Brands Bottled by MEI Bottler
(ads per thousand national ads)

Area	Mean Difference	T-Statistic
Omaha		
Hires Diet	+ 29.4	2.48
Hires Regular	+ 10.6	2.30
St. Louis		
A&W Root Beer Diet	+ 1.8	0.31
A&W Root Beer Regular	+ 4.4	1.89
A&W Megabrand[a]	+ 2.0	0.99

[a]Root beer and cream soda products.

case of relative raw weighted value for regular root beer, the measured
positive effect is statistically significant.

Based on the statistical analysis, the results indicate that PepsiCo's acquisition of the MEI bottlers was not anticompetitive. In no instance was the
acquisition found to have a statistically significant effect supportive of vertical
foreclosure. Moreover, in several instances, the measured effect was statistically significant and procompetitive. Overall the results support the conclusion
that PepsiCo's MEI acquisition increased consumer welfare.

Empirical Test of the Hypothesis That
Vertical Symmetry Facilitates Collusion

Measurement and Evaluation of
Carbonated Soft Drink Performance

An examination of the relative effects of competition in symmetric versus
asymmetric franchise areas can be used to test whether vertical symmetry
facilitates collusion. Output and advertising frequency are examined for evidence of restricted output. Geographic franchise areas were chosen where
PepsiCo operated a company-owned bottler (COBO) and where CCE purchased the independently owned Coca-Cola bottler, thus transforming the
geographic area from an asymmetric to a symmetric franchise area. Structuring the statistical analysis in this manner allows testing for the significance of
the CCE ownership transfer as the relevant event.

Nielsen Audit and Nielsen MAJERS bimonthly data on volume and feature advertising were collected for five geographic areas—Los Angeles, Phoenix, Detroit, Orlando, and Houston—and the overall total United States. The
choice of these five areas was dictated by the availability of data to analyze

recent CCE acquisitions in areas where a PepsiCo COBO competed against an independently owned Coca-Cola bottler prior to these acquisitions.

Statistical Methodology

A mean difference statistical analysis was used to test for the competitive effects resulting from symmetric franchise organization. Relative volume and, alternatively, relative feature advertising are the dependent variables in the two regression models estimated. In each model, a binary (dummy) variable, S, is defined to capture the increase in seasonal demand for carbonated soft drinks during the summer. A binary variable, X, distinguishes the periods of asymmetric and symmetric competition. Before September 1986 in the geographic areas examined, a PepsiCo COBO competed with an independently owned Coca-Cola bottler ($X = 0$), and after September 1986, a PepsiCo COBO and CCE-owned bottler (a Coca-Cola COBO) were in direct competition in these areas ($X = 1$). For both the volume and promotion regression models, bimonthly observations were pooled across the five areas. The regression models were specified to allow for area-specific averages in the performance variables with respect to asymmetric vertical integration and area-specific effects of the changes in franchise organization that resulted in symmetric vertical integration in the local areas.

Results

Volume Effects. The null hypothesis tested is that carbonated soft drink volume in each of the five geographic areas, relative to U.S. volume, rose or did not decline following Coca-Cola's acquisitions resulting in direct PepsiCo/Coca-Cola COBO/COBO competition. The estimated equation is,

$$\text{CSD volume} = f\,(C, \, XDORLF, \, XDHOUMM, \, XDPHXMM,$$
$$XDLAMM, \, X, \, S, \, DORLF, \, DHOUMM,$$
$$DPHXMM, \, DLAMM),$$

where,

$$C = \text{constant term,}$$

$$XDORLF = \text{interaction term between } X \text{ and Orlando relative volume,}$$

$$XDHOUMM = \text{interaction term between } X \text{ and Houston relative volume,}$$

$$XDPHXMM = \text{interaction term between } X \text{ and Phoenix relative volume,}$$

XDLAMM = interaction term between X and Los Angeles relative volume,

DORLF = intercept dummy variable for Orlando relative volume,

DHOUMM = intercept dummy variable for Houston relative volume,

DPHXMM = intercept dummy variable for Phoenix relative volume,

DLAMM = intercept dummy variable for Los Angeles relative volume,

X = dummy variable for change in franchise ownership, (0 if independently owned Coca-Cola bottler, 1 if CCE-owned Coca-Cola bottler), and

S = seasonal dummy variable (0 if October to March, 1 if April to September).

The results are presented in table M–7 along with relevant test statistics.[5] Table M–8 presents the results of this analysis in terms of the difference in average relative volume for each area.

The results indicate that the relative volume of carbonated soft drinks did not decline (in a statistically significant sense) after the PepsiCo COBO began competing against a Coca-Cola COBO in Los Angeles, Phoenix, Houston, Detroit, and Orlando. In two of the five areas, relative volume was higher when PepsiCo and CCE's company-owned bottlers competed than when

Table M–7
Relative Volume of Carbonated Soft Drink Sales

Variable	Parameter Estimate	Standard Error	T-Statistic
C	0.019654	0.00051026	38.517
XDORLF	0.000232	0.00090775	0.256
XDHOUMM	0.002618	0.00090775	2.884
XDPHXMM	0.000110	0.00090775	0.121
XDLAMM	0.000782	0.00090775	0.862
X	−0.000396	0.00064187	−0.617
S	0.000776	0.00028304	2.741
DORLF	−0.010993	0.00069330	−15.856
DHOUMM	−0.001498	0.00069330	−2.160
DPHXMM	−0.006602	0.00069330	−9.523
DLAMM	0.022774	0.00069330	32.848
Adjusted R^2	0.9831		
F-statistic	694.478		

Table M–8
Difference in Average Relative Volume
(number of 192-ounce cases per million of 192-ounce cases sold in the United States)

Area	Mean Difference	T-Statistic[a]
Los Angeles	+ 386	0.27
Phoenix	− 286	− 0.20
Houston	+ 2,222	1.55
Detroit	− 396	− 0.62
Orlando	− 164	− 0.11

[a]The t-statistic for each area except Detroit is the square root of the estimated variance of the sum of the coefficients of X and the corresponding interaction term.

there was asymmetric competition between the bottlers. Only in Houston is the measured positive effect nearly statistically significant. In the areas with measured relative volume decreases, the measured decrements are not statistically different from zero.

The statistical analysis of the relative volume effects provides no basis for the hypothesis that symmetry in the vertical franchise ownership of PepsiCo and CCE bottlers is more likely to result in collusion than in asymmetric PepsiCo and CCE franchise ownership organizations.

Promotion Effects. Finally, an analysis was performed to test the null hypothesis that the relative number and raw weighted value of feature advertising for carbonated soft drinks did not decline following direct competition between the PepsiCo COBO and the CCE-owned bottler in the five geographic areas examined. Feature advertising is almost always used to advertise a price special on carbonated soft drinks. Therefore, feature advertising may provide some indication of relative price effects from vertical integration. The estimated equations are:

Number of CSD = f (C, XDORLF, XDHOUMM,
feature ads XDPHXMM, XDLAMM, X, S, DORLF,
DHOUMM, DPHXMM, DLAMM)

and

Raw weighted = f (C, XDORLF, XDHOUMM,
value of feature XDPHXMM, XDLAMM, X, S, DORLF,
ads DHOUMM, DPHXMM, DLAMM).

The estimated coefficients for the equations are presented in tables M–9 and M–10. These results are reported in terms of the difference in average

Table M–9
Relative Number of Feature Advertisements

Variable	Parameter Estimate	Standard Error	T-Statistic
C	0.057568	0.00158751	36.263
DORLF	− 0.052187	0.00219679	− 23.756
DHOUMM	− 0.031788	0.00219679	− 14.470
DPHXMM	− 0.036002	0.00219679	− 16.388
DLAMM	− 0.029862	0.00219679	− 13.593
X	0.013090	0.00176135	7.432
S	0.001246	0.00065496	1.902
XDORLF	− 0.013423	0.00249093	− 5.389
XDHOUMM	− 0.013903	0.00249093	− 5.581
XDPHXMM	− 0.012718	0.00249093	− 5.106
XDLAMM	− 0.006544	0.00249093	− 2.627
Adjusted R^2	0.9785		
F-statistic	406.43		

Table M–10
Relative Raw Weighted Value of Feature Advertisements

Variable	Parameter Estimate	Standard Error	T-Statistic
C	0.031673	0.00316242	10.015
DORLF	− 0.026809	0.00437614	− 6.126
DHOUMM	0.001293	0.00437614	0.295
DPHXMM	− 0.009654	0.00437614	− 2.206
DLAMM	0.127507	0.00437614	29.137
X	0.010499	0.00350872	2.992
S	0.000723	0.00130471	0.554
XDORLF	− 0.011385	0.00496208	− 2.294
XDHOUMM	− 0.013913	0.00496208	− 2.804
XDPHXMM	− 0.007919	0.00496208	− 1.596
XDLAMM	− 0.004653	0.00496208	− 0.938
Adjusted R^2	0.9884		
F-statistic	761.299		

relative number and raw weighted value of feature advertisements in tables M–11 and M–12, respectively.

In the Phoenix, Houston, and Orlando areas, neither average relative number of feature advertisements nor average relative raw weighted value of feature advertisements was affected in a statistically significant manner by the change in franchise ownership of the Coca-Cola bottler from an independently owned to a CCE-owned bottler. In Los Angeles and in Detroit, the difference in average relative number of feature advertisements increased significantly (in a statistical sense) as a result of symmetric franchise owner-

Table M–11
Difference in Average Relative Number of Feature Advertisements
(ads per thousand national ads)

Area	Mean Difference	T-Statistic[a]
Los Angeles	+ 6.5	3.714
Phoenix	+ 0.4	0.205
Houston	− 0.8	− 0.447
Detroit	+ 13.1	7.432
Orlando	− 0.3	− 0.183

[a]The t-statistic for each area except Detroit is the square root of the estimated variance of the sum of the coefficients of X and the corresponding interaction term.

Table M–12
Difference in Average Relative Raw Weighted Value of Feature Advertisements
(ads per thousand national ads)

Area	Mean Difference	T-Statistic[a]
Los Angeles	+ 5.8	1.665
Phoenix	+ 2.6	0.735
Houston	− 3.4	− 0.949
Detroit	+ 10.5	2.990
Orlando	− 0.9	− 0.248

[a]The t-statistic for each area except Detroit is the square root of the estimated variance of the sum of the coefficients of X and the corresponding interaction term.

ship between PepsiCo and CCE bottlers. The ownership change in September 1986 also resulted in a statistically significant increase in the relative raw weighted value of the feature advertisements in these two areas.

Notes

1. The MEI acquisition involved more than the three areas for which data were available. For most areas, Nielsen data were not available for the time period when the corresponding bottler was owned by MEI. In other instances, data for the earlier time period pertained to a broad geographic area, including several non-MEI bottler franchises in addition to the bottler acquired from MEI.

The initial bimonthly period is the earliest date for which Nielsen Audit data were available. The final bimonthly period was the most recent observation available.

2. Best Food Day represents that day of the week used most frequently to advertise food products. Raw weighted value is a Nielsen construct that weighs feature

advertisements according to several dimensions of significance, including size of ad, number of stores covered, and size of market.

3. Nielsen collects shelf prices, by package type and brand, that are in effect on the day of the Nielsen audit. These prices are multiplied by the volume of carbonated soft drinks sold during the two-month period to calculate total revenue. Because prices of carbonated soft drinks are highly variable, often changing weekly, the prices gathered for one day during the two-month period may not reflect the average prices paid for carbonated soft drinks at the point of purchase during the period. So-called Nielsen Scantrack data, representing retail prices as scanned by a retailer's computer, were not prepared by Nielsen until 1987 and 1988.

4. In Minneapolis/St. Paul, the MEI bottler also bottled Seven-Up, Dr Pepper, A&W, Crush, Hires, Vernor's, and Squirt. In Omaha, the MEI bottler bottled Crush and Hires. The St. Louis bottler distributed A&W and Crush in addition to its Pepsi products.

5. The statistical insignificance of the interaction terms for Orlando, Phoenix, and Los Angeles implies that the effects of symmetric vertical integration occasioned by Coca-Cola's bottler acquisitions in these areas are no different from the measured effect in Detroit (the arbitrarily chosen benchmark area). When the regression model is respecified to reflect these equalities, the statistical results have the same implications as those inferred from the estimates in table M–7.

Index

About the Authors

Robert D. Tollison is the Duncan Black Professor of Economics and director of the Center for the Study of Public Choice at George Mason University in Fairfax, Virginia. Tollison served as director of the Bureau of Economics at the Federal Trade Commission from 1981 through 1983. He received his Ph.D. from the University of Virginia.

David P. Kaplan is president of Capital Economics, an economic consulting firm located in Washington, D.C. Kaplan, a specialist in antitrust economics and commercial damage analysis, holds an M.A. in economics from the George Washington University and a J.D. from the George Washington University School of Law. Kaplan is also a lecturer in economics at George Mason University.

Richard S. Higgins is a senior economist with Capital Economics. He served as deputy director of the Bureau of Economics, first for Consumer Protection and Regulatory Analysis and subsequently for Antitrust at the Federal Trade Commission from 1982 through 1987. Higgins received a Ph.D. in economics from the University of Virginia.